"In this small volume, Kevin Corrigan shows convincingly that, far from exclusive preoccupation with escaping from the ambiguities of ordinary human experience in favor of the intellectual contemplation of remote transcendental realities such as the Forms, the Unmoved Mover, or the Neoplatonic One, Plato and his successors held that such experiences as love, pleasure, and desire are entirely compatible with divine transcendence, without which there can be no real immanence and no real love of individuals without the vertical dimension that makes this possible."

—John D. Turner
Cotner Professor of Religious Studies
and University Professor of Classics and History, University of Nebraska-Lincoln

"Kevin Corrigan, noted authority on both Plato himself and the later Platonist tradition, particularly Plotinus, has here produced a remarkable study of the role of love in both stages of that tradition. Against the prevailing view that Plato in particular, downgrades the status of individual love and eliminates love from the relations between God and humans, Corrigan reasserts the role of love at all levels of the Platonist universe."

—John Dillon
Regius Professor of Greek (Emeritus), Trinity College Dublin

"In this multifaceted, crafted gem of a book, Kevin Corrigan expertly guides us to understand more deeply and anew the perennial themes of love and friendship both in Platonism and in our own lives. A deeply knowledgeable and perceptive scholar, Corrigan gently corrects widely disseminated misunderstandings of the Platonic tradition and shows how, much more than is generally recognized, the Platonic-Pythagorean tradition can be understood as a whole, from Plato through Aristotle and Plotinus, right through Dionysius the Areopagite. This is a valuable book and a model of concision—read it and be guided to a clearer understanding, not only of Platonism."

—Arthur Versluis
author of *Platonic Mysticism, and Perennial Philosophy*

"This is an arresting revisionist essay. Corrigan offers a novel analysis of ancient Platonism, challenging entrenched scholarly accounts of the nature of love and intellect in Platonism and, more broadly, inviting his readers to discover the distinctive understanding of divine love developed by the Platonists of late antiquity. This book should be required reading for students of ancient philosophy and early Christian theology."

—John Peter Kenney
Professor of Religious Studies at Saint Michael's College

"Corrigan's *Love, Friendship, Beauty, and the Good* debunks the academic myth which has encased ancient philosophy and its later pagan and Christian permutations in a curio box, available for a sterile analytical examination, but devoid of relevance to the nitty-gritty psychology of our daily life. It takes a life-time of experience and expertise to re-examine the relationship between being and thinking in the most Cartesian of ways. Corrigan does just this with reason and passion."

—Svetla Slaveva-Griffin
Florida State University

Love, Friendship, Beauty, and the Good

VERITAS
Series Introduction

"... the truth will set you free" (John 8:32)

In much contemporary discourse, Pilate's question has been taken to mark the absolute boundary of human thought. Beyond this boundary, it is often suggested, is an intellectual hinterland into which we must not venture. This terrain is an agnosticism of thought: because truth cannot be possessed, it must not be spoken. Thus, it is argued that the defenders of "truth" in our day are often traffickers in ideology, merchants of counterfeits, or anti-liberal. They are, because it is somewhat taken for granted that Nietzsche's word is final: truth is the domain of tyranny.

Is this indeed the case, or might another vision of truth offer itself? The ancient Greeks named the love of wisdom as *philia*, or friendship. The one who would become wise, they argued, would be a "friend of truth." For both philosophy and theology might be conceived as schools in the friendship of truth, as a kind of relation. For like friendship, truth is as much discovered as it is made. If truth is then so elusive, if its domain is *terra incognita*, perhaps this is because it arrives to us—unannounced—as gift, as a person, and not some thing.

The aim of the Veritas book series is to publish incisive and original current scholarly work that inhabits "the between" and "the beyond" of theology and philosophy. These volumes will all share a common aspiration to transcend the institutional divorce in which these two disciplines often find themselves, and to engage questions of pressing concern to both philosophers and theologians in such a way as to reinvigorate both disciplines with a kind of interdisciplinary desire, often so absent in contemporary academe. In a word, these volumes represent collective efforts in the befriending of truth, doing so beyond the simulacra of pretend tolerance, the violent, yet insipid reasoning of liberalism that asks with Pilate, "What is truth?"—expecting a consensus of non-commitment; one that encourages the commodification of the mind, now sedated by the civil service of career, ministered by the frightened patrons of position.

The series will therefore consist of two "wings": (1) original monographs; and (2) essay collections on a range of topics in theology and philosophy. The latter will principally be the products of the annual conferences of the Centre of Theology and Philosophy (www.theologyphilosophycentre.co.uk).

Conor Cunningham and Eric Austin Lee, *Series editors*

Love, Friendship, Beauty, and the Good

Plato, Aristotle, and the Later Tradition

KEVIN CORRIGAN

CASCADE *Books* • Eugene, Oregon

LOVE, FRIENDSHIP, BEAUTY, AND THE GOOD
Plato, Aristotle, and the Later Tradition

Veritas 26

Copyright © 2018 Kevin Corrigan. All rights reserved. Except for brief quotations in critical publications or reviews, no part of this book may be reproduced in any manner without prior written permission from the publisher. Write: Permissions, Wipf and Stock Publishers, 199 W. 8th Ave., Suite 3, Eugene, OR 97401.

Cascade Books
An Imprint of Wipf and Stock Publishers
199 W. 8th Ave., Suite 3
Eugene, OR 97401

www.wipfandstock.com

PAPERBACK ISBN: 978-1-5326-4549-5
HARDCOVER ISBN: 978-1-5326-4550-1
EBOOK ISBN: 978-1-5326-4551-8

Cataloguing-in-Publication data:

Names: Corrigan, Kevin, author.

Title: Love, friendship, beauty, and the good : Plato, Aristotle, and the later tradition / Kevin Corrigan.

Description: Eugene, OR: Cascade Books, 2018 | Series: Veritas 26 | Includes bibliographical references and index.

Identifiers: ISBN 978-1-5326-4549-5 (paperback) | ISBN 978-1-5326-4550-1 (hardcover) | ISBN 978-1-5326-4551-8 (ebook)

Subjects: LCSH: Plato | Platonists | Neoplatonism | Aristotle—Criticism, interpretation, etc. | Aesthetics | Metaphysics | Friendship—Philosophy

Classification: B395 C67 2018 (print) | B395 (ebook)

Manufactured in the U.S.A.   JULY 26, 2018

Contents

Acknowledgements | vii
Abbreviations | viii
Introduction | ix

1. Desire, Love, and Ascent through the Beautiful to the Good | 1
    1.1 Love and desire | 4
    1.2 Intellect and desire | 9
    1.3 Ascent to the beautiful and the good: Aristotle, *Metaphysics* 12.7 | 12
    1.4 Ascent to the beautiful and the good: Plato, the *Symposium* and *Republic* | **23**
    1.5 Plato and Aristotle | 27
    1.6 Alcinous | 31
    1.7 Plotinus (and Porphyry) | 32
    1.8 Proclus | 37
    1.9 Marsilio Ficino | 44
    1.10 Conclusions | 45

2. Friendship and Love of the Individual | 50
    2.1 Friendship in the Platonic tradition: The *Lysis*, *Alcibiades I*, and *Symposium* | 53
    2.2 Loving individuals | 59
    2.3 The ambiguities of ordinary experience | 60
    2.4 The *Symposium* and Pausanias' speech | 62
    2.5 Different models of erotic friendship in the *Symposium*, *Phaedrus*, and later Platonism | 65
    2.6 Plotinus: lateral attachment and reflexivity | 67
    2.7 Proclus: Pausanias' speech in light of the *Phaedrus* | 69
    2.8 Marsilio Ficino: Pausanias' speech and the *Symposium* as a whole | 71
    2.9 Conclusions | 75

3. The Problem of Divine Love | 82
    3.1 Pleasure, pre-inclusion, joy, and vulnerability | 82
    3.2 Self-relatedness, inclusion, pre-inclusion? | 83
    3.3 Pleasure and indivisible wholeness | 86

3.4 Plotinus: the joy of existence | 96
3.5 Implicate and explicate orders in Plotinus: Divine love? | 102
3.6 Later Neoplatonism: Iamblichus and Proclus | 105
3.7 Dionysius and Divine loving | 111

Conclusion | 114
Select Bibliography | 127
Index Locorum | 135
Index of Subjects and Names | 145

Acknowledgements

OUT OF RESPECT FOR my teacher and guide, Professor A. H. Armstrong, I have for the most part used his superb translations of Plotinus in this book. When I first came to study with him in Canada, he was working on Volumes VI and VII of the *Enneads* and had been corresponding regularly with Paul Henry and Hans-Rudolph Schwyzer, who established the first modern critical text of Plotinus' works on sound philological principles. It was an exciting time to be his student and to be able to read Plato, Plotinus, and the later Neoplatonists with him in person. I am grateful to him more and more as time passes, and I hope he would have approved of this little book. All other translations are my own unless otherwise indicated.

My special thanks to Robin Parry, editor with Cascade Books and Pickwick Publications, for his good advice, support, and friendship. I am also grateful to Conor Cunningham and Eric Austin Lee for including this book in their Veritas series, and to Ian Creeger, Matthew Wimer for help in the editing and production process. To my students, Madeline Long and Syed Zaidi, who read through the proofs and made many timely suggestions, my thanks. I also want to thank John Turner for our friendship and collaboration. Over the past year we have been working on two books and several projects together. My daughter, Sarah, helped me with formatting the manuscript and Elena, my wife, read the book through at an earlier stage with excellent critical suggestions. To Elena, and to my children, John and Peggy, Yuri and Arielle (and their children, Rafael and Natalya), Maria and Joaquin, Sarah and Jason—I am deeply grateful for everything.

Abbreviations

AJP	*American Journal of Philology*
Ast	*Lexicon Platonicum*
Bonitz	*Index Aristotelicus*
CQ	*Classical Quarterly*
DA	Aristotle, *De Anima*
DK	Diels-Kranz, *Fragmente der Vorsokratiker*
DM	Iamblichus, *De Mysteriis*
DN	Pseudo-Dionysius, *Divine Names*
EE	Aristotle, *Eudemian Ethics*
EN	Aristotle, *Ethica Nicomachea*
ET	Proclus, *Elements of Theology*
IJPT	*International Journal of the Platonic Tradition*
In Alc.	Proclus/Olympiodorus, *Commentary on the First Alcibiades*
In Rep.	Proclus, *Commentary on the Republic* (*Commentaire sur la République*)
In Tim.	Proclus, *Commentary on the Timaeus*
LCL	Loeb Classical Library
LSJ	Liddell, H. G., and Scott, R., *A Greek-English Lexicon*
MM	Aristotle, *Magna Moralia*
MT	Pseudo-Dionysius, *Mystical Theology*
OSAP	*Oxford Studies in Ancient Philosophy*
PA	Aristotle, *De Partibus Animalium*
PT	Proclus, *Platonic Theology* (*Théologie Platonicienne*)
SVF	*Stoicorum Veterum Fragmenta*

Introduction

PLATO'S THOUGHT, AND THE later tradition built upon it, is often characterized by the ascent of the soul or mind to the Supreme Principle, described in different ways in different dialogues. In the *Phaedo*, the soul gathers itself into itself away from the body in order to perceive the forms of beauty, equality, etc. In the *Republic* there are several different ascents: the approach to being and the whole of wisdom in Book 5; the pursuit of the good in Book 6; and the ascent from the cave through the kinship of the different sciences to the synoptic view of dialectic in Book 7. Probably the most distinctive ascent of all occurs in the *Symposium*, in the greater mysteries of Diotima-Socrates' speech, where the apprentice ascends from bodies through souls, ways of life, sciences to the single science and, finally, the vision of the supremely Beautiful, which alone makes human life truly worth living.

Since the Platonic tradition is also often characterized as privileging mind or soul over body and the emotions, I want first to see in Plato, Aristotle, and Plotinus how far this is really true, and how reason and mind can be compatible with feeling and desire. Is the view of the *Phaedo*, in which feeling seems to be confined to the body, at odds with the *Symposium*, *Republic*, and *Phaedrus*, where feeling seems to run through everything? But how far does love or feeling really go? Can love or eros be intrinsic to intellect or mind, one of whose principal features—from the time of Anaxagoras through Aristotle and into late antiquity—is impassibility or freedom from feeling or passion?[1]

Second, because the 19th Century sharply distinguished an Ur-Plato from Aristotle, I want to see if there is anything in Aristotle that matches these ascents in Plato. Did Aristotle develop his own thought in significant ways out of insights in Plato's dialogues? And how can we detect this?

Third, since the nineteenth-century rediscovery of a pristine Plato drew an even sharper distinction between the "thought" of the dialogues

---

1. For Anaxagoras *DK* II 12 D (at least, on Aristotle's view); Aristotle, *De Anima* 429b23; cf. *Physics* 256b20; *De Anima* 429a15; 430a18; 24; Stoics *SVF* III 109, 12–13; III 448; on the notion in Plato, Aristotle, the Stoics, Plotinus, and patristic thought (and for further references) see Corrigan, *Evagrius and Gregory*, 54–61.

and the later tradition apparently initiated by Plotinus in the third century CE and known as Neoplatonism, I want to examine some works of Plotinus and the later Neoplatonists to see whether this later tradition gets anything fundamental about Plato's dialogues right. Modern scholarship tends to identify the beautiful of the *Phaedo* and *Symposium* with the good of the *Republic* as coincident classes, for instance, whereas the Neoplatonic tradition tends—on the whole—to distinguish the beautiful and the good, never to reduce them to classes, and to read the forms of the *Phaedo* and *Symposium* in the light of the good beyond being in *Republic* 6. Is this correct or is it simply a later uncritical view superimposed upon the dialogues? Is it supported by a reading of Plotinus' *Enneads* as a whole, for instance? Does Plotinus distinguish the beautiful and the good in early works, for example, but identify beauty with goodness later, as Massagli has argued.[2]

If we look at this from a broader perspective still, Neoplatonism has been variously characterized as the failure of reason or as mystical nonsense bearing little relation to Plato and Aristotle. Much work has been done in the past twenty to thirty years to redeem a more "rational" Plotinus from the much more "religious" thought of the later Neoplatonists, especially Iamblichus and Proclus. Do we then have anything to learn about Plato and Aristotle not only from Plotinus but also from the later Neoplatonic tradition? We know that Neoplatonists frequently claimed to be able to reconcile "Plato" and "Aristotle," but no matter on what bases they might have made such claims,[3] how far did they really understand the "Plato" and "Aristotle" that we claim to read with superior expertise today? Here I am not really interested in the question of the "reconciliation" of Plato and Aristotle, on which there has been some excellent recent work, so much as I am concerned to identify some significant hidden resonances in the thought of Plato and Aristotle that important thinkers in late antiquity, such as Plotinus and Proclus, so obviously recognize that they can be fairly easily detected in the "body language" of their approaches to different problems in their interpretations of Plato and Aristotle.

Two further crucial questions arise out of this enquiry. First, if love really does characterize mind or soul in the Platonic tradition, what *kind* of love is it? Is it a love that allows for friendship in a way that is meaningful to us today? We know that the Platonic-Pythagorean tradition emphasized the importance of love on every level of existence, so much so that major figures such as Empedocles, Theophrastus, and Porphyry argued for friendship not only among human beings, as the Stoics maintained, but among all living

---

2. Massagli, "L'Uno al di sopra del bello e della belleza," 111–31.
3. See recently Karamanolis, *Plato and Aristotle in Agreement? passim.*

creatures, plants included.⁴ But did this cosmic emphasis and the Platonic focus on the primary importance of forms eclipse or eliminate real love of other individual things for themselves? Recent scholarship has argued forcefully from different perspectives that Platonism has little sense of the ambiguities of ordinary experience and that it promotes love of spiritual entities against the obvious facts of our experience, that we love individuals for their own sakes not for the sake of abstract ideals.⁵ I shall examine if this is true.

In this book I restrict my focus to what have become known as Plato's "early" and "middle dialogues," from the *Lysis*, *Hippias Major*, and *Alcibiades I* up to the *Phaedo*, *Symposium*, *Republic*, *Phaedrus*, including occasional references to the *Timaeus*, *Theaetetus*, *Philebus*, *Sophist*, *Laws*, *Letters*, where necessary. Special attention to the later dialogues, especially the *Sophist*, *Parmenides*, *Statesman*, etc., would require a different treatment. On the authenticity of the *Alcibiades I*, see chapter 2.

Finally, Plato's forms and Aristotle's unmoved mover seem to bear no resemblance to a Jewish or Christian God who plainly loves and favors individuals, nations, and groups. One could hardly imagine a stately Platonic Form or Aristotle's impassible Intellect loving anything at all. Indeed, in the later Aristotelian tradition, Alexander of Aphrodisias maintained that divine providence only extended as far as the celestial spheres down to the moon,⁶ leaving the sublunary world to its own nexus of causality, certainly dependent upon the movement of Intellect, but not intimately provided for by it. In this picture, individual things like you and me seem infinitely removed from the life of "God" and, certainly, from any possibility of real "friendship" with the gods, despite Plato and Aristotle's use of language suggesting the possibility of such friendship.⁷ We mortal beings might love the gods, but do they love us back?

One might reply that Plato and Aristotle were confronted with a horrific earlier tradition that privileged all kinds of divine favoritism of particular mortals, a tradition that saw a genetic necessity in deriving human from divine beings by sexual intercourse. Plato and Aristotle evidently needed to overcome such myths. Diotima, for instance, in the *Symposium* makes it perfectly clear that "god does not have sex with human beings."⁸ Fur-

---

4. For this history, see Sorabji, *Animal Minds and Human Morals*; Clark, *Animals in Classical and Late Antique Philosophy*, 35–60; Corrigan, *Unmoved Mover*, 372–90.

5. See note 11 below.

6. In the Arabic *De Providentia*, 1, 1–9, 2, translated by Ruland, in Sharples, *Alexander of Aphrodisias on Divine Providence*, 198–211.

7. On this see chapter 3.

8. If this is how we should translate *Symposium* 203a1–2: θεὸς δὲ ἀνθρώπῳ οὐ

thermore, Aristotle is compelled to overcome the anthropomorphicisms of Plato's own myths, conspicuously, of course, the myth of the making of the world in the *Timaeus* in which the Master Craftsman or Demiurge does all kinds of "human" things: he deliberates, thinks, and makes.[9] So maybe there is no place for any quasi-anthropomorphic feelings in thought after Plato? And, indeed, any reciprocal friendship seems even less likely given the inequality, or rather incommensurability, between gods and human beings.

This book aims to determine whether this is a fair picture for the whole of antiquity and whether there is anything in Plato—and Aristotle—that subverts this picture or suggests a different understanding. Did the later Platonic tradition develop an entirely different picture of divine love out of important elements in the thought of Plato and Aristotle—undoubtedly in competition with Judaism, Christianity, and some of the so-called hybrid gnostic groups that we know Plotinus engaged with in some of his most important works (if not throughout the whole of his writing career)?[10]

I shall take up these sets of questions then under three major headings as follows.

Chapter 1, entitled "Desire, Love, and Ascent through the Beautiful to the Good," examines three principal questions. First, the question of reason and desire: is feeling compatible with reason and mind in Plato, Aristotle, and Plotinus? Second, the specific case of Aristotle: is there anything in Aristotle that matches the ascents to the beautiful and the good in Plato and, if so, how is this to be seen in relation to Plato? Third, how is the beautiful, the highest form of the *Symposium*, to be related to the good, the highest form beyond being of the *Republic*? Can we give a definitive answer to this question in Plato and, if so, is there any evidence that key thinkers in later antiquity and even the Renaissance read Plato in this way? How did they see the forms of justice, equality, holiness, etc., in this configuration?

Chapter 2, entitled "Friendship and Love of the Individual," asks a series of questions that have become truly pressing questions over the last hundred years of scholarship and still remain contested. Is love of, and friendship with, the individual for the individual's own sake really a part of the Platonic tradition or does this tradition ignore the ambiguities of ordinary experience in favor ultimately of love of god? Significant modern scholarship has denied real love of the individual in Plato, and also Aristotle, on the one

---

μείγνυται.

9. *Timaeus* 28a–37d; *Statesman* 271d–274e.

10. On this question, see Narbonne, *Plotinus in Dialogue with the Gnostics*; Corrigan and Turner, *Plotinus, Ennead VI 8*.

hand,[11] and any real lateral relationship to other individuals in Plotinus, on the other hand, in favor of anagogic relations only.[12] This chapter will look at all of the major dialogues relevant to this topic and challenge the scholarly consensus about the inauthenticity of the *Alcibiades I*, unchallenged by anyone in antiquity before Schleiermacher in the nineteenth century.

Chapter 3, entitled "The Problem of Divine Love: Pleasure, Joy, Pre-inclusion, and Vulnerability," examines a question to which any reader of Plato, Aristotle, and the later tradition might reasonably want a good answer: in loving the divine, are we in some way loved in return? Is loving god in any real sense being god-beloved? Is there, perhaps, a way that the love of god pre-includes everything else? And what would it mean if we said that god loves you or me in god's own way, as somehow pre-included in god's being? Would this amount to loving *you* in any genuine sense and not some effigy or idealized version of what you *should* be? Where does pleasure fit into this picture? And how do Aristotle and the later Neoplatonic tradition think about these issues? Finally, is there any major development of this theme of divine love in later antiquity that can be realistically traced back to Plato and Aristotle?[13]

In this book, I will focus upon the pagan side of the Platonic tradition—except for Dionysius the Areopagite (fifth-sixth century CE) and Marsilio Ficino in the Renaissance. This is not to exclude the rich Jewish and Christian contributions, especially Philo and Origen of Alexandria, but rather to examine for the most part how pagan antiquity treated these issues and responded in its own ways to major questions that have become problematic and have been so misunderstood in modern times.

Finally, a word on capitalization: academic convention often capitalizes words such as Being (when not speaking of an individual being), World Soul (when not referencing the individual soul), Intellect (if the divine intellect or unmoved mover is intended), and transcendental forms, such as, the Good, Beauty. However, there are numerous texts in the Platonic tradition in which it is ambiguous whether the author speaks of Soul or soul, Intellect or intellect, Beauty or beauty, and so on. Indeed, sometimes this ambiguity is deliberate and pregnant with meaning. One problem with following the convention of capitalizing such words is that on each occasion they appear one must remove any ambiguity and opt for either Soul or soul, Intellect or intellect, etc. Now very often this is not a problem because the text clearly

11. On this see Vlastos, "The Individual as an Object of Love," 3–42; Nygren, *Agape and Eros*, 186; Dover, *Symposium*, 113, 152; Grube, *Plato's Thought*, 87–119; Nussbaum, *Fragility of Goodness*, 178ff.; and chapter 2.

12. See Mortley, *Plotinus, Self and the World*, 108–9; and chapter 2 (2.7).

13. For this see chapter 3.

indicates one or the other. However, when the text is deliberately ambiguous the common convention requires that one must shut down that ambiguity (or adopt inconsistent use of caps, which is itself confusing). My preference is thus to cut through all this and to use lower case in all instances, and as far as is possible I have stuck to it. This should not create undue perplexity because the literary contexts usually make clear when the author is speaking of transcendental forms, say, or divine intellect. And when it is not clear whether intellect or Intellect, soul or Soul, etc., is referred to this is because the texts themselves are ambiguous. In my view, it is wiser to wrestle with ambiguity than to try to short-circuit it.

1

Desire, Love, and Ascent through the Beautiful to the Good

SINCE DESIRE, FRIENDSHIP, AND love, together with the search for truth, beauty, and goodness, are necessary for any human life, and yet nothing is more likely to get us into trouble, more enigmatic in the final analysis, and more potentially fatal, I want to examine some of these issues in Plato, Aristotle, Plotinus, and some other major figures in the later history of thought. This is important because we in the modern world are divided about these ancient figures, so many convinced that Plato, Aristotle, and especially Plotinus rigidly divorced mind and feeling and thereby left a fatal legacy from which we are still trying to recover. It is important, too, because even in the various fields of contemporary scholarship it is still unusual to link the study of early and late antiquity directly. From Schleiermacher on, we have inherited a conviction that Plato, Aristotle, the Stoics, etc., should be separated from the preoccupations of the Neoplatonists, who, on some interpretations, invented the one as their highest Principle and introduced religious and ethical perspectives of an otherworldly character into what should be a world unencumbered by extraneous considerations. For most modern scholarship, the "good" is not a transcendental principle, but something we have to negotiate in the ambiguities of ordinary experience. In fact, if we can do without truth, according to truth-redundancy theory, perhaps we need the "good" even less, since even the Romantics could apparently get by without it. Keats appealed only to beauty and truth in the final lines of his famous poem *Ode on a Grecian Urn*: "Beauty is truth, truth beauty,—that is all/ Ye know on earth, and all ye need to know." But is it really true that "beauty is truth and truth beauty," as the *Symposium* (apparently) and Keats' *Ode on a Grecian* Urn might have us believe?[1] Or is this simply "all" we re-

---

1. *Ode on a Grecian Urn*, final stanza: O Attic shape! Fair attitude! with brede/ Of marble men and maidens overwrought,/ With forest branches and the trodden weed;/

ally need to know? But even if it is all we need, it seems unlikely that beauty is truth in any simple sense or that what is true is beautiful and that what is beautiful true, no matter how powerful the conjunction or identity of truth and beauty might be. What is true can be petty and crippling; what is beautiful can be deceptive—a path to destruction, like the figure of Alcibiades in Plato's *Symposium*; and what is good can be brilliant but empty inventiveness, like Agathon's speech in the *Symposium*. So how should the true, the beautiful, and the good be configured if what I shall, for convenience, call the "Romantic" interpretation of the erotic ascent is to be avoided? Can we, in other words, avoid petty truth, deceptive beauty, and empty good?

In this chapter, I will first examine the commonly supposed divide between reason and feeling, love and intellect in ancient thought. For Plato, Aristotle, and Plotinus, is desire lower than reason and always subordinated to reason, or does desire have its own reasons? Does reason generate its own desire? And can desire really characterize intellect? These are important life questions in themselves, since desire and its consequences ruin lives so easily and the question of how we are to live and from what perspective is so easily submerged by practical economic, social, and technological concerns. They are also important questions because even when they do arise, Platonism[2] and the ancient and medieval worlds are frequently dismissed as of

---

Thou, silent form, dost tease us out of thought/ As doth eternity: Cold Pastoral!/ When old age shall this generation waste,/ Thou shalt remain, in midst of other woe/ Than ours, a friend to man, to whom thou say'st,/ "Beauty is truth, truth beauty,—that is all/ Ye know on earth, and all ye need to know." For the *Symposium*, we ascend from beauties of body, soul, etc. to the "truth" of the supreme beauty (211–12).

2. For one recent broader definition of Platonism, see Lloyd Gerson, who has argued (in his book *From Plato to Platonism*, 2013) for what he calls Ur-Platonism, of which Plato's own philosophy is a version. Since Platonism is not limited to Plato's views as found in his dialogues, nor to other philosophers' presentations of them (primarily Aristotle's), nor to later philosophers' contributions to what is found in Plato's works, Platonism as a term must be flexible enough to signify all three of these aspects severally and collectively. To distinguish this all-inclusive meaning of Platonism from each of the individual renditions, Gerson hypothetically construes Ur-Platonism (UP) as a matrix-like collection of all possible meanings of Platonism. In his words, UP "is the general philosophical position that arises from the conjunction of the negations of the philosophical positions explicitly rejected in the dialogues" (9). These positions are anti-materialism, anti-mechanism, anti-nominalism, anti-relativism, and anti-skepticism. Holistically considered, these five pillars of UP amount to a foundation of Platonic metaphysics. If UP is accepted, Plato's philosophy and the philosophy of all generations of self-identified Platonists after him present different versions of UP. Each version draws from the same five pillars of UP to a different degree and with a varying, if not sometimes different, result (Slaveva-Griffin, review, *Notre Dame Philosophical Reviews*, 2013, 345). Gerson has since gone on to argue that philosophy *as such* is constituted in some sense by a rejection of one or all of these positions (materialism, mechanism, nominalism, relativism, skepticism). Philosophy, therefore, in some sense

no value, relics of elitist ages that have little relevance to modern thought. Platonism itself is often identified as the extirpation of feeling or the radical subordination of desire to reason and intellect or a refusal to engage with the ambiguities of ordinary experience.[3] These questions also arise for anyone who wants to study Plato's dialogues with an open mind. Already in Homer we find the frequent formulaic expression about the precondition of proper exchange: he, "thinking well to them," addressed or even harangued his audience (e.g., *Iliad* 1, 73, of Calchas to Achilles). This book is addressed to anyone who wants to understand what these important ancient thinkers might have been saying, "thinking well" of them even as one encounters real difficulties of interpretation and apparent contradictions. While the *Symposium* and the *Phaedrus* may recognize the need for feeling to be directed by reason, for instance, the *Phaedo* appears to banish all feeling to the body and to make the soul the exclusive intellectual core of what it means to be a human being.[4] So what are we to think about these issues? They are also important questions because the predominant model of mind since Descartes, a model that has colored our interpretation of much earlier thought, is arguably an intellectualist model that opposes mind and feeling. One striking example of this can be seen in the late ancient Christian ascetic thought of Evagrius of Pontus, where an intellectualist model of mind, borrowed in part from Plato and Aristotle, has been thought to lead to the "extirpation"

---

is identical or equivalent to a broader view of the Platonism-tendency.

3. For a strong expression of this view, see Hugh Trevor-Roper: the essence of Platonism is its abstract idealism, that is, "its determination to identify the universal spirit which informs matter and, having identified it, to disengage it from the bewildering variety, the inert machinery, the practical compromises in which, in practice, it is trapped and buried" (*Renaissance Essays*, 35). Or again, Richard Rorty: "the Platonic quest, the attempt to get behind appearance to the intrinsic [essential] nature of reality, is hopeless" (*Philosophy and Social Hope*, 48). Or, more recently, Martha Nussbaum: "Plato's ascent leaves out of account and therefore out of love, everything about the person that is not good and fine, . . . the flaws and the faults, the neutral discrepancies, the bodily history, . . . the very fact of difference" (*Upheavals of Thought*, 499). Human need and imperfection, therefore, play no role in such love (500).

4. See the assessment of the great scholar and translator of Plato, G. M. A. Grube: "To regard philosophy as a training for death is a dangerously *negative* point of view in which *no allowance is made for the development of the human emotions*. There is good reason to regard the teaching of the *Phaedo*, splendid though it be, as *pure intellectualism divorced from life*, its final aim being *the eternal preservation of the soul in the cold storage of eternally frozen absolute Forms*" (*Plato's Thought*, 129).

of any real subjectivity,[5] despite the fact that, for Evagrius, mind or *nous* is interchangeable with heart or *kardia*.[6]

Finally, in this chapter, I want to see if the ascent to the beautiful or the good is only a feature of Platonic thought. Is there anything in Aristotle that is in any way an ascent to the beautiful and the good? When we stress the difference between Plato and Aristotle, we can often miss the sympathies and resonances we might find in their thought, despite the major differences. And an important related question: does Plato really distinguish the forms of the beautiful and the good or are they simply indiscernible, and, if they are indiscernible, does Plotinus have a similar view? In other words, I want to see if Plotinus and other major figures from late antiquity can sometimes be a better guide to interpretation of Plato and Aristotle than some or most modern scholarship.

1.1 Love and desire

First, let me take up the question of desire and reason? While from one perspective Plato makes desire the lowest part, kind, or power[7] of soul in *Republic* 4, all the functions of soul or kinds of lives have their own desires in *Republic* 9: "Just as there are three [forms] of soul, so there also appear to me to be three pleasures (*hedonai*), one form appropriate to each; and desires (*epithymiai*) and rules in the same way . . ." (*Republic* 9.580d7–8). Thus, as with eros in the *Symposium* and *Phaedrus*, so in the broader argument of the *Republic*, desire as a love of something—love of wisdom, victory, or profit (*philosophos, philonikos, philokerdes*; *Republic* 9.581c)—is a single fount of

---

5. See, for example, Rowan Williams: "The flight from contingency triumphs; Evagrius is profoundly concerned with the fight against temptations and passions, but the goal tends to appear as extirpation, not integration, the reduction of the human subject" (*The Wound of Knowledge*, 76–77).

6. For heart-mind equivalence, see Corrigan, *Evagrius and Gregory*, 67, and Evagrius, *Praktikos* 47, where the heart is equivalent to the depth of mind: ". . . only God who made us knows our mind and has no need of indications to know what is hidden in the heart"; and catching the biblical equivalence of mind and heart, *Thoughts* 37: ". . . the Lord alone is a 'knower of hearts' [cf. Acts 1:24; 15:8], 'who knows the mind of human beings' [Job 7:20], and 'who alone fashioned their hearts' [Ps. 32:15]." (For translation, see Sinkewicz, *Evagrius of Pontus*.)

7. Plato uses several terms: *merē, eidē, genē, dunameis*. Socrates calls the tripartite structure *dynameis* (443b), *eidē* (435c–439e; 440e), and *genē* (435b; 441a–d; 443d) more often than *merē* (442b–c) in *Republic* 4, and in the famous definition of inner and outer justice he recognizes the possibility of other kinds or modulations in between the ones for which he has argued.

energy that can be focused in different ways. Such a view is already implicit in *Republic* Book 6:

> When someone's desires are strongly directed to some one thing, we know, don't we, that they are thereby weaker in other directions, like a stream that has been channelled. . . . In one whose desires flow toward learning and anything like that, don't you think, they would be concerned with pleasure of the soul itself in relation to itself, and would leave behind the pleasures that come through the body, if he isn't a pretender but a true philosopher. (6.485d6–e1).

For Plato, then, desire is crucial to the life of wisdom. The central challenge of such a life is to leave behind body-directed pleasures, which ultimately weaken or fragment human life, and to awaken instead a higher axis of desire-pleasure into which the *whole* of one's desire can be focused. To live only a profit-loving life, for Socrates in *Republic* 9, is not to live a bad life, but rather an impoverished one. Wisdom is a richer, more comprehensive life. Is this merely sublimation or the failure to recognize that we are simply substituting one pleasure for another? No, this is not the case since, as we shall see below in the *Phaedo*, this higher axis is a more fully willed, agent-focused activity, whereas the body-directed axis is more passive, an object-driven focus.

Aristotle therefore follows Plato[8] when he distinguishes three kinds of desire (*orexis*): *epithymia*, *thymos*, and *boulesis*, the former two situated in the irrational soul and the last differentiated by the presence of reason or logos (*De Anima* 2.3.414b2; 3.9.432b5–6). I suggest that, for Aristotle, desire, reason, and will converge in the life of rational agency. The highest form of desire, namely, the will, takes on a new energy in the life of the practical intellect, and reason itself both transforms and is transformed by this convergence: "if the choice is to be seriously good (σπουδαία), both the reason must be true and the desire correct (τόν τε λόγον ἀληθῆ εἶναι καὶ τὴν ὄρεξιν ὀρθήν), and . . . reason and desire must pursue the same aims" (*EN* 1139a22–25; cf. *De Anima* 3.10.433a26). When we are driven by passion, desire does not have a proper or "correct" focus. Only when reason and desire work together is there the possibility of proper focused or unified aims. Is desire here subordinate to reason? This is at first unclear. All Aristotle says at the outset is that "of the practical and discursive intellect the truth is in agreement with correct desire (τοῦ δὲ πρακτικοῦ καὶ διανοητικοῦ ἀλήθεια ὁμολόγως ἔχουσα τῇ ὀρέξει τῇ ὀρθῇ)," but he later makes it very clear that in this agreement a new form of rational desire emerges; this is

---

8. For a good account of this see Gerson, *Plotinus*, 151–55.

no longer desire subordinate to reason or vice versa, but effectively a new form of being: "choice is desiring intellect or reasoning desire and such an origin is a human being" (ἢ ὀρεκτικὸς νοῦς ἡ προαίρεσις ἢ ὄρεξις διανοητική, καὶ ἡ τοιαύτη ἀρχὴ ἄνθρωπος) (1139b). Desire, therefore, is fundamental to what we mean by real agency. This is, moreover, the point of convergence where the dispositions of soul in the serious or good person (the *spoudaios* or *phronimos*) rise to the level of intellect or *nous*: "All the states of soul are tending to the same point—quite reasonably so, for when we speak of judgment, understanding, practical wisdom, and intellect, we refer to the same people as having judgment and intellect and as being practically wise and understanding" (*EN* 1143a25–28).[9] Here Aristotle is, of course, speaking of "intellect" in the sense in which someone might be said *echein noun*, to have a mind or to be minded to do something, that is, the sense of having a natural *dynamis* that can be developed in the practically wise person (*phronimos*),[10] but at the same time this is where a natural *hexis* and its subsequent development coincide. Intellect "is concerned with ultimates in both directions;" that is, "the unchangeable, first terms," and the last terms, "variable facts," things that are to be done (*EN* 1143b). The naturally gifted intelligent person grasps both: "of these we must have perception, and this perception is intellect" (1143b). So the developed intellect of the *phronimos* would presumably have an equally immediate but deeper grasp of firsts and lasts, and intellect is the point of convergence where all the states of soul meet, including thought and proper feeling, and emerge onto a new threshold of being, that is, the point where the human being becomes an agent, an ἀρχή or originative principle.

But is this apparent transformation of reason and desire in Aristotle true in any way of Plato? And can it be found even in a dialogue such as the *Phaedo* that is so often taken to characterize the "intellectualist" character of Plato's thought? As we have noted above, this character of Platonism tends to get figured into accounts of the major difference between intellectualist "Platonist" thought and different emphases on virtue and its primacy in early Christianity. Anthony Meredith, for instance, quite plausibly identifies a new emphasis upon virtue over the primacy of reason in Gregory of Nyssa.[11] Here I can only touch upon a few elements in the *Phaedo* to show that, while patristic thought might well bring its own emphasis to traditional ascetic, philosophical, and theological issues (something we might expect

---

9. *EN* 1143a25–28: Εἰσὶ δὲ πᾶσαι αἱ ἕξεις εὐλόγως εἰς ταὐτὸ τείνουσαι· λέγομεν γὰρ γνώμην καὶ σύνεσιν καὶ φρόνησιν καὶ νοῦν ἐπὶ τοὺς αὐτοὺς ἐπιφέροντες γνώμην ἔχειν καὶ νοῦν ἤδη, καὶ φρονίμους καὶ συνετούς.

10. Cf. *EN* 1143b6–7.

11. Meredith, *The Cappadocians*, 60–61.

to be the case anyway), this is entirely the wrong contrast to draw, even from the *Phaedo*, between a supposedly new practical Christianity and an intellectualist Platonism.

Let me take up, at the outset, a misapprehension about "separation," a misapprehension typical again of scholars who see the separation of soul from body in the *Phaedo* as the privileging of intellect and the ultimate rejection of body and feeling. Socrates argues, in fact, for a rather different, more nuanced position. Just as the forms are separate, pure, and by themselves— and we cannot hope to see them purely as long as "we have a body and our soul contaminated with such an evil," so the *practice* of dying (67d8-10) is a progressive purification, in order to separate the soul from the body as far as possible (67c-d). Socrates spells out in the subsequent argument what is involved in this separation. Separation means (1) *turning away*[12] from body (64e: καθ' ὅσον δύναται ἀφεστάναι αὐτοῦ, πρὸς δὲ τὴν ψυχὴν τετράφθαι), not *associating* with or *touching upon* it (65c: καὶ καθ' ὅσον δύναται μὴ κοινωνοῦσα αὐτῷ μηδ' ἁπτομένη),[13] not *participating beyond necessity* in its possessions and adornments (64d-e: καθ' ὅσον μὴ πολλὴ ἀνάγκη μετέχειν αὐτῶν), but (2) *desiring* what is real (ὀρέγηται τοῦ ὄντος); and this also means (3) that we make it a matter of *habitual practice* to gather and collect the soul by itself (67c: ἐθίσαι ... συναγείρεσθαί τε καὶ ἀθροίζεσθαι); to purify it as a *practical occupation* (67b: πραγματεία; cf. 64e); (4) lovers of wisdom "are in training for dying" (67e); (5) they *desire* to have their soul by itself, but this involves not extinguishing but awakening a different axis of desire, not for wealth or body, or even thought only, but thought with *hope* (68a1: ἐλπίς), *desire* (66b; 66e; 67e; 68a), *gladness*, joyfulness, *love and longing* (*eros*) for wisdom (68a1-2: εἰ μὴ ἄσμενοι ἐκεῖσε ἴοιεν, οἷ ἀφικομένοις ἐλπίς ἐστιν οὗ διὰ βίου ἤρων τυχεῖν· ἤρων δὲ φρονήσεως).

This range of feeling inscribed in the notion of separation and the pursuit of practical wisdom is hardly the extirpation of desire or an exclusively intellectualist pursuit, according to common readings of the *Phaedo*, but plainly the *joyful practice of moral excellence*; just as in the *Theaetetus*, "becoming like the divine" is not to contemplate abstractly but *"to become just and holy with the help of wisdom"* (176b: ὁμοίωσις δὲ δίκαιον καὶ ὅσιον μετὰ φρονήσεως γενέσθαι.). In other words, as Pierre Hadot has well pointed out, philosophy in antiquity is not an abstract discipline, but a way of life, a way of purgation of passion and a training or purification of desire. And

---

12. Compare *Republic* 7.518c-519a.

13. For "community" and "touching upon" compare the language used at *Phaedo* 100d5-6; *Republic* 6.484b; 490b-c; 7.531d; *Symposium* 212a4 and 5.

such purification of desire is a way of integrated living by separation[14] in accordance with the proper ordering of things: not to be just or brave *because of* deficiency or cowardice, that is, in a market exchange of "pleasures for pleasures, pains for pains, and fears for fears" (69a–b); instead, Socrates argues, wisdom makes "true virtue" possible. It is not cowardice that causes courage or an exchange of bronze for gold;[15] *wisdom* is the only real basis for any buying or selling (69a–b)—the purgation of pleasures and desires and "a kind of purification" (69c). This is the polar opposite of sublimation or covert substitution. Human beings live between two possible poles: the loves and desires of the body and the higher erotic focus of the soul (just as in the *Symposium* and *Phaedrus*, but muted here);[16] and the ultimate focus of the latter is the awakening of a transcendental, but eminently practical, organization of one's being, focused not upon some *part* of oneself but rather upon *something bigger than* oneself. This is what the practice of living thought means, and it is noteworthy in the *Phaedo* that desire plays a crucial role in the sphere of body *and* soul. Just as particulars strive for or desire the forms (at 75a2; b1)—that is, individual things or anything that resembles the forms—so here the soul "desires what is real" (65c–d: ὀρέγηται).[17] It is no wonder that Aristotle considered participation to be a poetical way of talking about the motive organizational force of love or desire, both within and outside of organisms, that he saw as operative throughout the cosmos. At the same time, however, the real germ of Aristotle's later theory of movement by *desire* is already present in the *Phaedo*.[18] Desire is therefore fundamental to the views of Plato and Aristotle; and desire and virtue characterize the life of philosophy in the *Phaedo*, just as they do in the *Symposium*, *Republic*, and *Phaedrus*. We shall return to this in later sections.

---

14. Compare *Republic* 6.485d–486a for the contrast between concentrating upon the pleasures of soul "itself by itself" (d11), leaving those of the body behind, such as money and lavish expense (d12–e1), on the one hand, and the complementary position of "not participating in any meanness of spirit, which would be utterly opposed to a soul that is going to desire *as a whole and in its totality the divine and the human*" (486a5–6: τοῦ ὅλου καὶ παντὸς ἀεὶ ἐπορέξεσθαι θείου τε καὶ ἀνθρωπίνου). The movement away from body is a movement of desire for the whole.

15. The emphasis is upon things being exchanged for money. I cannot help thinking of the exchange of gold for bronze in the Glaucus-Diomedes episode in *Iliad* 6, 119–236, though this does not directly appear in the *Phaedo*.

16. Rowe, *Phaedo*, 145–46 on *Phaedo* 68a1–2.

17. Compare *Republic* 6.486a4–10, especially the phrase at 486a5–6: τοῦ ὅλου καὶ παντὸς ἀεὶ ἐπορέξεσθαι θείου τε καὶ ἀνθρωπίνου.

18. On this important theme see Nussbaum, *Aristotle's De Motu Animalium*, 57–106; Lear, *Aristotle*, 1–54 and 152ff.

1.2 Intellect and desire

But can intellect—even the divine intellect—really desire anything at all? For Aristotle and for Plotinus, intellect surely is pure, unmixed, and impassible. Famously in the *De Anima*, intellect has a double power: as passive, it "becomes" everything;[19] as active, it "makes" everything, being an instantaneously actualizing energy. Only this latter active aspect, Aristotle says in the *De Anima*, survives death.[20] So what about the power to become everything—the developmental, receptive aspect? Is there nothing of the divine in the developmental aspect of intellect? And how is the intellect of the wise person, the *phronimos*, related to the divine intellect? In Aristotle, the divine intellect or unmoved mover moves by being desired, not desiring; and if so, the intellect of the *phronimos* must be a desiring intellect. And if divine things are things we cannot so much learn as experience and receive (as fragment 15 of *De Philosophia* seems to indicate[21]), then surely in relation to the unmoved mover our intellects must not only be loving but also receptive, even if such a relation cannot be construed as passivity in the sense of undergoing physical change? Moreover, according to Aristotle, there are forty-seven or fifty-five unmoved movers to account for the motion of the celestial spheres.[22] But if all unmoved movers after the primary mover must be moved by love of the first, then surely they themselves must be loving activities and also "receptive" of motion in some sense? All of these questions do not receive clear answers in Aristotle (though we shall return to them below).

A similar problem can be felt in the thought of Plotinus, for in this case, it has been observed that Plotinus' emphasis on the "impassibility" of intellect (see especially *Ennead* III.6[26]) makes it impossible that there should be "any desire or *orexis* in the life of intellect" (as Plotinus does say, in fact, in IV.7[2].13, 3).[23] However, this cannot be the case since Plotinus formulates intellect's "desire" in striking ways: intellect "is always desiring

19. *De Anima* 3.5.430a1–16.
20. Ibid., 430a16–25.
21. Compare Aristotle, fr. 15 (Rose/Ross, https://archive.org/details/worksofaristotle12arisuoft), preserved in Synesius and Michael Psellus: ". . . as Aristotle claims, that those who are being initiated into the mysteries are to be expected not to learn anything, but to suffer some change, to be put into a certain condition, i.e. to be fitted for some purpose." Compare Plato, *Phaedrus* (and Simmias in the *Phaedo*); Hebrews 5:8; and Dionysius the Areopagite's famous dictum about learning from sacred writers, or discovering the truth oneself, or not only learning but "experiencing the divine things" (*pathein ta theia*) (*DN* 2.9).
22. Cf. *Metaphysics* 12.8, especially 1073b1–3 and 1074a10–17.
23. G. Leroux, *Plotin. VI 8*, 256–57.

and always attaining" (he says in III.8[30].11, 22–24: καὶ ἐφιέμενος ἀεὶ καὶ ἀεὶ τυγχάνων), and this certainly seems at odds with much else in the *Enneads*. A. H. Armstrong, for instance, thought that it, in fact, contradicted the rest of Plotinus' thought.[24] But I wonder if this is really true for Plotinus or for Aristotle. One might argue in relation to Aristotle that it is soul, or world soul in some sense, that desires or loves, not the intellect that acts as the final cause. But, on the other hand, as we noted above, surely our intellects too must be moved impassibly by love of the first mover? Indeed, surely all secondary intellects (including those forty-seven or fifty-five intellects that are introduced to account concretely for the movements of the heavenly spheres in *Metaphysics* 12.8) must be moved by love for the primary unmoved mover? Whether or not this is the case for Aristotle, it seems to me that, for Plotinus, intellect cannot be conceived as a static, fixed essence; when Plotinus examines the nature of intellect in itself, intellect may appear to be self-contained, but its real nature is dynamic—to be in search of its being, its *ousia*, and to be drawn out of itself incessantly into itself and into the good.[25] Therefore, desire in some sense must characterize both its longing for that which is beyond it and its search for its own identity. This is, in fact, what Plotinus explicitly states in VI.7[38].35: "intellect . . . has one power for thinking by which it looks at the things in itself, and one by which it looks at what transcends it[;] . . . the one is the contemplation of intellect in its right mind, and the other is intellect in love, . . . drunk on the nectar[;] . . . better for it to be drunk . . . than . . . more respectably sober."[26] Desire, love—even the undoing of its own sober nature—are crucial then to the being and the coming-to-be of intellect from the one in Plotinus.

However, if this is just too much to accept about the divine intellect, one might plausibly try to distinguish desire (*orexis, epithymia*) from love or *eros*, and, therefore, conclude that Plotinus might admit love in intellect, even "drunken" love as a metaphor, but not the lowliest kinds of desire, like *epithymia*, for instance, the lowest form of the tripartite soul in *Republic* Book 4. Certainly, in some works, Plotinus distinguishes desire qua desire from substance or *ousia*. He distinguishes *epithymia, thymos*, and *boulesis*,

24. Armstrong, "Eternity, Life and Movement," 67–74.

25. See VI.7[38].37, 20. This is one source, I suggest, of Gregory of Nyssa's doctrine of *epektasis*, according to which the soul is continually drawn out of herself into God (see Daniélou, *Platonisme et Théologie mystique*, 309–26).

26. VI.7[38].35, 19–27 (trans. Armstrong): καὶ τὸν νοῦν τοίνυν τὴν μὲν ἔχειν δύναμιν εἰς τὸ νοεῖν, ᾗ τὰ ἐν αὐτῷ βλέπει, τὴν δέ, ᾗ τὰ ἐπέκεινα αὐτοῦ ἐπιβολῇ τινι καὶ παραδοχῇ, καθ' ἣν καὶ πρότερον ἑώρα μόνον καὶ ὁρῶν ὕστερον καὶ νοῦν ἔσχε καὶ ἕν ἐστι. καὶ ἔστιν ἐκείνη μὲν ἡ θέα νοῦ ἔμφρονος, αὕτη δὲ νοῦς ἐρῶν, ὅταν ἄφρων γένηται μεθυσθεὶς τοῦ νέκταρος· τότε ἐρῶν γίνεται ἁπλωθεὶς εἰς εὐπάθειαν τῷ κόρῳ· καὶ ἔστιν αὐτῷ μεθύειν βέλτιον ἢ σεμνοτέρῳ εἶναι τοιαύτης μέθης. Cf. Plato, *Phaedrus* 244d2–5; 245a5–9.

DESIRE, LOVE, AND ASCENT THROUGH THE BEAUTIFUL   11

for example, as forms of desire (*orexis*), but implies that this tripartition is a division of *desires*, not a feature of the *substance* of soul (IV.4.28, 70–73). So far we can see that *boulesis* is a rational desire of the soul, and we can feel confident that the lowest forms of desire could never be admitted into the rarefied atmosphere of the divine intellect; but we would be wrong, for Plotinus is prepared to go far beyond this. In V.3[49], for instance, he seems to suggest that there is even a pre-intellectual *epithymia* involved in the full coming-to-be of intellect itself, that is, not simply *eros* or *orexis*, but *desire* right at the very root of intellect's coming to be that is there implicitly even in any *epithymia* or dim divination of the good (to use Socrates' term from *Republic* 6.505d–e): "so that it [pre-intellect in some sense] moved to it not as intellect but as sight not yet seeing . . . so that it desired something else having dimly an image in itself, but came out having grasped something else that it made many in itself" (V.3[49].11).[27] If the uses of words and their resonant meanings are anything to go by, then I suggest that V.3[49].11 proposes a more radical view of desire, namely, that *epithymia* (the lowest form of the tripartite soul in Plato's *Republic* Book 4)—probably not as a species of qualitative *orexis*, *ephesis*, *eros*, but rather as a pre-substantial anticipatory form of what in intellect proper will become thought—reaches right down into the substantial articulation of intellect's being, desire, and love.

However we are to interpret such passages in Plotinus, we can already see that love and desire are the cause of movement not only in the sublunary and celestial worlds of Aristotle; that they seem to forge a new emergent collaborative identity in our intellects, even discursive reason, and point beyond themselves to the natures of all secondary intellects in Aristotle; and that love and desire radically pervade the nature of divine mind or intellect itself in Plotinus. In other words, the life of mind is pervaded in these thinkers by a whole range of feeling that has not been properly appreciated precisely because these feelings are attached to mental activity, and this does not fit some preconceived notions of mind in the modern world or our readings of what mind might have meant in antiquity. We need now to look at one of the most famous passages from Aristotle's theology[28] to see

27. V.3[49].11, 5–9: ὥστε ὥρμησε μὲν ἐπ' αὐτὸ οὐχ ὡς νοῦς, ἀλλ' ὡς ὄψις οὔπω ἰδοῦσα, ἐξῆλθε δὲ ἔχουσα ὅπερ αὐτὴ ἐπλήθυνεν· ὥστε ἄλλου μὲν ἐπεθύμησεν ἀορίστως ἔχουσα ἐπ' αὐτῇ φάντασμά τι, ἐξῆλθε δὲ ἄλλο λαβοῦσα ἐν αὐτῇ αὐτὸ πολὺ ποιήσασα.

28. For the sake of simplicity, by "theology" I do not mean anything more than the movement of Aristotle's thought from physics to metaphysics to "first philosophy" as we find, for example, in *Metaphysics* Book 12 as a whole, especially the later chapters 7–10. There are many other texts traditionally assumed to be representative of Aristotle's natural theology, such as *Metaphysics* 6.1 and 11.7, together with perhaps earlier texts (e.g., *De Coelo, Physics*), some lost (e.g., *De Philosophia*), but it is traditionally thought that *Metaphysics* 12 is Aristotle's mature thought on the subject. For a rejection

what more we can reasonably discover about the nature of intellect and its relation to everything in the cosmos.

1.3 Ascent to the beautiful and the good: Aristotle, *Metaphysics* 12.7

Is there anything then in Aristotle that involves an ascent to the beautiful and the good? I shall argue here that Aristotle's thought is structurally developed—at least in part—out of the lesser and greater mysteries of Socrates-Diotima's speech in the *Symposium*. I shall, first, set out Aristotle's notion of the unmoved mover (in the *Physics* and *Metaphysics*), next compare this with what I shall argue is its first recognizable precursor in Plato's *Symposium*,[29] and then chart out some of the consequences of this in later thought, consequences that clearly arise from an interpretation of crucial texts in Plato and Aristotle.

For Aristotle, on H. H. Joachim's account,[30] god is the first originative source of motion, the only cause adequate to account for the unceasing continuity of change in the universe; God is the ultimate object of desire, that is, the ultimate final cause that moves "as being loved."[31] god is also the ultimate ideal towards which all things strive to assimilate themselves, because god is the only absolutely real activity (i.e., form without matter) or the only completely self-fulfilled and self-fulfilling activity without potentiality. According to Aristotle, the unmoved mover, identified as god, unlike the good and the beautiful in Plato, eternally thinks (but this is not self-movement), and god thinks about the best thing, which is his thought (since thinking is the best of activities), so that thought and its object are the same: god's life is a thinking of thinking.[32] Here there is no hint of things that make human life valuable such as feelings, emotions, and loves. The unmoved mover is impassible, unmixed, separate from everything, on the one hand. Yet, on

---

of this general assumption, see Bodéüs, *Aristotle*, passim, who argues that Aristotle is more closely in tune with popular Greek religion, that theology is not a science for him and that his theoretical philosophy about the unmoved mover is not actually a part of theology. I welcome Bodéüs' inclusive approach to the study of Aristotle, but I see no reason not to include "the first" (*Metaphysics* 12.1072a13); the unmoved mover (1072a24–25); that moves as being loved (1072b3); and that is designated "*archē*" and "the god" (at 1072b14; 25; 28–29; 30).

29. On this see also Chang, "Plato's Form of the Beautiful," 431–46.
30. Joachim, *Aristotle. The Nicomachean Ethics*, 291.
31. *Metaphysics* 12.7.1072b3: κινεῖ δὴ ὡς ἐρώμενον.
32. *Metaphysics* 12.9.1074b34–5.

the other hand, it is the ideal of love and of all striving, in what seems to be a deeply puzzling way.

Another way of expressing this puzzlement might be to ask whether the unmoved mover is in any sense an efficient cause—a real mover. Simplicius in late antiquity points out that the unmoved mover fits the definition of an efficient cause—"whence the first source of change or rest" (*Phys.* II.3.194b29–30; Simpl. 10.1361.12ff.), but Aristotle never acknowledges this or specifies in what sense the unmoved mover might be an efficient cause (a problem of which Simplicius is well aware: 10.1363.12–14). Even more puzzling is H. H. Joachim's comment that Aristotle's god is "the real coalescence of formal, final, and efficient causes."[33] How can this be so, if notions of efficiency or directing agency are all derived from the natural, technical, and anthropomorphic realms? What kind of coalescence might there be in this case? And how could any efficient notion of divine moving or divine craftsmanship escape the anthropomorphic way Plato makes his demiurge in the *Timaeus,* and *Statesman* "deliberate" and *do* various things?

Let me look first at one of the most famous passages from Aristotle's *Metaphysics* and then compare it with what I argue is its model—at least in part—in the *Symposium* and *Republic*. As we have seen above, the unmoved mover in *Metaphysics* 12.7 moves the first heaven unceasingly just as "the object of desire and the object of thought" move without being moved. God as pure act is the prime mover who moves the sphere of the fixed stars immediately by non-reciprocal contact (e.g., in the case where a mover moves without itself being moved, just as a person who grieves us "touches" us, but we do not "touch" him, Aristotle observes),[34] and imparts to it a uniform, continuous, and eternal motion that is closest to the immobility of the unmoved mover itself. The other spheres, in their turn, are moved eternally and continually, but not uniformly, because of the growing number of intermediary movers between them and the prime mover; and this continues down to the sphere of the sublunary world, where the circular movement of the upper spheres gives way to the cyclical transformation of the elements and the generation, destruction, growth, and change of animals, and where individual animals are so far removed from the prime mover that they cannot even attain to the continuous eternity of the upper spheres.[35]

So far, the unmoved mover is as remote as it would appear nearly 2000 years later in the words of Shakespeare's Julius Caesar, who cannot be moved like ordinary mortals: "I am constant as the northern star, Of

---

33. Joachim, *Aristotle. The Nicomachean Ethics,* 291n1.
34. *Physics* 3.2; *De Gen. et Corr.* 2.6.323a25.
35. See Tricot, *La Métaphysique,* Vol. 2, 672–4n2.

whose true-fixed and resting quality/There is no fellow in the firmament."[36] Yet Aristotle's unmoved mover is plainly *not* like Julius Caesar altogether, because, in *Metaphysics* 12, chapter 7, its capacity to move appears to reach into every desire, every willed action and every thought, for the object of desire and the object of thought, Aristotle argues, move in one and same way: "... they move without being moved. And the primary objects of desire and of thought are the same. For the apparent beautiful/good is the object of appetite, and the real beautiful/good is the primary object of rational wish" (ἐπιθυμητὸν μὲν γὰρ τὸ φαινόμενον καλόν, βουλητὸν δὲ πρῶτον τὸ ὂν καλόν). The movement of pure thought, therefore, reaches dynamically into every desire (ἐπιθυμητὸν) and every willed action (βουλητὸν)—even, one might say, into desire as *epithymia*, namely, the lowest part or power of the tripartite soul in *Republic* Book 4!

Aristotle concludes this section by arguing implicitly that "the beautiful," namely, something that in his thought denotes final causality (οὗ δ' ἕνεκα ... τὴν τοῦ καλοῦ χώραν),[37] points ultimately to the first or supreme *best*,

36. Shakespeare, *Julius Caesar*, Act 3, 1, 68–70.

37. See *De Partibus Animalium* 645a23-36, which I cite here because it catches something profound in Aristotle's view of nature as a whole ranging from the highest to the supposedly lowest things: "For in all physical things there is something wonderful; and just as Heraclitus, when the strangers who came to visit him found him warming himself at the furnace in the kitchen and hesitated to go in, reported to have bidden them not to be afraid to enter, as even in that kitchen divinities were present, so we should venture on the study of every kind of animal without distaste; for each and all will reveal to us something natural and something beautiful. Absence of haphazard and conduciveness of everything to an end are to be found in Nature's works in the highest degree, and the resultant end of her generations and combinations is a form of the beautiful. If any person thinks the examination of the rest of the animal kingdom an unworthy task, he must hold in like disesteem the study of man. For no one can look at the primordia of the human frame—blood, flesh, bones, vessels, and the like—without much repugnance. Moreover, when any one of the parts or structures, be it which it may, is under discussion, it must not be supposed that it is its material composition to which attention is being directed or which is the object of the discussion, but the relation of such part to the total form. Similarly, the true object of architecture is not bricks, mortar, or timber, but the house; and so the principal object of natural philosophy is not the material elements, but their composition, and the totality of the form, independently of which they have no existence" (trans. Peck and Forster, adapted [Loeb]). (Ἐν πᾶσι γὰρ τοῖς φυσικοῖς ἔνεστί τι θαυμαστόν· καὶ καθάπερ Ἡράκλειτος λέγεται πρὸς τοὺς ξένους εἰπεῖν τοὺς βουλομένους ἐντυχεῖν αὐτῷ, οἳ ἐπειδὴ προσιόντες εἶδον αὐτὸν θερόμενον πρὸς τῷ ἰπνῷ ἔστησαν (ἐκέλευε γὰρ αὐτοὺς εἰσιέναι θαρροῦντας· εἶναι γὰρ καὶ ἐνταῦθα θεούς), οὕτω καὶ πρὸς τὴν ζήτησιν περὶ ἑκάστου τῶν ζῴων προσιέναι δεῖ μὴ δυσωπούμενον ὡς ἐν ἅπασιν ὄντος τινὸς φυσικοῦ καὶ καλοῦ. Τὸ γὰρ μὴ τυχόντως ἀλλ' ἕνεκά τινος ἐν τοῖς τῆς φύσεως ἔργοις ἐστὶ καὶ μάλιστα· οὗ δ' ἕνεκα συνέστηκεν ἢ γέγονε τέλους, τὴν τοῦ καλοῦ χώραν εἴληφεν. Εἰ δέ τις τὴν περὶ τῶν ἄλλων ζῴων θεωρίαν ἄτιμον εἶναι νενόμικε, τὸν αὐτὸν τρόπον οἴεσθαι χρὴ καὶ περὶ αὑτοῦ· οὐκ ἔστι γὰρ ἄνευ πολλῆς δυσχερείας ἰδεῖν ἐξ ὧν συνέστηκε τὸ τῶν ἀνθρώπων γένος, οἷον αἷμα, σάρκες, ὀστᾶ, φλέβες καὶ τὰ τοιαῦτα

namely: "the first [that] is always *best*, or analogous to the *best*" (καὶ ἔστιν ἄριστον ἀεὶ ἢ ἀνάλογον τὸ πρῶτον). Aristotle therefore points to both the immanent good as "first best or analogous to the best" and the transcendent good as that to which everything else might be analogous. And as we know at the end of Book 12, the unmoved mover, explicitly in chapter 10 called "the good and the best," is present to everything *both* as transcendent, or separate, *and* as immanent, or as a function of internal order.[38] If this is the character of Aristotle's thought throughout the *Corpus Aristotelicum*, then the unmoved mover is not an infinitely remote final cause, but in producing motion "as being loved," is also an inner dynamic cause and an actual beginning of every impulse and thought—both immanent to, yet separate from, each thing. This is perhaps supported by the following well-known passage:

> On such a beginning, then, hang the heaven and nature. And it is a way of life such as the best that we enjoy for a short time (for it is always so, which for us is impossible), since its activity is also pleasure. And because of this waking, perception, and thinking are sweetest, and hopes and memories because of these. And thinking in itself is of that which is best in itself, and thinking in the fullest sense of what is best in the fullest sense. And intellect thinks itself by participation in the object of thought; for it becomes intelligible by touching and thinking, so that intellect and object of thought are the same. For that which receives the object of thought and the substance, is intellect, and it is active in having the object. Therefore, having rather than receiving is the divine that thought seems to have, and contemplation is the sweetest and best. If, then, god always has that good activity which we sometimes do, this is a thing of wonder; and if still more so, more wonderful still. And god is so better. And life too indeed belongs to god; for the activity of intellect is life, and god is activity; and god's acivity in itself is a best and eternal life. We

μόρια. Ὁμοίως τε δεῖ νομίζειν τὸν περὶ οὑτινοσοῦν τῶν μορίων ἢ τῶν σκευῶν διαλεγόμενον μὴ περὶ τῆς ὕλης ποιεῖσθαι τὴν μνήμην, μηδὲ ταύτης χάριν, ἀλλὰ τῆς ὅλης μορφῆς, οἷον καὶ περὶ οἰκίας, ἀλλὰ μὴ πλίνθων καὶ πηλοῦ καὶ ξύλων· καὶ τὸν περὶ φύσεως περὶ τῆς συνθέσεως καὶ τῆς ὅλης οὐσίας, ἀλλὰ μὴ περὶ τούτων ἃ μὴ συμβαίνει χωριζόμενά ποτε τῆς οὐσίας αὐτῶν.)

38. *Metaphysics* 12.10.1075a10–15: We must also examine in what sense the nature of the whole has the good and the best, whether as something separate and itself in itself or as the order. Or is it in both senses, like an army; for the well-being of an army is in the order and is the general; but more the general, for he is not the cause of the order, but the order is because of him. (Ἐπισκεπτέον δὲ καὶ ποτέρως ἔχει ἡ τοῦ ὅλου φύσις τὸ ἀγαθὸν καὶ τὸ ἄριστον, πότερον κεχωρισμένον τι καὶ αὐτὸ καθ᾿ αὑτό, ἢ τὴν τάξιν. ἢ ἀμφοτέρως ὥσπερ στράτευμα; καὶ γὰρ ἐν τῇ τάξει τὸ εὖ καὶ ὁ στρατηγός, καὶ μᾶλλον οὗτος· οὐ γὰρ οὗτος διὰ τὴν τάξιν ἀλλ᾿ ἐκείνη διὰ τοῦτόν ἐστιν.)

say therefore that god is a living creature, eternal, best, so that life continually lasting and eternal belong to god; for this is god (*Metaphysics* 12.7.1072b13-30).[39]

What is striking about this passage is that Aristotle weaves into the fabric of god's life the significance not only of human life at its highest but of *all* experience at whatever level of existence. God's way or mode of life (διαγωγή) is the purest pleasure, something we experience only intermittently. Furthermore, all animal activities throughout the cosmos—rational and non-rational, both intellect *and* feelings—are not only dependent on god's life; they are in a sense transfixed at the core by that life: "And because of this waking, perception, and thinking are sweetest, and hopes and memories because of these." First, the immediacy and pleasure of an activity such as waking up or hoping are *causally and internally* related to the activity of god's life. The pleasure of remembrance, however mysteriously, is a participation in the life of the unmoved mover. God's life is eternal, but it matches and exceeds the span of any lifetime, office, age, or epoch (αἰὼν συνεχής).[40] In other words, it somehow matches, measures, and yet exceeds our own lived experiences as a whole.

Second, even the passive, receptive side of human thought—namely, its participation in its object and its becoming, touching,[41] and having its object—seems somehow to be prefigured in divine thought itself, at least in the above passage. Or, in other words, something of human development

---

39. *Metaphysics* 12.7.1072b13-30: ἐκ τοιαύτης ἄρα ἀρχῆς ἤρτηται ὁ οὐρανὸς καὶ ἡ φύσις. διαγωγὴ δ' ἐστὶν οἵα ἡ ἀρίστη μικρὸν χρόνον ἡμῖν (οὕτω γὰρ ἀεὶ ἐκεῖνο· ἡμῖν μὲν γὰρ ἀδύνατον), ἐπεὶ καὶ ἡδονὴ ἡ ἐνέργεια τούτου (καὶ διὰ τοῦτο ἐγρήγορσις αἴσθησις νόησις ἥδιστον, ἐλπίδες δὲ καὶ μνῆμαι διὰ ταῦτα). ἡ δὲ νόησις ἡ καθ' αὑτὴν τοῦ καθ' αὑτὸ ἀρίστου, καὶ ἡ μάλιστα τοῦ μάλιστα. αὑτὸν δὲ νοεῖ ὁ νοῦς κατὰ μετάληψιν τοῦ νοητοῦ· νοητὸς γὰρ γίγνεται θιγγάνων καὶ νοῶν, ὥστε ταὐτὸν νοῦς καὶ νοητόν. τὸ γὰρ δεκτικὸν τοῦ νοητοῦ καὶ τῆς οὐσίας νοῦς, ἐνεργεῖ δὲ ἔχων, ὥστ' ἐκείνου μᾶλλον τοῦτο ὃ δοκεῖ ὁ νοῦς θεῖον ἔχειν, καὶ ἡ θεωρία τὸ ἥδιστον καὶ ἄριστον. εἰ οὖν οὕτως εὖ ἔχει, ὡς ἡμεῖς ποτέ, ὁ θεὸς ἀεί, θαυμαστόν· εἰ δὲ μᾶλλον, ἔτι

θαυμασιώτερον. ἔχει δὲ ὧδε. καὶ ζωὴ δέ γε ὑπάρχει· ἡ γὰρ νοῦ ἐνέργεια ζωή, ἐκεῖνος δὲ ἡ ἐνέργεια· ἐνέργεια δὲ ἡ καθ' αὑτὴν ἐκείνου ζωὴ ἀρίστη καὶ ἀΐδιος. φαμὲν δὴ τὸν θεὸν εἶναι ζῷον ἀΐδιον ἄριστον, ὥστε ζωὴ καὶ αἰὼν συνεχὴς καὶ ἀΐδιος ὑπάρχει τῷ θεῷ· τοῦτο γὰρ ὁ θεός. Compare *EN* 1154b24-28. For a different reading of the text and its meaning see Bodéüs, *Aristotle*, 22–29.

40. For the range of meaning for *aiōn* see *LSJ* sv.

41. See Ross, *Metaphysics*, vol. 2, 277 (on 1051b24): "The metaphor of contact in the description of simple apprehension recurs [at] 1072b21. Its implications are (1) the absence of any possibility of error.... (2) The apparent... absence of a medium in the case of touch. [It] means an apprehension which is infallible and direct." Cf. Tricot, *La Métaphysique*, vol. 2, 1986, 682n1 (on θιγγάνων and κατὰ μετάληψιν). Compare *Symposium* 212a4-5 (ἐφαπτομένῳ) and *Republic* 7.534c. For both terms together see Plotinus VI.9[9].4, 27; V.3[49].10, 43.

and of the achievement of thought appears to be pre-figured in divine thinking. They are not pre-contained as developmental processes, however, but only to the degree that they are active and self-complete energies. If god's life is a "thinking of thinking," as Aristotle characterizes it in *Metaphysics* 12.9, then such thinking must be self-dependent contemplation, not in a private, solitary sense, as it might be for us, but rather supremely active and present dynamically to the cosmos. And if love and desire characterize our lives as developing, never-fully-realized energies, then why should their *telos* and ultimate cause not be the fullest energy of love and desire possible?

This way of interpreting the above passage, I suggest, also casts light upon Aristotle's complex notion of actuality or energy. Just as teaching and learning involve two different subjects, but constitute a single activity (*energeia*) from different perspectives,[42] so also what is an action or an external motive force from one viewpoint is a manifestation of the deepest reality from another viewpoint. The same activity involves two distinct subjects[43] but is nonetheless a single activity seen from two different points of view. What is divine from one aspect may be quite human from another! At the same time, the Aristotelian scale of nature embodies a hierarchy of different developmental forms, the lower forms always requiring the higher forms for their fuller actualization and explanation. All lower forms, therefore, require the energy of higher-order forms to give them their meaning. God is not therefore an explanation or cause remote from worms, butterflies, hopes, and thoughts, but their ultimate and yet proper meaning present to them from the beginning.[44]

42. Aristotle, *Physics* 8.255a33–b5; 3.202a13–21.

43. Aristotle, *Physics* 202b7–8; Cf. Plotinus, VI.8[39].6, 19–22; compare the argument of IV.4[28].28 culminating in 28, 69–72; for the two-act theory, Rutten, "La Doctrine des Deux Actes," 100–106; Lloyd, *Anatomy of Neoplatonism*, 98–101; Emilsson, *Plotinus on Intellect*, 22–68.

44. This is not only so in the case of the parts of animals, even "unworthy" parts (see *De Partibus Animalium* (*PA*) 645a23–36, cited above note 37); and from a developmental viewpoint, even the case with the quality of a fluid like blood, since the blood as the "matter of the body" has a major developmental influence upon the formation of tissue and the quality of "natural" intelligence in different animals, and therefore, has a part to play in the development of higher order functions, such as the active virtues, intelligence, wisdom, and the spiritual life (on the role of natural virtues, see *EN* 1144b32–1145a2; 1151a15–20; *EE* 1234a27; *MM* 1198a2ff.; on the blood and the development of lower and higher functions, see *PA* 647b29–648a11; *DA* 421a20ff.). It is also true more profoundly still for Aristotle, I suggest, from a top-down perspective that god's activity reaches into bare potencies, into movements that are incomplete—even into irrational hopes or joys. Divine motive power in the cosmos holds not only for activities or energies, but also pervades *all* movement, even incomplete movements that do not necessarily rise to the level of formal intelligibility or purpose—such as good-fortune and orientations to the good that, strictly speaking, fall below the level of intelligibility,

according to one important text from the *Eudemian Ethics* (for difficulties in the text and related issues, see Bodéüs, *Aristotle*, 158–68; van der Eijk, *Medicine and Philosophy*, 238–58. (The vexed question of divination in Plato and Aristotle is certainly relevant, but is beyond the scope of the present enquiry.)

We can agree, Aristotle argues, that virtue and wisdom create well-being, but what gives rise to good fortune or "hitting well upon the good" (*eutychia*)? Surely, some people are just lucky, just as other people have blue or brown eyes, Aristotle observes. But what makes them lucky? It's clearly not wisdom or skill since lucky people cannot explain why they get things right. In fact, some lucky people are foolish in those matters in which they have good fortune. Can this be because they are loved by a god, as in popular thought, and so their fortune is externally directed for them?

Aristotle rules this possibility out because it would be absurd for a god or divinity to love a lucky but foolish person rather than the best or wisest person. Is good fortune, then, in any way because of nature or chance? Aristotle ultimately answers that the starting point of every movement in the soul, of all natural desire both of reasoning/thought and irrational impulses/desires is the god; and because of this, people who are without rational activity can make the right fortunate choice because of the movement of the god in them, while wise people also have the movement of the god whereby, together with experience and habit, they can calculate the future. Both rational and irrational divination "use" god, but god moves more strongly and more immediately in beings whose reasoning faculty is "disengaged," whereas in wise people god moves through the intermediary of "the divine in us." Aristotle puts this as follows:

> Is there some starting point which does not have another starting point outside, which can do this sort of thing because it is of such a kind (ἡ ἀρχὴ ... ἄλλη ἔξω, αὕτη δὲ [διὰ τί] τοιαύτη τῷ εἶναι τὸ τοιοῦτο δύναται ποιεῖν)? ... This is what we are looking for: what is the starting point of movement in the soul? And what it is is clear. Just as in the whole the starting point is the god, so too in the individual (τίς ἡ τῆς κινήσεως ἀρχὴ ἐν τῇ ψυχῇ. δῆλον δὴ ὥσπερ ἐν τῷ ὅλῳ θεός, [καὶ] κἂν ἐκείνῳ). For in a way the divine in us (τὸ ἐν ἡμῖν θεῖον) moves everything, but the starting point of reason is not reason, but something greater. What then could be greater than science except the god; for virtue is an instrument of intellect. And for this reason, they are called fortunate who when they have impulses succeed though they lack reason (οἳ ἂν ὁρμήσωσι, κατορθοῦσιν ἄλογοι ὄντες), and it is not profitable for them to deliberate, for they have such a starting point which is stronger than intellect and deliberation; the others have reason, but they do not have this, and they have divine inspiration (ἐνθουσιασμόν), ... they hit the mark, though they do not have reason (ἄλογοι γὰρ ὄντες ἐπιτυγχάνουσι). The divination of those who are intelligent and wise is also swift, and it may almost be said that we must distinguish divination founded on reason, but some people use this by experience, others by habituation in observation. These forms make use of God; and he well sees both the future and the present, and in those whose reason is disengaged (καὶ ὧν ἀπολύεται ὁ λόγος οὗτος). That is why melancholic people have clear dreams too, for the starting point seems to have more strength when reason is disengaged (ἔοικε γὰρ ἡ ἀρχὴ ἀπολυομένου τοῦ λόγου ἰσχύειν μᾶλλον), just as the blind recall more, because being disengaged from visible things, their power of memory is stronger. There are two forms of good fortune then, the one divine, which is why the fortunate person seems to get things right because of the god [and by nature]; and this is the one who succeeds in

Their *telos* really is their *archē*.⁴⁵

While from the viewpoint of the *Nicomachean Ethics*, therefore, the contemplative life may seem solitary and scarcely reconcilable with the life of practical, moral action, as many scholars have argued,⁴⁶ from the viewpoint of theology, by contrast, and also in light of the above passage in the *Eudemian Ethics*, a broader and deeper insight seems to emerge. God's life is the fullest and most complete energy, a prefiguring energy "separate" from "the nature of the whole" and yet simultaneously an immanent energy that gives meaning to every detail in cosmic life, rational and irrational, especially to the desire and love that all things experience. This is why, Aristotle observes at the end of the above passage, "we say" that God is a *zoon*—a living creature or animal.

To sum up and also to take this analysis somewhat further, several features of this famous passage in Aristotle's *Metaphysics* need emphasis.

First, it is striking, as we shall see below, that for both Plato in the *Symposium* and Aristotle in the *Metaphysics*, the beautiful and the good (intellect for Aristotle) move as final causes:⁴⁷ *Symp.* 204c2: τὸ ἐρώμενον; *Meta*physics 1072b3: κινεῖ δὴ ὡς ἐρώμενον.

---

accordance with impulse, while the other is the one who succeeds against his impulse. But both are irrational, the one is more a continuous good fortune, the other not continuous. (*EE* 1248a23–41; trans. Inwood and Woolf, altered)

This remarkable passage shows that, for Aristotle, "the god" is not a starting point outside the cosmos (as Aristotle might suppose a Platonic form to be); nor is the god a cause only of fully formed activities, but the originary cause of every motion in the universe, including irrational impulses. Good fortune is possible not only because the wise person harnesses experience, habit, observation, and wisdom to the initial movement of the god in his or her being, but even more because the strength of the god's movement in all beings, however irrational they may be, and however more powerful the god's movement might be for their being "disengaged," prompts the right kind of action instinctively. What is an irrational impulse or desire from one perspective is a divine movement from another. An apparently blind impulse or purposeless instinct from below the level of any final causality can be simultaneously potentially intelligible from above—and neither is strictly rational: the impulse is below reason, and the potential intelligibility apparently above or outside reason or immediate rational plausibility. In other words, the ascent of impulse and desire is simultaneously the descent of new forms).

45. Cf. Aristotle, *EN* 6.1143b10; see also Plotinus, *Ennead* III.8[30].7, 1–15.

46. Cf. Joachim, *Aristotle. The Nicomachean Ethics*, 241–43 (on the divide between both lives in the *Nicomachean Ethics* and the *Republic*), 293–97; Guthrie, *History of Greek Philosophy*, VI, 390–93.

47. *Symp.* 208b5 (ἀθανασίας γὰρ χάριν), 210a1 (ὧν ἕνεκα), 210e6 (οὗ δὴ ἕνεκεν), 211c2–3 (ἀρχόμενον ἀπὸ τῶνδε τῶν καλῶν ἐκείνου ἕνεκα τοῦ καλοῦ ἀεὶ ἐπανιέναι; cf. Aristotle, *Meta*physics 1072b1–2, τὸ οὗ ἕνεκα; *De Anima* 433a14–15; it is the goal, end [*Symp.* 210e4 (τέλος), 211b7], perfect in itself [*Symp.* 204c4, τέλεον] and, strikingly, the

Second, Aristotle, like Plato, defines participation in the divine as a range of activities and pleasures (cf. *Republic* 9.580dff.), from waking up[48] to perception, thought, and hopes,[49] and memories[50] through them. Moreover, just as Socrates stresses in *Republic* 9 that the best way of life that most truly belongs to who we really are is "sweet" and "most pleasurable,"[51] so for Aristotle pre-eminently, god's "way of life" is pleasure and that is why contemplation or living insight is "sweetest."

Two further details from *Metaphysics* 12.7 have escaped attention and need some emphasis. First, according to Aristotle, the heaven and the world of nature "hang" from god's "way of life":

> On such a beginning, then, hang the heaven and nature. And it is a way of life such as the best that we enjoy for a short time (for it is always so, which for us is impossible), since its activity is also pleasure. And because of this waking, perception, and thinking are sweetest, and hopes and memories because of these.[52]

In the above passage, I suggest, the verb "depend" (ἤρτηται), or better "hang on or from," is a deliberate reminiscence of Plato's famous image of "art" as a "divine power" that forms a chain from which everything else *hangs* (*Ion* 533d–e): the gift of speaking well, like the gift of the Muse, is not an art, but "a divine power" like that of the magnet stone, imparting the power to attract another ring "so that sometimes a pretty long chain of iron rings hang from one another; but for all of them the power hangs from that stone" (ὥστ' ἐνίοτε ὁρμαθὸς μακρὸς πάνυ σιδηρίων καὶ δακτυλίων ἐξ ἀλλήλων ἤρτηται· πᾶσι δὲ τούτοις ἐξ ἐκείνης τῆς λίθου ἡ δύναμις ἀνήρτηται). The verbs *artasthai* and *anartasthai* do not appear in Ast's *Lexicon Platonicum*; and, what is perhaps even stranger, Bonitz' *Index Aristotelicus* provides no mention of this passage in *Metaphysics* 12.7, which is *the* most important passage for Aristotle's theology and one where Aristotle virtually cites Plato with approval. Indeed, the notions of "holding onto," "touching upon," or "hanging from" are fundamental also to Plato's view of dialectic and participation; and perhaps after the *Ion*, the most famous example occurs at the end of *Republic* 6, where the sense of the text is difficult, but one may reasonably translate as follows:

---

object of love [*Symp.* 204c2, τὸ ἐρώμενον; *Metaphysics* 1072b3, κινεῖ δὴ ὡς ἐρώμενον].

48. Cf. *Republic* 7.524d5: ἐγερτικὰ τῆς νοήσεως.

49. Cf. *Phaedo* 67b–c; 68a; *Apology* 40c; *Republic* 6.494c; 6.496e; 7.517b.

50. Cf. *Philebus* 11b–c: rather than pleasure etc. "wisdom and thought and *memory* and their kindred, right opinion and true reasonings, are for those who can partake of them . . . the most beneficial of all things"; *Republic* 6.490c.

51. *Republic* 9.583a; 585b–587a.

52. *Metaphysics* 1072b14–18.

[M]aking the hypotheses not beginnings but really hypotheses, as it were stepping stones and launching points, in order to get up to that which is beyond hypothesis, the beginning point of the all, touching upon it, again in turn holding on to/being held up by the things that hold to/are held by that (i.e., the first principle), [the power of dialectic] comes down to a conclusion . . . (511b5–8: τὰς ὑποθέσεις ποιούμενος οὐκ ἀρχὰς ἀλλὰ τῷ ὄντι ὑποθέσεις, οἷον ἐπιβάσεις τε καὶ ὁρμάς, ἵνα μέχρι τοῦ ἀνυποθέτου ἐπὶ τὴν τοῦ παντὸς ἀρχὴν ἰών, ἁψάμενος αὐτῆς, πάλιν αὖ ἐχόμενος τῶν ἐκείνης ἐχομένων, οὕτως ἐπὶ τελευτὴν καταβαίνῃ . . .)

As noted above, this is a difficult passage to construe, and there is an ambiguity that should be retained between the passive and middle forms: holding onto/being held up by. But the point I wish to make is that hanging from, holding to, being held by, etc., are distinctive notions in Plato that Aristotle implicitly references in his use of ἤρτηται: "From such an originative principle, the heaven and nature hang."

Second, Aristotle develops his own distinctive noetic theory, of course, but, like Plato, he frames participation in terms of real generative contact, namely, mind touching, becoming, and thinking its object, with the primary emphasis upon *having* rather than *receiving*, yet the receiving and participation are *included* in the whole movement of thought:

And thinking in itself is of that which is best in itself, and thinking in the fullest sense of what is best in the fullest sense. And intellect thinks itself by participation in the object of thought; for it becomes intelligible by touching and thinking (αὐτὸν δὲ νοεῖ ὁ νοῦς κατὰ μετάληψιν τοῦ νοητοῦ· νοητὸς γὰρ γίγνεται θιγγάνων καὶ νοῶν), so that intellect and object of thought are the same. For that which receives the object of thought and the substance, is intellect, and it is active in having the object. Therefore, having rather than receiving is the divine that thought seems to have, and contemplation is the sweetest and best.[53]

Here it is perhaps natural to emphasize the difference between Plato and Aristotle because of Aristotle's intellect theory, but touching by participation and coming-to-be are most characteristic of participation as the highest moment of real apprehension or contact in Plato too. J. Tricot in his note to the above passage remarks that the verb *thigganein* means to touch

---

53. *Metaphysics* 1072b18–24: ἡ δὲ νόησις ἡ καθ' αὑτὴν τοῦ καθ' αὑτὸ ἀρίστου, καὶ ἡ μάλιστα τοῦ μάλιστα. αὑτὸν δὲ νοεῖ ὁ νοῦς κατὰ μετάληψιν τοῦ νοητοῦ· νοητὸς γὰρ γίγνεται θιγγάνων καὶ νοῶν, ὥστε ταὐτὸν νοῦς καὶ νοητόν. τὸ δεκτικὸν τοῦ νοητοῦ καὶ τῆς οὐσίας νοῦς. ἐνεργεῖ δὲ ἔχων· ὥστε ἐκείνου μᾶλλον τοῦτο ὃ δοκεῖ ὁ νοῦς θεῖον ἔχειν, καὶ ἡ θεωρία τὸ ἥδιστον καὶ ἄριστον.

or apprehend immediately by intuition and is more or less a synonym for *metalepsis* at line 20, "that indicates, in fact, more than a 'participation' in the way Plato understood the term."[54] But Tricot's emphasis on the difference in participation between Plato and Aristotle is simply incorrect. Certainly, Plato does not use the verb *thigganein*, and this, it might be argued, marks a different emphasis in Aristotle since Aristotle's philosophy is a philosophy of movement by desire and touch or contact.[55] But Plato's thought equally emphasizes final causality as *desire* and *touch* of the desiring subject in real apprehension. Indeed, Plato uses the verbs *haptesthai* and *ephaptesthai* and several clusters of ordinary language verbs and nouns that help to articulate what this means;[56] and at the highest level of participation, Socrates emphasizes the touching upon or grasping the intelligible and the generative coming-to-be that ensues. In the *Symposium*, the apprentice "gives birth" to true virtue by such contact;[57] in the *Republic*, he or she touches upon the nature of "each itself what it is," mingles with it, gives birth.[58] These passages articulate a vision of participation as touching that genuinely anticipates Aristotle: in Aristotle, mind *becomes* an object of thought by its *having* the "divine" in *touching* and *thinking*; for Aristotle we become divine, as it were, not so much by receiving as by having, that is, the actualization of a natural capacity; and this actualization is in the *De Anima* a disposition "like light" (430a15). In fact, this is the one instance in the *Corpus Aristotelicum* that is closest to Plato's own thought. So while the two positions are of course different, it is striking that Aristotle should immediately emphasize the continuity between them:

---

54. Tricot, *La Métaphysique*, Vol. 2, 682n1. The original reads: "qui marque, en fait, plus qu'une 'participation' telle que l'entendait Platon."

55. By this, I mean that a mover moves without itself being moved, just as a person who grieves "touches" us, but we do not "touch" him, Aristotle observes (*Physics* 3.2; *De Gen. et Corr.* 2.6.323a25).

56. For vocabulary see Allen, "Participation and Predication," 43–60; Pradeau, *Platon*, 30–45; Brisson, "Comment render compte de la participation," 55–86; Hermann, "*Metechein, metalambamein*," 19–56; and on the distinction between the intelligible reality or *ousia* and its form or *eidos* participated by sensible things, see 45ff., and Dixsaut, "*Ousia, eidos et idea*," 71–91 (in Pradeau, *Platon*, 46–47n3). For comprehensive analysis of *eidos, idea*, and related words, see Ritter, "*Eidos, idea* und verwandte Wörter," 228–326; Baltès, "Idee (Ideenlehre)," 213–46; Pradeau, *Platon*, 23–54; Fronterotta, *Methexis. La Teoria Platonica delle Idee*, 3–47; Motte, Rutten, and Somville, *Philosophie de la Forme*, passim, but especially 272–80. *Eidos* and *idea*, in my view, do not have a different sense, as Pradeau argues, *Platon*, 20–54.

57. *Symposium* 212a.

58. *Republic* 6.489e–490a.

And life too indeed belongs to god; for the activity of intellect is life, and god is activity; and god's activity in itself is a best and eternal life. *We say* therefore that god is a living creature, eternal, best, so that life continually lasting and eternal belong to god; for this is god (*Metaphysics* 12.7.1072b13–30).[59]

Here I italicize the words "we say" above to note that in this case Aristotle speaks as a member of the Platonic School. He is in fact referring to the intelligible living creature of the *Timaeus*: "we say" that god is a living creature. We moderns have a tendency to overstate the differences rather than the resonances, because we find it quaint that Neoplatonists like Porphyry should have tried to "reconcile" Plato and Aristotle,[60] but the use of common language tends to show some genuine continuities in language and thought, as Jonathan Barnes has so effectively argued about later antiquity,[61] no matter how different the thought might be on occasion.[62] To sum up, Aristotle developed his very different theology out of what he took to be the heart and impulse of Plato's thought.

1.4 Ascent to the beautiful and the good: Plato, the *Symposium* and *Republic*

As we have seen above in Aristotle, everything desires τὸ καλόν (the apparent or real beautiful/good) as the final cause of its movement, development, and completion, but ultimately we desire the *one* good or "best" as the ultimate object of any active love: "one ruler let there be" (*Metaphysics* 12.10). This theory should be compared, as I have suggested, with Plato's

---

59. *Metaphysics* 1072b26–30: καὶ ζωὴ δέ γε ὑπάρχει· ἡ γὰρ νοῦ ἐνέργεια ζωή, ἐκεῖνος δὲ ἡ ἐνέργεια· ἐνέργεια δὲ ἡ καθ' αὑτὴν ἐκείνου ζωὴ ἀρίστη καὶ ἀΐδιος. φαμὲν δὴ τὸν θεὸν εἶναι ζῷον ἀΐδιον 30 ἄριστον, ὥστε ζωὴ καὶ αἰὼν συνεχὴς καὶ ἀΐδιος ὑπάρχει τῷ θεῷ· τοῦτο γὰρ ὁ θεός.

60. On this see Barnes, *Porphyry*, 338, and especially Karamanolis, *Plato and Aristotle in Agreement?* 243–330, who argues persuasively that Porphyry wrote two works on this question, both now lost: his work on the "division" between Plato and Aristotle must have been a shorter introduction to his bigger work arguing that Plato and Aristotle have one *hairesis*, that is, that they belong to the same school of thought, a relation which is not *symphonia* or comprehensive agreement, but one that allows for differences between them, though Porphyry thinks the differences are (a) perspectival or trivial, or (b) misunderstandings of Plato by Aristotle or (c) misunderstandings of Aristotle by later interpreters (322–23).

61. Barnes, *Porphyry*, 136–41.

62. For examples of *metechein* and cognates in Aristotle, see Bonitz, *Index Aristotelicus*, ad loc. and Corrigan, "The Place and Scope of 'Participation' in the thought of Plato and Aristotle" (forthcoming).

Symposium and *Republic*, since Aristotle's theory is first intimated in these two dialogues and, because, as I shall argue, there are very good reasons for reading the *Symposium* and *Republic* together.

As any reader of Socrates' speech may see, according to Diotima's lesser mysteries, the final object of love (that is, what the lover is attracted to) is different from the ultimate goal of love (that is, what the lover aims at). The final object of love is the form of the beautiful, whereas the ultimate end of love is the eternal possession of the good, that is, procreation in the beautiful. We do not love the beautiful for its own sake, Diotima argues, as we love the good, but we love it because of our desire to procreate and beget bodily and psychic children in the beautiful.[63] The form of the beautiful, like Aristotle's unmoved mover, is the final cause of desire: it is that "for the sake of which" (*Symp.* 208b5 [ἀθανασίας γὰρ χάριν], 210a1 [ὧν ἕνεκα], 210e6 [οὗ δὴ ἕνεκεν], 211c2–3 [ἀρχόμενον ἀπὸ τῶνδε τῶν καλῶν ἐκείνου ἕνεκα τοῦ καλοῦ ἀεὶ ἐπανιέναι]; cf. Aristotle, *Metaphysics* 1072b1–2 [τὸ οὗ ἕνεκα]; *De Anima* 433a14–15; it is the goal, end [*Symp.* 210e4 (τέλος), 211b7], perfect in itself [*Symp.* 204c4, τέλεον] and, strikingly, the object of love [*Symp.* 204c2, τὸ ἐρώμενον; *Metaphysics* 1072b3, κινεῖ δὴ ὡς ἐρώμενον]).[64]

Because the form of the good does not appear in the *Symposium*, it has been suggested that either the beautiful and the good are coincident classes[65] or the lover aims only at "the particular good of a particular being," not the good itself.[66] However, neither of these alternatives is plausible: the first because Diotima expressly distinguishes the beautiful and the good in the lesser mysteries and the second because it would render the "higher mysteries" or ladder of ascent fundamentally irrelevant as a completion of the lesser mysteries. Indeed, part of the purposive result of the ascent is *not* to generate only the particular *good* of a particular being, but "to give birth to *logoi* that will make the young *better*"[67] (i.e., goodness more broadly or universally conceived; 210c1–2) and to generate "not images of virtue" but "*true things*," "*true excellence*" (i.e., goodness or "bestness" more completely realized; 212a3–6).

Second, whatever a form may be, it is surely not a class. Is the *eidos* a species, genus, or universal, as Aristotle supposed in criticizing Plato for

---

63. *Symposium* 204d–207a.

64. Cf. Chang, "Plato's Form of the Beautiful," 440.

65. Dover, *Symposium*, 136; Rowe, *Symposium*, 179.

66. Neumann, "Diotima's Concept of Love," 37–38.

67. *Symposium* 210c1–2: ἐξαρκεῖν αὐτῷ καὶ ἐρᾶν καὶ κήδεσθαι καὶ τίκτειν λόγους τοιούτους καὶ ζητεῖν, οἵτινες ποιήσουσι βελτίους τοὺς νέους . . . ; 212a3–6: τίκτειν οὐκ εἴδωλα ἀρετῆς, ἅτε οὐκ εἰδώλου ἐφαπτομένῳ, ἀλλὰ ἀληθῆ, ἅτε τοῦ ἀληθοῦς ἐφαπτομένῳ· τεκόντι δὲ ἀρετὴν ἀληθῆ καὶ θρεψαμένῳ . . . .

separating universals from particulars? Or is the *eidos* an idea in the sense of a thought content or concept, as the Neo-Kantians and a significant portion of modern readers have supposed?[68] For the Plato of the dialogues, at least, the *eidos* cannot be a universal, genus, or concept, since while it informs everything, it is simultaneously separated from everything and is the only truly singular, individual reality that can be conceived.[69] Moreover, if the form is generic, then it will not be fully real, but something abstracted and empty without the species and the things in which it finds itself instantiated. Therefore, a form cannot be a universal in this sense.[70]

Whatever the "good" in question may be, then, it is consequently a bigger good than simply my or your particular good, and it is not a coincident class. But if this detail early in Diotima-Socrates' speech points in some way to a form of goodness that is something real, then it must be more intrinsically involved in the design of the *Symposium*. And yet, since the primary emphasis of the *Symposium* is upon the beautiful, is Diotima's mention of the "good" anything more than a coincidence in the earlier part of the dialogue? Could the good be a final, motive cause, as we also find in Aristotle in the progression of his thought in *Metaphysics* 12, 7 that we have outlined above?

Certainly, the "good" plays a tantalizing and incidental role throughout the *Symposium*. It occurs in the first form of the proverb "of their own accord do the good go to the tables of the good" (172b) that Socrates immediately erases or "destroys."[71] It occurs in the pun of Agathon's own name, Agathon, that is, the person who is the host or prime mover of the get-together! And when Agathon acknowledges in the elenchus or cross-examination by Socrates that in presenting his own vision of Love as all-perfect and all-good "he did not know what he was talking about" (201b11–12), Socrates replies: "Never mind, you spoke *beautifully*; but tell me one little thing more: do you think that good things are not also beautiful things?" It is evident already by this point that the good and the beautiful cannot simply be identical or coextensive classes. And the early parts of Diotima's speech only re-emphasize

---

68. As R. E. Allen, a great twentieth-century Platonic scholar observed: "In late antiquity, Plato became a Plotinian. In the middle ages, he became a Christian. In the last century [i.e., nineteenth] he first became a Kantian and a Hegelian. In this century [i.e., twentieth] he became a realist, and he moved toward conceptual analysis" (*Studies in Plato's Metaphysics*, introduction, xii).

69. See *Philebus* 15d–17a. On this see Pradeau, *Platon*, 12; Brisson, "Comment rendre compte de la participation," 60n1; Fronterotta, *Methexis. La Teoria Platonica delle Idee*, 13–21; 33–42.

70. Allen, "Participation and Predication," 52–59; Pradeau, *Platon*, 12; Brisson, "Comment rendre compte de la participation," 60n1.

71. *Symposium* 174b3: διαφθείρωμεν.

this. Love is not exactly longing for the beautiful itself but for the conception and generation that the beautiful brings about—a longing for the good to belong to one eternally, namely, the different species of immortality in body and soul (205e–207a) that will be given a vertical application in relation to the highest beautiful at the end of Diotima's speech. It would therefore appear that neither happiness nor the beautiful are the ultimate goals of all human longing. In other words, a distinction between the good and the beautiful is implicit but fundamental to all the early parts of the *Symposium* as well as to Socrates-Diotima's speech, and this distinction is subtly thematized by the presence of the gigantic pun of Agathon himself at the center of the dialogue and yet characterized, one might also say, on the other hand, by the absence of any explicit mention of the form of the good that is so centrally present in the *Republic*.

The good itself, however, plays a pivotal role in the *Symposium* that, as far as I know, has not been noticed by modern scholars—and this occurs in the final stages of the ascent to the beautiful. Let me first characterize the ascent before focusing upon this pivotal role of the good.

The ascent itself characterizes the nature of loving rather than that of the ultimate beloved: "What you thought love to be is not surprising. You supposed, if I take what you said as evidence, that the beloved and not the loving was love. That is why, I think, eros seemed completely beautiful to you. In fact, it is the beloved that is really beautiful . . . and blessed; but loving has this other character" (204b8–c6). Love is, therefore, characterized by need, progressive dialogical education, and the transformability of that need by desire for the truly beautiful, just as the study of the good in the *Republic* characterizes the development of the synoptic eye of the dialectician.[72] What is disclosed at each level "strengthens and increases" (cf. ῥωσθεὶς καὶ αὐξηθεὶς) the apprentice in a movement through beauties of bodies, souls, moral ways of life, sciences, and studies, in each case from many to one, up to the supreme beauty, which is ultimately the knowledge of the beauty yet untold (210d6–8). It is at this point, at the top of the ladder, that we read the following famous words that, in plain sight, indicate that beauty cannot be contemplated or seen except by what makes it visible:

> What then, she said, do we think it would be like if it were possible for somebody to see the beautiful itself entire, pure, unmixed . . . ? Do you think, she said, that it would be an inferior life for a human being to contemplate the beautiful *by that by which it is necessary to contemplate it and being with it*? Or do you not think, she said, that it will happen to him only here, seeing the

---

72. Cf. *Republic* 7.537c.

beautiful *by that which makes it visible*, to give birth not to images of virtue, since he does not touch upon an image, but true things, since he touches upon the true, and having brought forth true virtue and reared it, he shall be beloved of god, and if ever it is given to any human being to be immortal, it will be given to him (211d–212a).[73]

Dover, in his commentary, notes some striking parallels with the *Republic*: "contemplating it by that by which it is necessary," namely, he argues, by "the eye of the soul" in *Republic* 533d. And *Symp.* 212a3, ᾧ ὁρατὸν he compares with *Republic* 490b: "to touch upon the nature of each thing by that element of the soul by which it is appropriate." But we should ask the most important question of all. What is ᾧ ὁρατὸν τὸ καλόν? What is ᾧ δεῖ θεωμένου? What is *that by which the beautiful is visible*? What is *that by which it is necessary to contemplate it*? There is only one answer in Plato's works: the beautiful is evidently visible or able to be contemplated (not only by itself but) by the ultimate source of light and intelligibility, namely, the good itself, likened by Socrates in the *Republic* to the "sun" of the intelligible realm, final cause of all intelligible visibility,[74] and also in the *Symposium* the implicit but indispensable cause of the beautiful being seen. Plainly, the beautiful is not to be seen by virtue of the eye of the soul, as if the soul were to cause the beautiful. What causes the beautiful to be seen or contemplated must be the good. If this is so, as surely it must be, then the *Symposium requires* the *Republic* for its contextual interpretation of the ladder of ascent, since what makes the beautiful visible or thinkable has to be the good.

1.5 Plato and Aristotle

I suggest then that this is the way Aristotle interpreted the theory of love and motion in both the *Symposium* and *Republic* and applied it to his own view of motion, extending it, unlike Plato, to the physical universe as a whole. The unmoved mover as the final cause of motion for all beings in the cosmos, rational and irrational, is a kind of Aristotelian adaptation of Diotima's

---

73. Τί δῆτα, ἔφη, οἰόμεθα, εἴ τῳ γένοιτο αὐτὸ τὸ καλὸν ἰδεῖν εἰλικρινές, καθαρόν, ἄμεικτον, ἀλλὰ μὴ ἀνάπλεων σαρκῶν τε ἀνθρωπίνων καὶ χρωμάτων καὶ ἄλλης πολλῆς φλυαρίας θνητῆς, ἀλλ' αὐτὸ τὸ θεῖον καλὸν δύναιτο μονοειδὲς κατιδεῖν; ἆρ' οἴει, ἔφη, φαῦλον βίον γίγνεσθαι ἐκεῖσε βλέποντος ἀνθρώπου καὶ ἐκεῖνο ᾧ δεῖ θεωμένου καὶ συνόντος αὐτῷ; ἢ οὐκ ἐνθυμῇ, ἔφη, ὅτι ἐνταῦθα αὐτῷ μοναχοῦ γενήσεται, ὁρῶντι ᾧ ὁρατὸν τὸ καλόν, τίκτειν οὐκ εἴδωλα ἀρετῆς, ἅτε οὐκ εἰδώλου ἐφαπτομένῳ, ἀλλὰ ἀληθῆ, ἅτε τοῦ ἀληθοῦς ἐφαπτομένῳ· τεκόντι δὲ ἀρετὴν ἀληθῆ καὶ θρεψαμένῳ ὑπάρχει θεοφιλεῖ γενέσθαι, καὶ εἴπέρ τῳ ἄλλῳ ἀνθρώπων ἀθανάτῳ καὶ ἐκείνῳ;

74. *Republic* 6.507d–509c; 7, 517a–c.

lesser mysteries,[75] whereas the unmoved mover as the ultimate cause of the hierarchy of compounds, and enmattered and matterless forms—transfixed by desire, will, and thought[76]—is a complementary Aristotelian development of Diotima's greater mysteries[77] that range from the beauty or finality in bodies and souls, through ways of life, and sciences, to the beautiful itself and ultimately to the unmoved good ("beyond being and thought"[78]). Though Aristotle has a different conception of good and being, he moves as a point of practice from the unmoved mover as beautiful to the unmoved mover as good. In the *Symposium, Republic*, and in Aristotle's theology, this is an *embodied* ascent ("if ever it is given to a *human being* . . .")[79]—even if it leads in both to the grasp or touch of immaterial forms or the ultimate immaterial object of thought. In the *Symposium*, for instance, the apprentice travels with a guide with whom he or she gives birth at each level and then cares for and rears this offspring. Even the highest revelation is not given to a "soul," "mind," or science but to "a human being" (212a7). In the lesser mysteries of Diotima-Socrates' speech and in Aristotle's *Physics*, the motive

---

75. That is, the first part of Diotima-Socrates' speech, after the elenchus of Agathon, *Symposium* 201d1–209e4).

76. Compare, first, Tricot, *La Métaphysique*, vol. 2, 672–73n2: "Dieu, forme pure et transcendante, Individu supreme, est le sommet et le terme de la série des forms, qui se développent entre les deux poles de l' être, entre la matière et la Pensée pure. L'Univers aristotélicien est constitué par une hiérarchie de réalités, disposés selon une échelle continue . . . qui sont toutes, à des degrés divers, des composés de matière et de forme, et dont l'une sert de substrat et d' echelon à celle qui suit et qui la surpasse par son acte propre. Chaque forme substantielle trouve, en effet, dans une matière qui lui est extérieure la condition de sa realization. . . . La forme supérieure, par la richesse plus grande de ses determinations est la raison d' être et le principe d' intelligibilité de la forme inférieure. La forme absolument pure, à laquelle on arrive aisi graduellement, par elimination progressive de l' element material et de la puissance, n'a plus besoin de s'appuyer sur une matiére préexistante pour se realiser. Elle n'a d'autre condition qu'elle-même, elle est la Réalité par excellence, *Ens realissimum*, qui confère à toutes les autres existence et intelligibilité;" and, second, *Symposium* 211b6–d1: ὅταν δή τις ἀπὸ τῶνδε διὰ τὸ ὀρθῶς παιδεραστεῖν ἐπανιὼν ἐκεῖνο τὸ καλὸν ἄρχηται καθορᾶν, σχεδὸν ἄν τι ἅπτοιτο τοῦ τέλους. τοῦτο γὰρ δή ἐστι τὸ ὀρθῶς ἐπὶ τὰ ἐρωτικὰ ἰέναι ἢ ὑπ' ἄλλου ἄγεσθαι, ἀρχόμενον ἀπὸ τῶνδε τῶν καλῶν ἐκείνου ἕνεκα τοῦ καλοῦ ἀεὶ ἐπανιέναι, ὥσπερ ἐπαναβασμοῖς χρώμενον, ἀπὸ ἑνὸς ἐπὶ δύο καὶ ἀποδυοῖν ἐπὶ πάντα τὰ καλὰ σώματα, καὶ ἀπὸ τῶν καλῶν σωμάτων ἐπὶ τὰ καλὰ ἐπιτηδεύματα, καὶ ἀπὸ τῶν ἐπιτηδευμάτων ἐπὶ τὰ καλὰ μαθήματα, καὶ ἀπὸ τῶν μαθημάτων ἐπ' ἐκεῖνο τὸ μάθημα τελευτῆσαι, ὅ ἐστιν οὐκ ἄλλου ἢ αὐτοῦ ἐκείνου τοῦ καλοῦ μάθημα, καὶ γνῷ αὐτὸ τελευτῶν ὅ ἔστι καλόν.

77. That is, the second part of Diotima-Socrates' speech, *Symposium* 209e5–212c3.

78. *Republic* 6.509b.

79. See, for example, *Symposium* 212a6–7 and *Republic* Books 5, 6, and 7, all of which deal with an *embodied* ascent that culminates in Book 9, where the man of intellect "will cultivate the harmony of the body for the sake of the symphony of his soul" (591c–d).

force in the whole of nature includes both rational and irrational things, and results in the eternal propagation of the species and the movement of the heavens; in the higher mysteries and Aristotle's theology, the motive force is transformative of one's whole being and of all the activities that make life worth living. In other words, it makes no sense to separate Aristotle rigidly from a "pristine" Plato, since Aristotle's physics and theology are developed consciously from the inspiration, and shadow, of the *Symposium* and *Republic*. The "light metaphysics" of the *Republic* may be missing from Aristotle's *Metaphysics* 12, but it plays a tantalizing role in the *De Anima*, where the active intellect is a "disposition, like light," that is, it actively and instantaneously illuminates;[80] and this illuminating power of active intellect will become a major feature in Alexander of Aphrodisias[81] (and, of course, later still in Pseudo-Alexander). The outpouring of light that makes the beautiful visible is also the lure of love and desire that leads back to the final cause itself, the good; and this will be true in different ways of both Peripatetic thought and Neoplatonism.

One of Aristotle's major criticisms of the Platonic forms is that they cannot *do* anything and they are not attainable: "nothing is gained even if one supposes eternal substances unless there is to be in them some principle which can cause movement" (*Metaphysics* 1071b14–16).[82] Here in the *Symposium* and the *Republic*, we find a principle of motion actually *in individual things and species* that causes all their ordinary movements, prompts their longing to attain what is at first unattainable, and even develops a method for this attainment. Just as in Aristotle, so also in Plato, the language of final

---

80. On Alexander's identification of the intellect of *Metaphysics* 12 with that of *De Anima* 3, see Armstrong (ed.), *The Cambridge History of Later Greek and Early Medieval Philosophy*, 117.

81. For Alexander on intellect, see Schroeder and Todd, *Two Greek Aristotelian Commentators*. See especially Alexander, *De Anima* 88, 26–89, 15 (Bruns): ἐν πᾶσιν γὰρ τὸ μάλιστα καὶ κυρίως τι ὂν καὶ τοῖς ἄλλοις αἴτιον τοῦ εἶναι τοιούτοις. τό τε γὰρ μάλιστα ὁρατόν, τοιοῦτον δὲ τὸ φῶς, καὶ τοῖς ἄλλοις τοῖς ὁρατοῖς αἴτιον τοῦ εἶναι ὁρατοῖς, ἀλλὰ καὶ τὸ μάλιστα καὶ πρώτως ἀγαθὸν καὶ τοῖς ἄλλοις ἀγαθοῖς αἴτιον τοῦ εἶναι τοιούτοις· τὰ γὰρ ἄλλα ἀγαθὰ τῇ πρὸς τοῦτο συντελείᾳ κρίνεται. καὶ τὸ μάλιστα δὴ καὶ τῇ αὐτοῦ φύσει νοητὸν εὐλόγως αἴτιον καὶ τῆς τῶν ἄλλων νοήσεως. τοιοῦτον δὲ ὂν εἴη ἂν ὁ ποιητικὸς νοῦς. εἰ γὰρ μὴ ἦν τι νοητὸν φύσει, οὐδ' ἂν τῶν ἄλλων τι νοητὸν ἐγίνετο, ὡς προείρηται. ἐν γὰρ πᾶσιν ἐν οἷς τὸ μὲν κυρίως τί ἐστιν, τὸ δὲ δευτέρως, τὸ δευτέρως παρὰ τοῦ κυρίως τὸ εἶναι ἔχει. ἔτι, εἰ ὁ τοιοῦτος νοῦς τὸ πρῶτον αἴτιον, ὃ αἰτία καὶ ἀρχὴ τοῦ εἶναι πᾶσι τοῖς ἄλλοις, εἴη ἂν καὶ ταύτῃ ποιητικός, ᾗ αὐτὸς αἴτιος τοῦ εἶναι πᾶσι (10) τοῖς νοουμένοις. καὶ ἔστιν ὁ τοιοῦτος νοῦς χωριστός τε καὶ ἀπαθὴς καὶ ἀμιγὴς ἄλλῳ, ἃ πάντα αὐτῷ διὰ τὸ χωρὶς ὕλης εἶναι ὑπάρχει. χωριστός τε γὰρ καὶ αὐτὸς καθ' αὑτὸν ὢν διὰ τοῦτο. τῶν γὰρ ἐνύλων εἰδῶν οὐδὲν χωριστὸν ἢ λόγῳ μόνον τῷ φθορὰν αὐτῶν εἶναι τὸν ἀπὸ τῆς ὕλης χωρισμόν. ἀλλὰ καὶ ἀπαθής, ὅτι τὸ πάσχον ἐν πᾶσιν ἡ ὕλη . . . .

82. Cf. 991a8–11, b3–9, 992a29–32, 1033b26–1034a5; *Nicomachean Ethics* 1.6.1096a11–1097a14.

causality—namely, the "beautiful," fine, or noble—finds its ultimate end in the sphere of the "good" and the "best." In fact, this is much more pronounced in *Metaphysics* 12.7–10 than in the *Symposium*: the language of the beautiful, τὸ καλόν (1072a28, b34, 11; 1074b24), in chapter 7 *gives way to the language of the good and the best* in chapters 7–10 (7.1072a35–1072b1, 12, 15, 24, 28, 29, 32; 9.1074b20, 33; 1075a8–9; 10.1075a12, 14, 36–38; 1075b, 2. 8, 11; 1076a4).

And just as in Aristotle through the causal role of the unmoved mover, as both external good and the principle of internal good in the universe, the ordered and teleological change of nature is maintained in a specific way through the medium of desire,[83] so too in the *Symposium* and *Republic* the beautiful and the good may be only dimly glimpsed at first, yet they are the goal of all striving, and, in the *Republic*, Socrates represents the good, not simply as the theoretical ground of everything but as *the* most practical and useful good of all: without it, nothing is truly beneficial.[84] It is, according to him, the regulative ground of all our judgments, dimly glimpsed or "divined" in all our experience (from perplexity[85] to sex—the latter, at least, according to Aristophanes in the *Symposium*);[86] and it is also what provides both the power and means of seeing, feeling, or thinking anything.[87] In short, the good is that by which the *best state* or capacity of anything is felt, seen, imagined, or thought reflexively.[88] There is a strong affinity, therefore, between Aristotle's theory of the unmoved mover, on the one hand, and Diotima's presentation of desire in relation to all forms of the beautiful (and hidden good) in the *Symposium*, on the other hand. It is an affinity intensified if we add the presentation of, and ascent to, the good in the *Republic*.[89]

---

83. Cf. Chang, "Plato's Form of the Beautiful," 442.
84. *Republic* 6.504e–505b.
85. *Republic* 6.505d11–e2; 506a6.
86. *Symposium*, 192c–d.
87. *Republic* 6.508e–509b.
88. By "reflexively" I mean that the good is the principle by which we are able to conceive the best state of anything, a principle disclosed in the acts of seeing or thinking themselves, just as in seeing we see the light of the sun, according to Socrates' analogy in *Republic* Books 6–7, and in thinking objects of thought we think of them as "good—form" (*Republic* 6.508d–509b). For the conception of forms as ideals or "what should be" and for understanding the form of the good as overcoming the modern dichotomy between being and value, see Ferber, *Platos Idee des Guten*, 30–33; and compare Gonzalez, *Dialectic and Dialogue*, 209–44.
89. See especially *Republic* 7.521c–537d.

1.6 Alcinous

What is striking (and the significance of this has not been appreciated in modern times) is that three major figures of the Platonic tradition in late antiquity interpreted Plato and Aristotle in just this way. First, we have direct testimony from the influential *Handbook of Platonism* or *Didaskalikos* by the Middle Platonist Alcinous. We used to think that Alcinous was actually a certain "Albinus," the teacher of Galen, who lived at some point in the middle of the second century CE. While there is not enough evidence to support this identification, the dates of Alcinous are also roughly mid-second century.[90] But whoever he was, he interprets Plato's *Symposium* and Aristotle's *Metaphysics* 12.7 in exactly this way. In the *Didaskalikos* he outlines three ways of conceiving God: by abstraction of attributes (as we conceive a point by abstracting surface and line); by analogy (from the sun simile in *Republic* 6: as the sun is to vision and sensible objects, so the first intellect is to intellect in the soul and to its objects); and by supereminence, as we see in the following passage that interprets the ascent of the *Symposium* in the light of *Republic* Book 6 and Aristotle's *Metaphysics*:

> The third way of conceiving him is the following: one contemplates first beauty in bodies, then after that turns to the beauty in soul, then to that in customs and laws, and then to the great sea of beauty, after which one gains an intuition of the Good itself and the final object of love and striving, like a light appearing and, as it were, shining out to the soul which ascends in this way; and along with this one also intuits God, in virtue of his pre-eminence in honor (*Didaskalikos* 10.3, trans. Dillon).[91]

As an exponent of what has become known as "Middle Platonism," of course, Alcinous conflates the good of the *Republic* with the demiurge of the *Timaeus*,[92] but this does not negate the central feature of his interpretation of the *Symposium* in the light of *Republic* 6 and Aristotle's *Metaphysics* 12.7. As Dillon notes,[93] in this passage, Alcinous also links the *Symposium* to the unmoved mover as "object of striving" (ἐφετόν, cf. *Metaphysics* 12.7, 1072a26; *Physics* 1.9.192a17ff.) and to the *Seventh Letter* 341c–d, where

---

90. For the problem of identification and dating, see Dillon, *Alcinous*, ix–xiii.

91. *Didaskalikos* 10.3: Τρίτη δὲ νόησις τοιαύτη τις ἂν εἴη· θεωρῶν γάρ τις τὸ ἐπὶ τοῖς σώμασι καλόν, μετὰ τοῦτο μέτεισιν ἐπὶ τὸ τῆς ψυχῆς κάλλος, εἶτα τὸ ἐν ἐπιτηδεύμασι καὶ νόμοις, εἶτα ἐπὶ τὸ πολὺ πέλαγος τοῦ καλοῦ, μεθ' ὃ αὐτὸ τὸ ἀγαθὸν νοεῖ καὶ τὸ ἐραστὸν καὶ ἐφετὸν ὥσπερ φῶς φανὲν καὶ οἷον ἐκλάμψαν τῇ οὕτως ἀνιούσῃ ψυχῇ· τούτῳ δὲ καὶ θεὸν συνεπινοεῖ διὰ τὴν ἐν τῷ τιμίῳ ὑπεροχήν.

92. See *Didaskalikos* 10.3 and Dillon, *Alcinous*, 106.

93. Dillon, *Alcinous*, 110.

understanding is described as "brought to birth suddenly, like a light that is kindled by a leaping spark from a fire." So the thought link in Alcinous between Plato and Aristotle is clear.

1.7 Plotinus (and Porphyry)

This is also the way Plotinus will interpret the *Symposium* and *Republic* together in later antiquity, though he, of course, sees this very differently from Alcinous:

> The knowledge or touching of the Good is the greatest thing, and he [Plato] says it is the greatest study (cf. *Republic* 505a2); ... up to here one has been led along (παιδαγωγηθείς, cf. *Symposium* 210e3; cf 210a6–7) and settled in beauty and up to this point, one thinks that in which one is, but is carried out of it by the surge of the wave of intellect itself and lifted on high by a kind of swell (ἐξενεχθεὶς δὲ τῷ αὐτοῦ τοῦ νοῦ οἷον κύματι καὶ ὑψοῦ ὑπ' αὐτοῦ οἷον οἰδήσαντος ἀρθείς) one sees suddenly (εἰσεῖδεν ἐξαίφνης), not seeing how, but the vision fills his eyes with light and does not make him see something else by it, but the light itself is what he sees (*Ennead* VI. 7[38] 36, trans. Armstrong).[94]

In other words, Plotinus sees that the beautiful leads in the *Symposium* to the good—and he is surely correct. Although in the passage above there is

---

94. I provide the larger passage for context: "The knowledge or touching of the Good is the greatest thing, and he [Plato] says it is the greatest study (cf. *Republic* 505a2), not calling the looking at it a study, but learning about it beforehand. We are taught about it by analogies, negations, and knowledge of the things that come from it and certain methods of ascent by degrees, but we are put on the way to it by purifications, virtues, adorning and by gaining footholds in the intelligible and settling ourselves firmly there and feasting on its contents. But whoever has become at once contemplator of himself and all the rest and object of his contemplation, and since he has become substance, intellect and the complete living being (*Timaeus* 31b), no longer looks at it from outside—when he has become this, he is near, and That is next and close, shining upon all the intelligible world. It is there that one lets all study go, up to here one has been led along (παιδαγωγηθείς) and settled in beauty and up to this point, one thinks that in which one is, but is carried out of it by the surge of the wave of intellect itself and lifted on high by a kind of swell (ἐξενεχθεὶς δὲ τῷ αὐτοῦ τοῦ νοῦ οἷον κύματι καὶ ὑψοῦ ὑπ' αὐτοῦ οἷον οἰδήσαντος ἀρθείς) sees suddenly (εἰσεῖδεν ἐξαίφνης), not seeing how, but the vision fills his eyes with light and does not make him see something else by it, but the light itself is what he sees. For there is not in That something seen and its light ... but a ray which generates these afterwards and lets them be beside it; but *he* himself is the ray which only generates intellect and does not extinguish itself in the generation, but it itself abides and that comes to be because this exists" (*Ennead* VI.7[38].36, 3–25, trans. Armstrong)

no direct link to Aristotle, Plotinus comes back immediately after this to Aristotle's theology at the end of the chapter when he concludes that it is the good and not intellect that is the real cause: "... Intellect has come to be by virtue of the existence of this Good; for if this were not of the kind it is, that would not have come into being." Aristotle, of course, expressly indicates in *Metaphysics* 12.7 that in some sense intellect "comes-to-be" (however we are to understand this). So Plotinus, naturally, since he is thinking of Aristotle's *Metaphysics*, pursues a critique in the passage immediately following, that is, VI.7, chapter 37, of the Peripatetic position that the "worth" of intellect is by virtue of *thinking* himself ("since those people found nothing more worthy than him, [they] gave him thinking of himself") rather than simply by virtue of *being* himself, without any need for thinking—along the lines of Aristotle's *aporia* about this matter in *Metaphysics* 12.9.1074b17–35.[95] And Plotinus therefore concludes: "But what has not come to be and has nothing before it, but is always what it is—what cause is there for it to have to think? This is why Plato rightly says that it is above Intellect" (VI.7[38].37, 22–24). Plotinus uses the pre-eminent "worth" language of Aristotle here from *Metaphysics* 12.9,[96] and also of Alcinous in the passage from the *Didaskalikos* cited above: "And in this way one intuits god in virtue of his pre-eminence in worth" (*Didaskalikos* 10.6.6–7).

Before coming to my third major figure in Antiquity, Proclus, I want to make two further suggestions in response to questions I raised at the beginning of this chapter: first, about the evolution of Plotinus' thinking about the beautiful and the good and about Keats' equation of beauty and truth, and, second, about the self-reflexive character of thought in both Aristotle and Plotinus.

First, against the view of a chronological evolution of Plotinus' thinking about the beautiful and the good,[97] I argue that from I.6[1], through V.5[32].12, VI.7[38], VI.2[43].18, 1–5, Plotinus can plausibly hold that the

---

95. Aristotle, *Metaphysics* 12.9.1074b17–35, especially "if it thinks of nothing, what would its dignity (*to semnon*) be? ... and if it thinks, but another is master of this ... it cannot be the best substance ... for it because of thinking that its worth (*to timion*) belongs to it. Further, if the faculty of intellect is its substance or its thinking, what does it think? Either it thinks itself or something different; and if something different, either the same always or something else. Does it matter then or not whether it thinks the beautiful or any chance thing? Or is it absurd for it to think about some things? It is clear then that it thinks the most divine and the most worthy (*to timiōtaton*), and it does not change...."

96. *Ennead* VI.7[38].37: "For by what does he have his worth, by thinking or by himself? If it is by thinking, he is in himself of no worth or lesser worth ...etc." (trans. Armstrong).

97. Massagli, "L'Uno al di sopra del bello e della belleza," 111–31.

forms are the place of beauty, that beauty can even be deceptive, leading us away from the good, and yet simultaneously that beauty itself must be traced ultimately to the good—"the super beautiful," "the primary beautiful," etc." This does not mean, however, that he has the same view of the beautiful of the *Symposium* and the good of the *Republic* throughout the *Enneads*. He can appear to identify them in the ascent of I.6[1].7, for instance, where the close identity between the two, so natural because intellect is illuminated by the good and also illuminates itself, permits him to "correct" Aristotle:[98] it is, rather, the *good* upon which "everything depends and to which all look and live and think; for it is cause of life and mind and being" (7, 10–12). Nonetheless, he also distinguishes the two in these later chapters of his earliest work, but the central point in these chapters is that whatever view one takes of reality—Middle Platonic, Peripatetic, or that of Plotinus (namely, either that beauty and good are identical or that the good is beyond the beautiful)—beauty ultimately has to be founded in the good, for Plotinus. So the Romantic interpretation of the *Symposium*, that truth is beauty and beauty truth, is false—at least, according to the Platonic tradition. But, of course, it may be enough to get by: "that is all ye need to know . . . ." According to the argument of Plotinus in I.6[1], the beauty of the *Symposium needs* the proper measure and *aretē* of the *Phaedrus*[99] and especially the light of the good of the *Republic*.[100]

And I suggest that this is true of all Plotinus' later works. In V.5[32].12, the good is sharply distinguished from the beautiful. In VI.2[43].18, 1ff. Plotinus argues that you might, if you wish, equate the two, but if the good is "that which, as it were, shines out upon the idea, then one would have to say that it is not the same in all the Ideas and that the shining upon them is posterior."[101] It is not entirely clear what Plotinus means, but implicitly he distinguishes intelligible beauty from its source in the good. The same is true in the earlier chapters of VI.7[38], where in chapter 22 he goes so far as to argue that the soul can be bored by intellect unless it is illumined by a light or grace from the good: "each is what it is by itself, but it becomes desirable when the good colors it, giving graces to them and passionate love to the desirers" (ἔστι γὰρ ἕκαστον ὅ ἐστιν ἐφ' αὑτοῦ· ἐφετὸν δὲ γίνεται ἐπιχρώσαντος

---

98. *Metaphysics* 12.7.1072b13: On such a principle, then, depend the heavens and the world of nature.

99. *Ennead* I.6[1].9, 7–15; cf. *Phaedrus* 252d; 254b.

100. *Ennead* I.6[1].9, 15–34; cf. *Republic* 6.508b–509a; I.6[1].9, 40–41; Cf. *Republic* 6.509b and 7.517b5. See my comments about the good as the source of beauty and as superbeautiful in chapter 2.8 on Proclus below.

101. *Ennead* VI.2[43].18, 4–5: καὶ εἰ τὸ ἐπὶ τῇ ἰδέᾳ οἷον ἀποστίλβον, ὅτι μὴ τὸ αὐτὸ ἐν πᾶσι, καὶ ὅτι ὕστερον τὸ ἐπιστίλβειν.

αὐτὸ τοῦ ἀγαθοῦ, ὥσπερ χάριτας δόντος αὐτοῖς καὶ εἰς τὰ ἐφιέμενα ἔρωτας) (VI.7[38].22, 5–7). So the beauty in anything secondary is ultimately given to it by the good. However, in the later chapters, he goes somewhat further to argue that the unbounded intensity of love in the soul is a gift from, and response to, the good:

> ... so his beauty is of another kind and beauty above beauty. ...Therefore the productive power of all is the flower of beauty, a beauty which makes beauty (δύναμις οὖν παντὸς καλοῦ ἄνθος ἐστί, κάλλος καλλοποιόν). For it generates beauty and makes it more beautiful by the superabundance of beauty which comes from it, so that it is the principle of beauty and the term of beauty. (*Ennead* VI.7[38].32, 28–34, trans. Armstrong)

Though Plotinus comes close here to identifying "the good" and "supreme beauty," he nonetheless retains some distinction: the good is the "originative principle and limit of Beauty, a beauty above beauty." This is surely a reasonable interpretation of Socrates' statement in *Republic* 6.508e4–6: "Both knowledge and truth are beautiful, but you will correctly think of the good *as other and more beautiful* than they" (οὕτω δὲ καλῶν ἀμφοτέρων ὄντων, γνώσεώς τε καὶ ἀληθείας, ἄλλο καὶ κάλλιον ἔτι τούτων ἡγούμενος αὐτὸ ὀρθῶς ἡγήσῃ). But in the final chapter of VI.7[38] he restates his fundamental position clearly: "But when Plato calls him [the King of Plato's *Second Letter* 312e] 'Cause of all Beauties' he is clearly putting beauty in the World of Forms, but the Good itself above all this beauty" (42, 15–17, trans. Armstrong).[102]

I think we can say definitively, then, that Plotinus distinguishes the good and the beautiful throughout the *Enneads* but that he also makes a case for the superior beauty of the good, on the basis of Socrates' statement above, if one understands properly what one *means*. This is also Porphyry's view in one of the fragments collected by Andrew Smith from Porphyry's *History of Philosophy*.[103] Porphyry says that Plato speaks about the good as follows: "... this ... is the primarily beautiful and the beautiful itself, *having the form of beauty derived from itself* ..." (ὃ δὴ καὶ πρώτως καλὸν καὶ αὐτοκαλὸν παρ' ἑαυτοῦ τῆς καλλονῆς ἔχον τὸ εἶδος). The distinction between "the beautiful itself" and "the form of beauty" might be a little confusing, but the thought is recognizably that of Plotinus and it anticipates distinctions that Proclus will make later, as we shall see.

---

102. Compare Porphyry, *History of Philosophy*, fragment 16, TLG; fragment 222, Smith.

103. Preserved in Cyril, *Contra Iulianum* I.32cd, 552b1–c8; translation by Gerson and Dillon; fragment 17, TLG.

Second (in relation to the self-reflexive character of thought in both Aristotle and Plotinus), in the middle of the long passage we cited above from VI.7[38].36, 3–25, one can see the after-image of Aristotle's theology transformed by Plotinus into a Platonic ascent (rooted primarily throughout the *Enneads*, of course, in Plato's *Symposium*, *Republic*, *Phaedrus*, and, as here, the *Timaeus*):

> But whoever has become at once contemplator of himself and all the rest and object of his contemplation, and since he has become substance, intellect, and the complete living being (*Timaeus* 31b), no longer looks at it from outside (Ὅστις γένηται ὁμοῦ θεατής τε καὶ θέαμα αὐτὸς αὑτοῦ καὶ τῶν ἄλλων καὶ γενόμενος οὐσία καὶ νοῦς καὶ ζῷον παντελὲς μηκέτι ἔξωθεν αὐτὸ βλέποι)—when he has become this, he is near, and That is next and close, shining upon all the intelligible world (VI.7[38].36, 10–15, trans. Armstrong).

As in III.8[30] and V.8[31], Plotinus insists that true thinking cannot involve looking at something as an object outside of oneself. Instead, thinking must be transformative of one's very being, a self-reflexive thinking. And surely, this is the point of the ladder of ascent in the *Symposium* and also of Aristotle's notion of what theoretical or contemplative science really means, namely, that such sciences no longer operate on an external instrumental level as in the productive sciences (that is, to make something other than us) or on an internal instrumental level as in the practical sciences (that seek to make us, our home, and our polis better—or, in other words, ethics, economics, politics, respectively). By contrast, if philosophical or contemplative wisdom is a genuine understanding of substance in the primary sense, then it must be divine understanding itself, however transformed. My contemplative understanding is myself transformed by, and into, what is supremely real. Here Plotinus therefore reasonably adapts Aristotle's interweaving of human-divine perspectives from *Metaphysics* 12.7.1072b20–30 into his argument: intellect "becomes intelligible," (νοητὸς . . . γίγνεται) is "receptive of the intelligible object and substance" (τὸ γὰρ δεκτικὸν τοῦ νοητοῦ καὶ τῆς οὐσίας) and is "we certainly say a best eternal living being" (φαμὲν δὴ τὸν θεὸν εἶναι ζῷον ἀΐδιον ἄριστον). As we have seen above, Aristotle is himself citing Plato's *Timaeus* here and Plotinus naturally does so too, but the thought progression in Plotinus is an adaptation of both Plato and Aristotle.

1.8 Proclus

Our third major figure is Proclus, but let me make the case carefully since he appears to say different things in different works that can appear inconsistent.

In the *Platonic Theology* his approach is twofold: first, he interprets the *Phaedo* and *Symposium* in the light of the *Republic*, that is, he subordinates beauty and other "forms," whether transcendental or immanent, to the good; and, second, he draws a distinction between the one as cause of procession or the outpouring of being, on the one hand, and the good as the principle or goal of conversion or return, on the other. *PT* II.40, 25–27: "So the good draws all the secondary beings through conversion, while the one makes them exist" (Ἐπιστρεπτικὸν ἄρα τὸ ἀγαθόν ἐστι τῶν δευτέρων ἁπάντων, ὑποστατικὸν δὲ τὸ ἕν). Dodds mentions this passage in his commentary on the *Elements of Theology*, proposition 13, and notes "its hint of dualism," unlike Proclus' treatment of propositions 1–11 in the *Elements*, on Dodd's view.[104] But I don't think this is really the case. Something else is in play in this passage. Plato, Proclus observes, uses two names for "the ineffable cause"—namely, the good as "the fountainhead of the truth that unifies intellect and the intelligibles" in the *Republic* and the one as the principle that makes the "divine henads exist" in the *Parmenides*—and this means that the *Parmenides* provides us with an image of the procession "of the wholes" whereas the *Republic* furnishes an image of conversion.[105] The good therefore is the object of desire through which all secondary beings convert to their cause, while the one is that which makes them exist. Here it is not clear at first which of the two is primary; but Proclus explains that these names do not grasp the ineffable (II.6.42, 6); they are names drawn from secondary beings according to two methods of ascent (II.6.42, 20–24), one by analogy that links up with the naming of the good (in the *Republic*) and the other by negation linking to the one (in the *Parmenides*). And so at the end of this section he observes that "the one transcends perfectly altogether the fertile processions, the converting powers, and the uniform realities in real beings" (II.6.43, 8–11), which seems to indicate that the first principle is a unity beyond even its names, but to suggest at the same time that the "one" is more originary. Nevertheless, in what follows Proclus identifies the good of the *Republic* with the supreme god and argues that the beautiful and other forms are secondary to it.

---

104. Dodds, *Proclus: Elements*, 200.

105. *PT* II.6.95, 8–96, 11.

From where does Proclus develop his distinction between the good as the cause of conversion (*epistreptikon*) and the one as the cause of the existence and subsistence of everything (*hypostatikon*)? There is one striking clue in the passage that, as far as I know, has escaped attention. He uses a distinctive phrase of the good that he also employs in two other places in the *Platonic Theology* (II.6.42, 2; cf. I.18.83, 27 and 87, 10). He writes as follows: "desire perfects the conversion of existing beings and the return to the ineffable. Therefore, since all beings are eternally united to the first, some further, others nearer, and through this unification receive both their existence and *their portion of the good*, we have undertaken to show by means of names the procession of wholes and their conversion" (II.6.41, 27–42, 4).[106] What does he mean by "portion of the good" (τὴν τοῦ ἀγαθοῦ μοῖραν)? The phrase is certainly distinctive and, in my view, Proclus takes it from one of Plotinus' most famous works (VI.8[39], *On What is Voluntary and On the Free Will of the One*) and, what is even more pertinent, from what is one of its most striking passages, VI.8, chapter 13, 16–19, which reads as follows: "the nature of the good is for itself a much greater priority of choice, if whatever portion (*moira*) of the good that is most to be chosen by another becomes its voluntary substantial being (*ousia hekousios*) supported by its will, and is one and the same with its will and is established through its will."[107] This is a remarkable sentence, part of a rapid-flowing argument, but profoundly important for understanding Plotinus' linking of human freedom and choice through the intelligible world of soul and intellect to the good.

Choosing the good itself and also choosing any portion (*moira*) of the good which is most to be chosen in our daily lives becomes the voluntary or free stuff of which we are really made and, in choosing which, we also make ourselves. Here choice is not between alternatives on a horizontal level (this house or that yacht, making this or that moral decision), but rather between alternatives on a depth level.

What does Plotinus mean? He appears to mean that whatever we do— in any circumstance or in choosing anything—should be a choosing, even among relative goods, of what is best in and for itself. So even when I have to choose among proximate means and ends, I should have the deeper ends in mind—the deepest, in fact. What then makes Proclus think of VI.8 as

---

106. PT II.6.41, 27–42, 4: ἡ δὲ ἔφεσις τὴν ἐπιστροφὴν τῶν ὑποστάντων καὶ τὴν εἰς τὸ ἄρρητον ἀνακύκλησιν τελειοῖ. Πάντων δὲ ἄρα καὶ ἡνωμένων ἀεὶ τῷ πρώτῳ, τῶν μὲν πορρώτερον τῶν δὲ ἐγγύτερον, καὶ διὰ τῆς ἑνώσεως ταύτης τήν τε ὕπαρξιν καὶ τὴν τοῦ ἀγαθοῦ μοῖραν ὑποδεχομένων, τὴν μὲν πρόοδον τῶν ὅλων καὶ τὴν ἐπιστροφὴν δι' ὀνομάτων δηλοῦν ἐπικεχειρήκαμεν·

107. For translation and comment see Corrigan and Turner, *Plotinus, Ennead VI 8, ad loc.*

a way of explaining two different usages of names derived from Plato: the one and the good? Strangely enough, Porphyry got the first half of the title that he devised for Plotinus' great work completely right: he emphasized *the voluntary* since that was exactly what Plotinus clearly intended. This, however, has been entirely missed in modern times since the title has invariably been translated not as "On What Is Voluntary..." but as "On Free Will ...," which rather misses the point Plotinus wants to make about *voluntary substance* in chapter 13.

On the other hand, Porphyry plainly got the second half of the title ("... and the Free Will of the One"), not so much wrong, as misleading in an interesting way, since, in tracing free human agency back through our intellect and the divine intellect to the first principle, Plotinus refers throughout *exclusively* to the good, only once mentioning the one (in the dative).[108] I suggest then that Proclus' distinction between the two names employed by Plato as a way of showing two different approaches to the first principle (conversion and cause of existence) was prompted in part by his reading of Plotinus and, in particular, by his implicit interpretation of the positive and somewhat shocking language Plotinus uses of the good in VI 8 to describe what has been called "the astonishing exploration of the inner life of the Good."[109] Proclus plainly thinks that while such language points beyond itself, its immediate reference is not to the true one or true good but to the level of *intelligible reality* or to pre-intelligible generation. So Proclus restricts speech about the existence-making one and the converting good (just like *eros pronoetikos* and *eros epistreptikos* in his *Alcibiades I Commentary*) to the intelligible realm. And presumably this would be his interpretation of Plotinus' shockingly positive language about the good in VI.8[39], chapters 13–21: namely, this language is not applicable to the first principle, but it is, instead, acceptable epistreptic (converting) language that can lead to the first principle.

Here in the *Platonic Theology*, he argues that both names, the one and the good, in fact, point beyond themselves, though the good of the *Republic*, he also insists, is perfectly appropriate "to lead up to the one science of theology" (*PT* II.7.43, 19–20). It is at this point that he goes on to argue that the forms of the *Phaedo* and the *Symposium* have to be interpreted in light of the *Republic*. He makes the following observation: "[In Book 6 of the *Republic*,] Plato teaches us in another way the resolution that leads to the first. For all the multiplicities in the cosmos depend on intelligible monads, for example, all the beautiful things depend on beauty itself, and all the good things on

---

108. See ibid., 358.
109. Bussanich, *The One and Its Relation to Intellect*, 206.

good itself, and all the equal things on equal itself" (*PT* II. 7, 45, 25-46, 1).[110] Here Proclus is evidently thinking of one of the early arguments in the *Phaedo* about equals, equality itself, and the puzzling phrase "the equals themselves" (*Phaedo* 74c1-2)[111]—just as he thinks of the many instances and kinds of beauty in the *Symposium* leading up the beautiful itself (as also in the *Phaedo*, *Hippias Major* etc.)[112] and the many good-form things leading to the good in the *Republic*. How are these to be related to each other?

"Let no one think," he says, "that Plato supposed the same rank of the good both in the intelligible forms and before them. On the contrary, the good that is ranked together with the beautiful, one must suppose this to be substantial and one of the forms in the intelligibles; . . . in the realm of the forms, the beautiful itself (τὸ αὐτοκαλόν) is at the head of the many beautiful forms and the good itself (τὸ αὐτοαγαθόν) at the head of the many goods, but the first good before all (τὸ πρώτιστον ἀγαθόν) is not only cause of the good forms but also of the beautiful forms, just as Plato says [in the *Second Letter*]: for the sake of That all things exist and That is cause of all the beautiful forms" (*PT* II.7.46, 13-47, 10; *Second Letter* 312e2-3).[113] Proclus therefore distinguishes the "good itself" and the many beautiful goods from the first good that transcends all intelligible forms (both "the good itself" and the many good forms). By contrast, "beauty itself" and the many beautiful forms, just like the good itself and the many good forms, remain on the level of intelligible reality, so that their source and principle is clearly the first good that gives them their light. For Proclus, the *Symposium* and the *Phaedo*, therefore, remain on the level of intelligible reality, whereas the *Republic* goes beyond both.

Surely this is a plausible interpretation of Plato's three works, particularly in relation to the *Symposium's* apparent claim that the beautiful is seen

---

110. *PT* II.7.45, 25-46, 1: Ἔτι τοίνυν καὶ καθ' ἕτερον τρόπον τὴν ἐπὶ τὸ πρῶτον ἡμῖν ἀνάλυσιν ἐν τούτοις ὁ Πλάτων ὑφηγεῖται. Πάντα γὰρ τὰ ἐν τῷ κόσμῳ πλήθη νοητῶν ἐξάπτει μονάδων, οἷον τὰ μὲν καλὰ πάντα τοῦ αὐτοκαλοῦ τὰ δὲ ἀγαθὰ πάντα τοῦ αὐτοαγαθοῦ τὰ δὲ αὖ ἴσα τοῦ αὐτοΐσου·

111. On which there is a considerable amount of modern scholarship. Rowe, *Plato: Phaedo, ad loc.*

112. For the *Hippias Major*, see Woodruff, *Plato: Hippias Major* and for both *Hippias Major* and *Minor*, see Pradeau and Fronterotta, *Hippias majeur et Hippias mineur*.

113. *PT* II.7.46, 13-47, 10: Μὴ δή τις οἰέσθω τὸν Πλάτωνα τὴν αὐτὴν ὑποτίθεσθαι τοῦ ἀγαθοῦ τάξιν ἔν τε τοῖς νοητοῖς εἴδεσι καὶ πρὸ τῶν νοητῶν. Ἀλλὰ τὸ μὲν ἀγαθὸν τὸ τῷ καλῷ συντεταγμένον ὄν, οὐσιῶδες καὶ τῶν εἰδῶν ἕν τι τῶν ἐν τοῖς νοητοῖς ὑπολαμβανέτω . . . Ἐν μὲν γὰρ τοῖς εἴδεσι τὸ αὐτοκαλὸν ἐξηγεῖται τῶν πολλῶν καλῶν καὶ τὸ αὐτοαγαθὸν τῶν πολλῶν ἀγαθῶν, καὶ τῶν ὁμοίων ἑκάτερον ὑποστατικόν ἐστι μόνον· τὸ δὲ πρώτιστον ἀγαθὸν οὐ τῶν ἀγαθῶν μόνον ἐστὶν αἴτιον, ἀλλὰ καὶ τῶν καλῶν ὁμοίως, ὥσπερ καὶ ἐν ἄλλοις ὁ Πλάτων ἔφη· Καὶ ἐκείνου ἕνεκα πάντα καὶ ἐκεῖνο αἴτιον πάντων καλῶν.

by that which makes it visible, as I have argued above. Proclus does not mention illumination here in the *Platonic Theology*, but he does in his Commentary on Book 6 of the *Republic*, where he distinguishes the good from both "the good in us" and "the good that is on the same level as the beautiful and the just" (*in Rep.* 1.271, 9–10; cf. 271, 18–29). "The beautiful and every form of virtue . . . are illuminated by the good" (*in Rep.* 1.275, 27–276, 5), as Proclus interprets Socrates' words at *Republic* 6, 508d5 ("whenever it is fixed on that upon which truth and being shine . . .") and as he views Socrates' analogy in this section of Book 6: "[Socrates] took being as the analogue of color, truth as analogous to light, the good as analogous to the sun, and intellect as analogous to the eye."[114] In other words, as the sun not only makes everything visible but also is cause of coming-to-be, so the good as the cause of everything makes everything not only visible but also knowable. "The good illuminates being by means of truth just as the sun illuminates color by light" (*in Rep.* 1.278, 13–14). Here there is an implicit interpretation of *Symposium* 212a, from a slightly different viewpoint. In the concluding step of the ladder of ascent in the *Symposium*, Socrates-Diotima implicitly lifts visibility (ὁρῶντι ᾧ ὁρατὸν τὸ καλόν) up into noetic contemplation and being (ἐκεῖνο ᾧ δεῖ θεωμένου καὶ συνόντος αὐτῷ), to the point where the apprentice gives birth no longer to images of truth, but to true things since she "touches upon what is true" (τίκτειν οὐκ εἴδωλα ἀρετῆς, ἅτε οὐκ εἰδώλου ἐφαπτομένῳ, ἀλλὰ ἀληθῆ, ἅτε τοῦ ἀληθοῦς ἐφαπτομένῳ). And according to Proclus' interpretation of Socrates' analogy in the *Republic*, truth and beauty as supreme forms in the intelligible, and also in a lesser mode "in us," cannot be identified with the first good that illuminates them primarily.

Again, Proclus provides a more plausible interpretation of Plato than some modern scholarship, and he concludes his account of Book 6 by bringing the reader back to the motif of final causality that we have outlined above in Plato's *Symposium* and Aristotle's *Metaphysics* 12.7–10. This good cannot be a part of substance since everything that is a part of substance has to be more imperfect than the substance of which it is a part—a thesis fundamental to Aristotle, of course, but also to Plato, especially in the *Timaeus*. For the former, if the "good" were a part of substance, this would make the good an incomplete *energeia* or *kinesis*;[115] for the latter, the paradigm cannot be imperfect or incomplete; otherwise it would not be the complete living creature.[116] So if the good were only a *part*, it wouldn't be the

---

114. *In Rep.* 1.278, 8–10.
115. *Physics* 201b16–202a12; 257b8–9; *De Anima* 417a16.
116. *Timaeus* 28a–b.

good we are looking for: "namely, that for the sake of which all things exist" (τοῦτο γάρ ἐστιν, οὗ ἕνεκα πάντα) (*in Rep.* 1.286, 22–25).

> Therefore, only that good of which we speak is the good, upon which every reality and perfection hangs, for the sake of which everything exists (μόνον οὖν ἐκεῖνο τἀγαθόν, εἰς ὃ καὶ ὑπόστασις ἀνήρτηται πᾶσα καὶ τελειότης, οὗ ἕνεκα πάντα ἐστίν), but itself exists for the sake of nothing, which neither belongs to anything as the eidetic good nor desires anything else in the way the substance of every being desires the good in order that it might exist and that it might exist completely (καὶ ἵνα ᾖ καὶ ἵνα τελέως ᾖ). (*in Rep.* 1.287, 5–10).[117]

Proclus clearly stands in a long tradition of interpretation of Plato and Aristotle here, emphasizing the οὗ ἕνεκα πάντα, the "hanging" of every reality upon the good (εἰς ὃ καὶ ὑπόστασις ἀνήρτηται πᾶσα), and the energetic perfection of being (ἵνα ᾖ καὶ ἵνα τελέως ᾖ) so characteristic of Plato's *Symposium* and *Republic*, Aristotle's *Metaphysics*, and the whole earlier tradition.

Of this tradition, Plotinus is a conspicuous example, someone who frequently uses *artasthai* and compounds to express the dependence of everything upon the good.[118] But the language Proclus uses in this context reveals his conviction that a similar spirit animates the theologies of both Plato and Aristotle, no matter how different their thought may seem, and that while the good may be for Plotinus not only the source of beauty but supremely beautiful itself, ultimately the good of the *Republic* has to be distinct from the beautiful of the *Phaedo*, the *Hippias Major*, and the *Symposium*, for it is the good alone that makes everything knowable and visible.

This I take to be a crucial, if small, point of difference between Plotinus and Proclus. Proclus insists that "good itself" and "beauty itself" are forms and therefore subordinate to the supreme good. Strictly speaking, therefore, the ultimate good should not be described as beautiful, whereas all derivative goods can also be beautiful. Early in his *Commentary on the Alcibiades I*, for instance, he speaks of the chain of love that creates friendship through its outpouring of providential *eros* and that brings everything back through converting *eros* to culminate in its principle, namely, *auto to kalon*.[119] However, this providential and converting *eros* that works concretely in the rela-

---

117. *In Rep.* 1.287, 5–10: μόνον οὖν ἐκεῖνο τἀγαθόν, εἰς ὃ καὶ ὑπόστασις ἀνήρτηται πᾶσα καὶ τελειότης, οὗ ἕνεκα πάντα ἐστίν, ἕνεκα δὲ οὐδενὸς αὐτό, οὔτε τινὸς ὂν ὡς τὸ εἰδητικὸν ἀγαθόν, οὔτε ἄλλου ἐφιέ- μενον, ὡς ἡ οὐσία παντὸς ὄντος ἐφίεται τοῦ ἀγαθοῦ, καὶ ἵνα ᾖ καὶ ἵνα τελέως ᾖ.

118. For example, see III.1[3].1, 10; VI.4[22].2, 5.

119. Proclus, *In Alc.* 26, 2–34, 10.

tionship between Socrates and Alcibiades, according to Proclus' subsequent interpretation,[120] is an intelligible chain of love that culminates in the *form of beauty*. And so later in the commentary he explicitly interprets the *Symposium* not as leading to the beautiful as its final goal but as culminating ultimately in the good. He argues that all good is beautiful as follows:

> if all the beautiful is desirable, all the lovable desirable and all the desirable good, then all the beautiful is good. Conversely, all the good is desirable, all the desirable is lovable (love and desire have the same object, but differ from each other in moderation or intensity of desire), since Socrates in the *Symposium* leads *love up to the good through the beautiful* and says that the good, just like the beautiful, is the object of love (ὁ ἐν Συμποσίῳ Σωκράτης διὰ τοῦ καλοῦ τὸν ἔρωτα καὶ πρὸς τὸ ἀγαθὸν ἀνάγει καὶ ἐραστόν φησιν εἶναι τὸ ἀγαθόν); so if all the good is desirable, all the desirable lovable, and all the lovable beautiful (since love is immediately of beauty) then all the good is beautiful. (*in Alc.* 329, 17–330, 1)

Here Proclus appears to argue for two conflicting positions. On the one hand, he maintains the primacy of the good on the grounds of Diotima's implicit distinction between the two in the lesser mysteries: the good is surely always to be preferred, she insists,[121] and it is also what most truly belongs to who we are, as Socrates argues in the *Republic*.[122] So Proclus asserts that the correct way to read the *Symposium* is an ascent *through* the beautiful *to* the good. On the other hand, he argues for the convertibility of good and beautiful that seems to run counter to the primacy of the good. But he clarifies what he means immediately: "Let no one object that the good is beyond Beauty or that the object of love is twofold, since the discourse is not about the primary principles but about what is beautiful and good in us" (*in Alc.* 330, 2–4). He then gives an interpretation of the ladder of ascent in the *Symposium* that leads us from our own experience of the good (which transcends perceptible beauties) to the intelligible form of beauty (that presupposes the good to be the ultimate transcendent object of desire):

> In fact, the good in us is simultaneously desirable and lovable; through love, then, and an intense pursuit of it, we acquire the

---

120. Proclus, *In Alc.* 42, 5–63, 11.

121. Plato, *Symposium* 205a; *Republic* 505d; and Plotinus V.5[32].12, 23–24.

122. *Republic* 9.586e: ἅτε ἀληθείᾳ ἑπομένων, καὶ τὰς ἑαυτῶν οἰκείας, εἴπερ τὸ βέλτιστον ἑκάστῳ, τοῦτο καὶ οἰκειότατον—in following the truth, all the parts of soul will reap their own truest pleasures, "if what is best for each is that also that most belongs to each."

> good, and if anyone has an intimate perception of himself, he doubtless knows that this good has a more piercing effect of love[123] than the beautiful objects of sense perception. The good then is also beautiful. That is why lovers are encouraged after perceptible beauty to lead their beloveds to the beauty that lies in actions, ways of life, scientific understanding and virtue, and there to practice the erotic impulse of the soul, then to stretch up in this way to intellect and the primary active divine Beauty there .... (*in Alc.* 330, 4–12)

Proclus then is, in fact, arguing that real beauty is always good, but that the good itself precedes intelligible beauty. Plotinus too will often make similar statements. As we have seen above, in what is clearly an interpretation of the great myth of the *Phaedrus* 246aff, Plotinus argues that the soul can be bored by intellect unless it is illumined by a light or grace from the good (VI.7[38].22). But later in the same work, he comes close to identifying the good and supreme beauty, but retains nonetheless a reasonable distinction since the good is the "originative principle and limit of beauty, a beauty above beauty," something that Proclus does not appear to approve, but which is a very reasonable interpretation of Socrates' statement in *Republic* 6.508e4–6 that while knowledge and truth are beautiful, "you will correctly think of the Good *as other and more beautiful* than they."

On the basis of all the evidence so far, therefore, both Plotinus and Proclus are firmly in agreement on two principles: the beautiful leads to the good and the good is that by virtue of which everything else, including the beautiful, is both thought and perceived. Nuances of interpretation apart, this is surely a plausible interpretation of all the earlier dialogues, including the *Hippias Major* and *Phaedo*, dialogues that set the scene in significant measure for the *Symposium*, *Republic*, and *Phaedrus*.

1.9 Marsilio Ficino

This overall interpretation will persist not only in late antiquity but also in the Renaissance. Even though in very late antiquity, Pseudo-Dionysius, for instance, identifies the beautiful and the good in the *Divine Names* (*DN* 704b) and proceeds in the *Mystical Theology* beyond names into the "brilliant darkness of hidden silence," nonetheless, there remains a priority of light over beauty: "amid the deepest shadow they pour overwhelming light

---

123. Proclus, *in Alc.* 330, 7: "more piercing" (*drimuteros*); the higher the principle, the more extensive or the more piercing is its effect; cf. *ET* prop. 57; for comment, see Dillon, *Iamblichi Chalcidensis Fragmenta*, 236–38 (on Olympiodorus, *in Alc.* 110, 13ff).

upon what is most manifest... and completely fill our sightless minds with treasures *beyond all beauty*" (*MT* 997b).[124] Marsilio Ficino's approach is even more striking in his Commentary on the *Symposium* and confirms this priority. Instead of the vision of the beautiful in the final revelation of the greater mysteries, at the end of his Sixth Speech (equivalent to that of Socrates-Diotima), in chapter 19, Tomasso Benci points in his concluding words not to the *Symposium* but instead to *Republic* Book 6 when he observes: "...we shall not only love God without limit as Diotima is depicted as commanding, but God alone. For as the eyes are to the sun, so the mind is to God. But the eye seeks not only light before other things, but the light alone."[125]

1.10 Conclusions

Contrary to common views that Platonism is responsible for a fatal divorce between the intellectual soul or mind and feelings or that at the heart of this tradition, in Aristotle, impassible or unfeeling mind is incompatible with any recognizable human feeling, this chapter argues that in both Plato and Aristotle the real divide is a choice between lives. It is a choice between a life that is object-driven, passive in the sense that it is led by uncontrolled feeling or passion, on the one hand, and a life that is subject-initiated, that is, a life that awakens a more integrated, higher focus of reason and desire; a life, in other words, that is not self-directed, but focused upon something bigger than itself, a world or worlds of wisdom.

Even in the most difficult case in Plato, namely, the *Phaedo*, where the intellectual soul seems most sharply divided, desire characterizes *both* body *and* soul. In the *Phaedo* lovers of wisdom "are in training for dying" (67e), but this means they *desire* to have their soul by itself, not by extinguishing but by awakening a different, more comprehensive axis of desire, not wealth or body, or even thought only, but, as we saw above, thought with hope (68a1: ἐλπίς), desire (66b; 66e; 67e; 68a), gladness, joyfulness, love, and longing (*eros*) for wisdom (68a1-2: εἰ μὴ ἄσμενοι ἐκεῖσε ἴοιεν, οἷ ἀφικομένοις ἐλπίς ἐστιν οὗ διὰ βίου ἤρων τυχεῖν· ἤρων δὲ φρονήσεως). This position becomes only more prominent in the *Symposium*, *Republic* and *Phaedrus*. So Grube's view that in the *Phaedo* "no allowance is made for the development of the human emotions," and that there is only "pure intellectualism

---

124. Dionysius, *MT* 997b3-4:...καὶ ἐν τῷ πάμπαν ἀναφεῖ καὶ ἀοράτῳ τῶν ὑπερκάλων ἀγλαϊῶν ὑπερπληροῦντα τοὺς ἀνομμάτους νόας.:

125. S. Reynolds Jayne, trans., *Marsilio Ficino*. Compare Laurens, *In Convivium*, 202-3.

divorced from life"[126] is not simply inaccurate, but a profound misreading of a more complex position.

But is Grube partially right in so far as the practice of dying is not a truly *human* goal and in so far as the life exemplified by Socrates in this dialogue is only a life for rare human beings, not a life that could be in any sense a *practical* ideal for ordinary people? The language of the *Phaedo* indicates clearly that this is a practical preoccupation, not some dry intellectual one. Neither here nor later in the *Theaetetus* does Plato make the life of wisdom a predominantly intellectual concern. Healthy virtuous action is not an adjunct or afterthought to the philosopher's quest to become "like to god" but altogether central. Instead, it is unbalanced for readers of Plato to disregard how important it is for Socrates or for anyone to confront the reality of death in a healthy way, not only in all the "deaths" that necessarily pervade the course of a lifetime, but especially in the case of Socrates as he confronts directly his own death. There are additional compelling reasons for this in the *Phaedo*: if action is to be agent-driven rather than simply circumstantial, and if we are to give good reasons for our actions rather than mechanical or purely physiological reasons, then formal causality must have some role to play. Whatever good hope or not one might have for an afterlife, wise action should surely spring as far as possible from a wise steadfast disposition, and not simply because of pleasure or pain in a privative sense or because we happen to be composed of bones and sinews. This does not eliminate good hope; instead, it constitutes its reality. The *Phaedo* is a dramatic representation of a remarkable human being facing in a remarkable way what every living creature has faced or must one day face. The vision of the dialogue is pervaded by what it means to be a subject-agent confronting death. It is not primarily a vision for a young person in love with his or her life still unveiling in front of her. Other dialogues are written from that viewpoint. But it is concerned most directly with how we should live our lives practically at any and every given moment. And in the *Republic* (Book 9), this apparently highest life most involves desire and pleasure.

In Aristotle, as we also saw, there is no divide between thought and feeling, but there is effectively, in cooperation between the two, a new emergent form of being or chiastic psychology in which the human being becomes an agent or originative principle: ὀρεκτικὸς νοῦς ἢ ὄρεξις διανοητική. Neither in Plato nor Aristotle is this state devoid of pleasure. On the contrary, it is only at the point where one can discriminate between pleasures with some experience of life—that is, Book 9 of the complex argument of the *Republic* and Book 10 of the equally complex argument of the *Nicomachean Ethics*—that

---

126. Grube, *Plato's Thought*, 129.

one can begin to see the complex trajectories of desire that lead one to the need for a choice of lives.

The chapter then goes on to argue that love and desire must be intrinsic to all intellects and unmoved movers after the primary mover in Aristotle and that, despite scholarly reservations about this in the *Enneads* of Plotinus, *orexis*, *eros*, and *epithymia* in different passages characterize the being of even the divine intellect or pre-intellect in relation to Plotinus' primary principle, the one or the good.

This first part of the chapter, then, helped to set the scene for the subsequent development of a series of important theses: I first argued that in perhaps the most important passage of Aristotle's theology, the apparently remote unmoved mover that moves everything "by being loved" but that looks utterly removed from anything resembling love itself is, in fact, almost exactly the opposite: the unmoved mover's "way of life" appears to reach down into every activity and emotion in the cosmos and to be a life of the purest pleasure. I then went on to argue for the following positions:

(1) That Aristotle's theology and physics were implicitly developed from the hierarchy of forms and final causality by desire and love from the "lesser" and "greater" mysteries of Diotima-Socrates' speech in Plato's *Symposium*.

(2) That features of Aristotle's presentation of participation in the divine life resonate demonstrably with Socrates' treatment in the *Republic* of a range of activities or powers—from thought, through perception, to memory and hope—that characterize the life of wisdom, and that Aristotle's famous statement that "the heaven and nature *hang from* such a principle" must surely be a deliberate reference to the *Ion*'s image of divine creativity from which a long chain of iron rings "hangs." In other words, Aristotle presents his theology consciously in the after-image of Plato's dialogues in order to highlight both the differences and the continuities.

(3) That both the *Symposium* and *Metaphysics* 12.7–10 present the ascent to god as a movement, first, to the beautiful of final causality and, finally, to the good. This has altogether escaped attention in both texts. In Aristotle, demonstrably, the language of the beautiful (τὸ καλόν[127]) in chapter 7 *gives way to the language of the good and the best* in chapters 7–10.[128] The *Symposium* is a more difficult case, since the good of the *Republic* seems almost entirely absent. However, at the conclusion of Socrates-Diotima's speech, something unsuspected in modern scholarship actually happens.

---

127. *Metaphysics* 7.1072a28, b34, 11; 1074b24.

128. *Metaphysics* 7.1072a35–1072b1, 12, 15, 24, 28, 29, 32; 9.1074b20, 33; 1075a8–9; 10.1075a12, 14, 36–38; 1075b, 2. 8, 11; 1076a4.

Diotima's words "*that by which the beautiful is visible*" and that "*by which it is necessary to contemplate it*" can only have one ultimate referent: the beautiful is evidently visible or able to be contemplated (not only by itself but) by the ultimate source of light and intelligibility, namely, *the good*. Consequently, even if we should be cautious about making chronological claims about these dialogues, the *Symposium* demonstrably has to be read in the light of the *Republic*, just as Aristotle's theology and physics have to be read in the light of both Platonic dialogues.

The following question, therefore, naturally emerged: if this overall interpretation, at odds with much modern scholarship and, in fact, virtually unsuspected in the modern world, is relevant to Plato and Aristotle, is there any trace of it in the later ancient tradition? And, more precisely, first, did the Neoplatonists genuinely find the good of the *Republic* in the ascent to the beautiful in the *Symposium* and, second, did they read Aristotle's theology in the light of this?

The chapter, therefore, went on to show that even a Middle Platonist like Alcinous and also the later Neoplatonists, Plotinus and Proclus, clearly read Plato and Aristotle in exactly this way. Indeed, even a major Renaissance figure like Marsilio Ficino automatically reads the conclusion of the ascent to the beautiful in the *Symposium* from the perspective of light in *Republic* 6—to the extent of not even mentioning the beautiful at this point!

This chapter then has uncovered new readings of some of antiquity's most important texts and demonstrated that major interpreters in late antiquity, thought by many contemporary scholars, after Schleiermacher, to be some of the most inferior readers of Plato, appear to have got Plato and Aristotle substantially right on these issues.

Finally, concerning what appears to be a Romantic identification of beauty and truth in Keats' *Ode on a Grecian Urn*, and perhaps to characterize a form of Platonism if Romanticism does build in part upon the Platonic tradition, as is often thought: this identification of beauty and truth would not be genuine for either Plato or Aristotle. As we indicated at the beginning of the chapter, it seems unlikely that beauty is truth in any simple sense or that what is true is beautiful and that what is beautiful true, no matter how powerful the identity of truth and beauty might be. What is true can be petty and crippling; what is beautiful can be deceptive; and we might add that what is good might turn out to be neither beautiful nor true. It would seem that in Plato, Aristotle, and the later Neoplatonists, all of these qualifications—true, beautiful, or good—can wander or admit of opposites, as Socrates puts it in the *Republic*. Only when the beautiful and the true are configured in and by the highest good do we have an ascent we can hold to in the shifting fortunes and appearances of ordinary life. Nowhere do Plato and Aristotle say exactly this, But this is their clear practice, a practice they bequeathed to later antiquity.

With all of this in mind, let us now turn to the questions of human friendship and love of the individual. Does Platonism understand anything about the human condition or are ordinary human relations subordinated and perhaps eclipsed in the ascent to the true/beautiful/good?

2

Friendship and Love of the Individual

THE PLATONIC-PYTHAGOREAN TRADITION PLACED strong emphasis upon friendship at all levels of reality—cosmic, hypercosmic, human, interspecies friendships, even friendship between body and soul. Empedocles believed that there was a golden age of friendship among all living creatures before the rise of strife.[1] Yet Plato and Aristotle, primary exponents of this tradition, have suffered at the hands of some of their critics who have shaped contemporary discourse on this issue. Famously, for Karl Popper, in the *Republic* one is loved in so far as, and only in so far as, one produces good for the community as a whole; and so "Plato recognizes only one ultimate standard [of justice], the interest of the state. . . . *Morality is nothing but political hygiene.*"[2] For Gregory Vlastos, perhaps the most influential figure in Plato scholarship of the last fifty years, "the cardinal flaw in Plato's theory [is that] it does not provide for love of whole persons, but only for love of that abstract version of persons which consists of the complex of their best qualities. . . . [P]ersons cannot compete with abstractions of universal significance, like schemes of social reform or scientific and philosophical truths, still less with the Idea of Beauty (*Symp.* 211e)."[3] More recently, for Martha Nussbaum, an equally influential figure and prolific scholar on some of the most important questions of our time, Plato's Diotima has "the object of her love as a seat of valuable properties, and therefore as a suitable vehicle for creation," and so "neglects in the process the other person's own agency and choice." This results in "an unpromising attitude toward another person" and in there being "ultimately no difference between loving a person and loving a scientific system."[4] Aristotle fares somewhat better, but not

---

1. *DK* 130b, 128b, 137b.
2. Popper, *The Open Society*, I, 113.
3. Vlastos, "The Individual," 3–42.
4. Nussbaum, *Upheavals of Thought*, 498–99.

much. Aristotle, on Vlastos' account, at least sees (a) that the active desire to promote the interest of the person we love "'for that person's sake, not ours' must be built into love at its best, but not as far as sorting this out from (b) appreciation of the excellence instantiated by that person; (b), of course, need not be disinterested and *could* be egoistic. The limits of Aristotle's understanding of love show up in his failure to notice the ambiguity in 'loving a person for himself.'"[5] In other words, for Vlastos, "A and B are good and A loves B for B's self" implies that "A loves B because and only because B is good." In this chapter, I will restrict myself to an examination of Plato and the later Neoplatonic tradition, leaving Aristotle to fare for himself because generally he seems to be holding his own with most readers, even though his notion of friendship is so often considered elitist or conditional.

I think that these criticisms fail to understand the depth and subtlety of Plato's treatments of love and friendship. I shall argue here then for the following theses: First, the *Alcibiades I*[6] has to be included in the series of dialogues that examine this crucial human issue, namely, the *Lysis, Symposium, Phaedrus*, and to lesser extent, the *Republic*. This is so for three reasons: because it fits thematically into this series of dialogues, adding a crucial element to the treatment of love and friendship, because its authenticity was never questioned until Schleiermacher in the nineteenth-century, and because it was long considered the first dialogue that anyone should read.[7] Second, the *Alcibiades I* fits the series of these dialogues not because it

---

5. G. Vlastos, "The Individual," 33n100.

6. On the question of the authenticity of *Alcibiades I*, see N. Denyer, *Plato. Alcibiades*, 14–26 (who on balance finds it authentic); N. D. Smith, "Did Plato Write the Alcibiades I?" 118–23, H. Tarrant, *Alcibiades and the Socratic Lover-Educator*, 223–233 (who on balance, for stylometric and other reasons, thinks it spurious: "The basic working vocabulary appears... more similar to... dialogues such as the *Phaedo* that already introduce the Forms...the balance of probability is tipped in favor of this work being a spurious dialogue" (232–33)); and O. Velásquez, *Alcibíades, Platón*, 24–32, for whom the most reasonable solution is to accept its authenticity. I think too that it is most probably authentic and closer to the "middle" than to the "early" dialogues—perhaps a dialogue that Plato started earlier but returned to later. Its authenticity was never doubted until the 19th century, and indeed it was thought to be the first dialogue of Plato that anyone should read (Diogenes Laertius, 3.37), and considered a useful introduction to Plato by the later Neoplatonists. Denyer aptly sums up the strangeness of Schleiermacher's view: "The *Alcibiades* maintained its place among Plato's dialogues unchallenged, until the early nineteenth century. Then Friedrich Schleiermacher (1836, 329) declared it to be 'very insignificant and poor, and that to such a degree, that we cannot ascribe it to Plato.' The *Alcibiades* fell out of favor. From being the one dialogue read by anyone who had read any Plato at all, it passed out of the canon, and almost completely out of sight" (6).

7. As prescribed by Iamblichus, in the *Anonymous Prolegomena to Platonic Philosophy*, 26. See for example Proclus, *Commentary on the First Alcibiades*, 4, 19–7, 8.

presents a less self-directed or egoistic view of love than they do but because these dialogues develop some of the themes of the *Alcibiades I* and bring them into a sharper reflexive and intersubjective focus. Third, a striking feature of these dialogues is that they do not simply provide an analysis of or teaching on love, as in Socrates-Diotima's speech, for instance, but that these analyses, speeches, or myths are set in living situations where the love experience of individuals cannot be separated from the actual characters with all their imperfections, limitations of vision, sophisticated discourses, and errors of judgment. In fact, Plato's refusal to ignore the complexities of the human predicament leads him to develop a new genre in the *Symposium*, above all, and this has not been properly appreciated, but rather sacrificed in favor of extracting segments of the dialogues that present limited versions, indeed caricatures, of Plato. In short, the modern critical view that Plato is all about perfection, with a woeful disregard of the imperfect, is a modern misreading: the nature of *eros* itself and even the *dramatis personae* of the dialogues paint an entirely different picture. These dialogues explore the ambiguities of ordinary experience in profound ways, provide models of love and friendship, and show who the individual as object and subject might really be.

Finally, if one goes more deeply into the history of interpretation in later antiquity and the Renaissance, one finds a history of reading Plato in this double-edged way, understanding the imperfections of the speakers but recognizing simultaneously the quest for love that reflects the deepest concerns of Plato. A history of readings of different speeches in the *Symposium*, for instance, and of cross-readings from the perspective of several dialogues, reveals a sophisticated sensitivity. In order to show this, I will take the speech of Pausanias from the *Symposium* as a test case for exploring the psychological ambiguities of ordinary experience and trace the after-life of this speech in the later tradition from Plotinus to Ficino in order to show how major figures from late antiquity to the Renaissance could do cross-readings of the *Alcibiades I*, *Symposium*, and *Phaedrus* with a profound understanding of Plato's thought. In all of this, I question a modern tendency to make Plato into a straw man for modern concerns and to simplify his thought in the process.

I leave Aristotle for the most part out of account only because my principal focus is upon the *Platonic* tradition, but he is, in fact, an integral part of this tradition; and if his view of the best form of friendship in the *Ethica Nicomachea* is that the quality of one's self-relatedness is important because this is what one gives to one's friend,[8] I will simply state here that this is

---

8. For an excellent treatment, especially on "primary" friendship, see Stern-Gillet,

neither simply elitist nor conditional but *dynamic* and developmental, on the one hand, and, on the other, should be read in the broader context of friendship in the *Eudemian Ethics*, where true friendship can well be non-elitist—at least, in the modern sense—since it is extended to include unequals, between gods and human beings, for example.

2.1 Friendship in the Platonic tradition: *The Lysis, Alcibiades I,* and *Symposium*

Plato discusses love (*eros*)[9] and friendship (*philia*)[10] primarily in two dialogues, the *Lysis* and *Symposium*, with significant treatment also in the *Phaedrus* and, as I maintain, earlier in the *Alcibiades I*.

While the *Lysis* is an aporetic dialogue and reaches no firm conclusions, it nonetheless serves one important preliminary task. Hippothales asks Socrates to tell him "what someone should do or say to get his prospective boyfriend to love him" (206c1–3). Through an elenchic examination of Hippothales, Socrates shows that one should not swell one's boyfriends up and spoil them, but "[draw] in their sails and [make] them humble" (210e2–5). But the *Lysis* does not perform a successful answer to Hippothales' original question. In fact, a successful performance of how one should approach an individual boyfriend in the appropriate way intimated in the *Lysis* occurs only in the *Alcibiades I*; and this, in my view, is one good reason to suggest that the *Alcibiades I*, whether genuinely Platonic or not, can be reasonably seen as an "in between" companion piece to the *Lysis* and *Symposium*, and, indeed, a dialogue that discusses love and friendship from a perspective apparently missing from other dialogues. As John Dillon has argued, "on the subject of the art of love Platonists turned for inspiration primarily, not to the *Symposium* or the *Phaedrus*, nor even to the *Lysis*, but to the *First Alcibiades*."[11]

There is a long tradition linking discussion of *eros* to that of friendship—something we see already in the *Lysis,* as also later in the second-century handbook of Platonism, the *Didaskalikos*, by Alcinous. As Dillon

---

Aristotle's Philosophy of Friendship, and for evaluation of Vlastos' account, see 175–77.

9. On *eros* and cognates, see Dover, *Plato: Symposium*, 1, 134–35; Rowe, *Plato: Symposium*, 168–71; 188; 190; Corrigan and Glazov-Corrigan, *Plato's Dialectic at Play*, 44–46.

10. For the range of meaning in *philia*, see Schroeder, "Friendship," 36n2; Rowe, *Plato: Symposium*, 147–48; generally Joachim, *Aristotle. The Nicomachean Ethics*, 243–61; Stern-Gillet, *Aristotle's Philosophy of Friendship*, 11–58.

11. Dillon, "Ars Amatoria," 387–92, quotation from 391.

notes, in chapter 33 of the *Didaskalikos*, on friendship, there is attached a discussion of erotic love (187, 20ff.), which "leads in turn to the propounding of a sort of *ars amatoria*,"[12] such as we find in Ovid's *Ars Amatoria* (I.35–40).[13] The Greek phrase *erotikē technē* is, of course, mentioned already in the *Phaedrus* 257a, as Dillon points out, and this suggests a connection between this *ars amatoria* and Plato's dialogues. The characteristic of true friendship, for Alcinous, is reciprocal good will (κατ' εὔνοιαν ἀντίστροφον) (as in Aristotle) among people of similar or equal good character. Other kinds of friendship are not always reciprocal or among equals and may therefore be more superficial (such as the natural affection of parents for children, of kinsfolk for one another, or political or club friendships). Erotic love, Alcinous observes, is also a form of friendship and admits of three degrees: good, median, and bad, relating respectively to the soul alone, the compound, and the body alone. Only the love of the good is a true *technē*, admitting of three aims or *theorēmata* (similar to those we find in Ovid's *Ars Amatoria*): "Its aims are to discern the worthy object of love, to gain possession of it, and to make use of it" (θεωρήματα δ' αὐτῆς τὸ γνῶναί τε τὸν ἀξιέραστον καὶ κτήσασθαι καὶ χρήσασθαι) (187, 41). So there is a triad of aims here: *gnōsis, ktēsis, chrēsis,* or knowledge, acquisition, and use. This means, according to Alcinous, first selecting someone on the basis of his noble, strong, and fiery aims and impulses directed to the beautiful; second, working to acquire him not by spoiling but by restraining him and showing him that life in its present state is not worth living; and, finally, after capturing the beloved, to use him: "pledging guarantee of these things through which he might become perfectly exercised in virtue and the goal for this pair is to progress from being lover and beloved to becoming friends" (ὅταν δ' ἕλῃ τὸν ἐρώμενον, χρήσεται αὐτῷ παρεγγυῶν ταῦτα, δι' ὧν ἀσκηθεὶς ἔσται τέλειος, τέλος δὲ αὐτοῖς τὸ ἀντὶ ἐραστοῦ καὶ ἐρωμένου γενέσθαι φίλους). In other words, true friendship is the goal to which genuine erotic love aspires. (This is one way to read *Phaedrus* 255e–256e.)

Dillon points out that, in the light of the theorizing of Aristotle and of the Stoics about perfect friendship (the latter perhaps, indeed, itself influenced by a reading of the *Alcibiades*), this account in later Platonists fits the

---

12. Ibid., 388.

13. Ovid, *Ars Amatoria*, I.35–40: *Principio, quod amare velis, reperire labora,/ Qui nova nunc primum miles in arma venis./ Proximus huic labor est placitam exorare puellam:/ Tertius, ut longo tempore duret amor./ Hic modus, haec nostro signabitur area curru:/ Haec erit admissa meta terenda rota.* "First, strive to find an object for your love, you who come now for the first time as a new soldier to battle. The next job is to win the girl who pleases you. Third, to make love last for a long time. This will be the limit, this the field that will be marked by my chariot, the goal that will be worn by my wheel."

more altruistic portrayal of Socrates' amatory procedure in the *Alcibiades I* rather than the apparently self-directed accounts of love in the *Symposium* and the *Phaedrus*.¹⁴ I think the case is more complex still, but I suggest we can see this love of the individual directly in the above passage of Alcinous' *Didaskalikos*, which goes back to the enquiry between Socrates and Alcibiades in the *Alcibiades I*.

The *Alcibiades* situates the search for self-knowledge, first, through the distinction between the soul alone, on the one hand, and the compound of soul and body and the body alone, on the other, as in Alcinous above. Second, the outcome of the relationship is, at first, a pledge of the lover that leads secondarily to reciprocal friendship, in the *Didaskalikos*: "he will use him pledging guarantee (χρήσεται αὐτῷ παρεγγυῶν ταῦτα) of these things through which *he* might become perfectly exercised in virtue, and the goal *for them* is to progress from being lover and beloved to becoming friends." The *Alcibiades* employs a similar "pledge" language (134d: ἐθέλω ἐγγυήσασθαι) leading to a new mutuality or love in return, *anteros*, in its concluding pages, as we will see (134d–135d).¹⁵ Let me first put this correlation between the treatments of love in the *Didaskalikos* and the *Alcibiades* into the immediate context of the *Alcibiades*.

The famous eye-soul analogy in the section previous to this, though complicated by the Christian Bishop Eusebius' external god testimony,¹⁶ must surely involve Alcibiades looking not to an external god but *into Socrates' soul*, that is, into Socrates himself—on the understanding that the soul *is* most directly the individual—and uncovering there what is best in Socrates, on the analogy of the eye and its pupil, in which the one sees both oneself and the other:

> if an eye is to see itself, it must look at an eye, and to that place of the eye in which the excellence of an eye happens to be, ... and if the soul is to know herself, she must look to a soul, and especially to this place of the soul in which soul's excellence dwells ... wisdom ... can we say there is anything more divine than this? ... Then this place of soul resembles god, and anyone looking to this and coming to know all the divine, god and wisdom, will in this way most know himself.¹⁷

---

14. Dillon, "Ars Amatoria," 392.

15. A more distant form of this pledge can be seen at *Phaedrus* 256d1–2.

16. *Alcibiades* I.133c8–17 (Eusebius with variants in Stobaeus).

17. *Alc.* 133b–c: Ὀφθαλμὸς ἄρ' εἰ μέλλει ἰδεῖν αὑτόν, εἰς ὀφθαλμὸν αὐτῷ βλεπτέον, καὶ τοῦ ὄμματος εἰς ἐκεῖνον τὸν τόπον ἐν ᾧ τυγχάνει ἡ ὀφθαλμοῦ ἀρετὴ ἐγγιγνομένη· ἔστι δὲ τοῦτό που ὄψις; {ΑΛ.} Οὕτως.
{ΣΩ.} Ἆρ' οὖν, ὦ φίλε Ἀλκιβιάδη, καὶ ψυχὴ εἰ μέλλει γνώσεσθαι αὑτήν, εἰς ψυχὴν αὐτῇ

For all the religious or spiritual connotations of this passage, what is remarkable about the analogy is that one sees oneself and the god not in a purely external way but in and through another human being. As Harold Tarrant has plausibly argued,[18] the text of the *Alcibiades* available to Proclus and Olympiodorus, whatever it might have been, did not include the external god testimony, but rather enjoined, as Olympiodorus makes clear in his prologue to the commentary,[19] that Alcibiades look into Socrates' soul: "*look into me*, i.e. into Socrates' soul, and not into any random part of it but into the highest, and you will see *in me* intellect and god" (ἀπόβλεψον εἰς ἐμέ, τουτέστι τὴν Σωκρατικὴν ψυχήν, καὶ ταύτης μὴ εἰς τὸ τυχὸν μέρος, ἀλλ᾽ εἰς τὸ ἀκρότατον, καὶ ὄψει ἐν ἐμοὶ νοῦν καὶ θεόν'). Olympiodorus goes on to view this direct individual focus as a process of ascent with four different levels—political, kathartical, theoretical, and enthusiastical—as is implied in Alcinous' statement about moving from simple erotic love to true friendship and in the conclusion of the *Alcibiades*, but as is actually spelled out in the higher mysteries of the *Symposium* and in the scale of virtues in later Neoplatonism:[20]

> So through his saying "look into me" he showed that the target [of the dialogue] is about knowing oneself constitutionally; through his saying "not into any random part" that it is also [about knowing oneself] cathartically, since purifying oneself belongs to the highest part of the soul; through the [words] "you will see intellect in me," that it is also [about knowing oneself] theoretically, since engagement with things at an intellectual level belongs to the theoretic faculty; and through the [words] "and [a] god" that it is also [about knowing oneself] inspirationally, for it is in accordance with the divine within us—something

---

βλεπτέον, καὶ μάλιστ᾽ εἰς τοῦτον αὐτῆς τὸν τόπον ἐν ᾧ ἐγγίγνεται ἡ ψυχῆς ἀρετή, σοφία, καὶ εἰς ἄλλο ᾧ τοῦτο τυγχάνει ὅμοιον ὄν; {ΑΛ.} Ἔμοιγε δοκεῖ, ὦ Σώκρατες. {ΣΩ.} Ἔχομεν οὖν εἰπεῖν ὅτι ἐστὶ τῆς ψυχῆς θειότερον ἢ τοῦτο, περὶ ὃ τὸ εἰδέναι τε καὶ φρονεῖν ἐστιν; {ΑΛ.} Οὐκ ἔχομεν.

{ΣΩ.} Τῷ θεῷ ἄρα τοῦτ᾽ ἔοικεν αὐτῆς, καί τις εἰς τοῦτο βλέπων καὶ πᾶν τὸ θεῖον γνούς, θεόν τε καὶ φρόνησιν, οὕτω καὶ ἑαυτὸν ἂν γνοίη μάλιστα.

18. Tarrant, "Olympiodorus and Proclus," 3–29.

19. For discussion of the passages in Olympiodorus, *in Alc.*, see Tarrant, "Olympiodorus and Proclus," 6–15.

20. See, for example, Porphyry, *Sententia* 22 (civic, purificatory, contemplative, paradigmatic; cf. Plotinus I.2.1, 16–21; 3, 11–19; 6, 22–27; 7, 1–6); Macrobius *In Somn. Scip.* I. VIII; Marinus, *Life of Proclus*; Olympiodorus *In Phaed.* 45–49, 113–14; Wallis (Gerson), *Neoplatonism*, 98n2. And also from the perspective of the beloved in the *Phaedrus* 255d5–6: "and [he] is unaware that he is seeing himself in his lover as in a mirror."

simple like the divine itself—that we are inspired (ἐνθουσιῶμεν). (Olymp. *In Alc.* 8.2-12; trans. Tarrant).[21]

In other words, remaining true to the spirit of individual, intersubjective loving in the *Alcibiades I*, this later version reads the *Alcibiades* already in the ascent mode of the *Symposium*, the political mode of the *Republic*, and the inspirational mode of Socrates' myth in the *Phaedrus*.

What we see in the closing pages of the *Alcibiades* is the practical outcome of Alcibiades seeing the divine in Socrates. The reference of τὸ θεῖον καὶ λαμπρὸν at 134d—"the divine and bright" that Alcibiades will look to in action—is unclear, but since this was agreed between them earlier (134d4: ὅπερ γε ἐν τοῖς πρόσθεν ἐλέγομεν), it should refer to their internal mutual agreement as the sequel makes clear: in looking to the divine in Socrates "you will see and know both yourselves and your goods" (134d5), "you will act rightly and well" (134d7-8), and so be "god-beloved"(134d2), and "I [Socrates] will be your *pledge* that you will be happy," to which Alcibiades replies "you are *a secure pledge*" (134e1-3: Ἀλλὰ μὴν οὕτω γε πράττοντας ὑμᾶς ἐθέλω ἐγγυήσασθαι ἦ μὴν εὐδαιμονήσειν. Ἀσφαλὴς γὰρ εἶ ἐγγυητής). All of this is on the clear understanding that "before having virtue, it is better for a man to be ruled than rule" (135b7-8),[22] and that this is not according to the wish of Socrates, but of god (135d3-6). On the basis only of this mutual pledge under god, the result that Socrates wants is actually brought about when an explicit responsive love, as of other *self* or agent, is born in Alcibiades himself: "Then *I* say it . . . and this besides, that *we are* likely to change the shape of things, Socrates, so *that I shall have yours and you mine.* For from this day forward, *I must lead you and you will be led by me*" (135d7-10). Here self-realization clearly depends on the presence and mutuality of friendship. However we are to interpret the αὐτὸ τὸ αὐτό[23] or

---

21. Olympiodorus, *In Alc.* 8, 2-12: διὰ μὲν οὖν τοῦ εἰπεῖν ἀπόβλεψον εἰς ἐμὲ' δεδήλωκεν ὅτι περὶ τοῦ γνῶναι πολιτικῶς ἑαυτόν ἐστιν ὁ σκοπός· διὰ δὲ τοῦ εἰπεῖν 'μὴ εἰς τὸ τυχόν', ὅτι καὶ καθαρτικῶς, τοῦ γὰρ ἀκροτάτου τῆς ψυχῆς τὸ καθαίρειν ἑαυτόν· διὰ δὲ τοῦ 'ὄψει ἐν ἐμοὶ νοῦν', ὅτι καὶ θεωρητικῶς, πρέπει γὰρ τῷ θεωρητικῷ τὸ κατὰ τὸν νοῦν τοῖς πράγμασιν ὁμιλεῖν· διὰ δὲ τοῦ 'καὶ θεόν', ὅτι καὶ ἐνθουσιαστικῶς, κατὰ γὰρ τὸ ἐν ἡμῖν θεῖον ἐνθουσιῶμεν, ἁπλοῦν ὂν ὥσπερ καὶ τὸ θεῖον αὐτό.

22. The need for a recognition that there be ruler and ruled in each person is emphasized at *Laws* 5.726-727a.

23. The contrast between αὐτὸ τὸ αὐτό and αὐτὸ ἕκαστον cannot, in my view, be a contrast between a property or characteristic and a generic, universal ideal or between an individual and a generic, impersonal idea, because the soul (i.e., Alcibiades or Socrates as souls) is neither a property nor an individual in any ordinary, material sense. The contrast is rather between the indwelling reality that makes Socrates himself as Socrates and the ultimate reality that by being itself is the standard according to which all other individuals are themselves. If we should be careful not to project

the identification of self with the soul,[24] there could not be a more concrete mutual exchange of pledges for the better or of reciprocal individual love. The images Socrates employs—conversation, love, looking into the eye of the other, one's beloved friend—indicate the personal, individual, and intersubjective. Thus, the exchange of pledges involves a chiastic change of guidance: with all the ironies that this must involve, Alcibiades will lead Socrates. Indeed, the appropriate direct love of the individual is what the *Lysis* aspires to but the *Alcibiades* actually performs: "I alone was a lover of *you*, Alcibiades, whereas the rest were lovers of *what belongs to you*"(131e).[25]

---

any modern notions of "self" onto the *Alcibiades*, then it is even more suspect surely to cast the entire discussion into a personal/impersonal dichotomy, as Annas ("Self-Knowledge"), Brunschwig ("La deconstruction du 'connais-toi toi-même'") and even Gill ("Self-Knowledge") do. Nonetheless, I prefer Gill's "triangular" interpretation, according to which the two psyches are actively related to each other on one horizontal axis, "while their converging axis is directed to god" ("Self-Knowledge," 109). What is at stake here, I suggest, is the question not so much of the "subject," as Foucault puts it—though I do not think Foucault is entirely wrong, or of the "self" anachronistically conceived, but rather of what makes each individual unique as the bearer of other related properties and of what uniqueness itself makes other things unique. This, I also suggest, anticipates the "final argument" of the *Phaedo* (soul as the bearer of properties) (105dff.) and the description of Socrates by Alcibiades in the *Symposium* as *atopos* (221c), unlike any other individual being, by virtue of his search for the divine reflected in the divine images in him.

24. Rather than looking at the soul as a disembodied entity distinguished from the compound and the body, I prefer to regard all three as different dimensions of lived experience, with the richest, most comprehensive being the soul-dimension. This makes sense of what we actually find in the *Alcibiades I* and middle dialogues such as the *Symposium* and *Republic*. Christopher Gill distinguishes two conceptions in Plato's dialogues as a whole of "what is essential to us," embodied minds in shared search for truth, on the one hand, and essentially disembodied minds in which knowledge of truth and god-like status are realized; and he situates the eye analogy in the *Alcibiades* as "lying on the cusp between these two ideas" ("Self-Knowledge," 110). There is some truth to this, perhaps, insofar as both conceptions overlap each other significantly—except for the fact that in the *Alcibiades*, as in the ladder of ascent in the *Symposium* and the dialectical ascent to the synoptic view in *Republic* 7, the vision analogy remains *embodied*. The dimension of self-knowledge in what is best in two souls is an embodied experience of divine wisdom in the soul by which "anyone" (*tis*) (i.e., not a disembodied soul) knows "all the divine" and "himself . . . above all" (133c) and, furthermore, by which one knows each thing as a result (133c–135c), not only oneself, but determinate practical things that "our belongings are our belongings" (133d). All of this results in temperance and just *action* both for the city (134a) and for oneself (134dff.). In my view, therefore, the soul-dimension is more comprehensive than those of the compound or body simply. This is not unlike the later epistemological models—according to the different capacities of the knower—that we find in Proclus (*in Timaeum* I 352, 16–27; *Elements of Theology* 118) and Boethius (*Consolation* Book 5).

25. *Alcibiades I*.131e10–11: Τοῦτο τοίνυν αἴτιον, ὅτι μόνος ἐραστὴς ἦν σός, οἱ δ' ἄλλοι τῶν σῶν.

2. 2 Loving individuals

Does Vlastos' distinction between loving the person for his sake or loving only the excellence in the person still apply here? I think Vlastos' distinction is simply false. In loving Alcibiades, rather than what belongs to Alcibiades, Socrates loves Alcibiades both for himself *and* for his best flourishing. And if what makes Alcibiades flourish is his soul, then in loving Alcibiades' good or best flourishing, one is loving Alcibiades for his own sake. Even in Alcibiades' deteriorating state, as Plato depicts this in the *Symposium*,[26] when love and hate, praise and censure nestle within him,[27] one can still love the Alcibiades who is and who might have been, even if we cannot embrace without reserve the fatal ruin that threatens to kill both him and Socrates. This fatal imbalance is what Socrates' closing words in the *Alcibiades* foreshadow: "yet I am apprehensive, not because I distrust anything in your nature, but because I see the sheer force of the city, lest it overwhelm both me and you" (135e). Ambiguity, the potentially fatal consequences of loving other individuals, and ultimate failure, despite present best intentions, are precisely what Plato depicts in the *Alcibiades I* but dramatizes so poignantly in the *Symposium*.

In other words, a model of individual love and friendship is articulated first in the *Alcibiades I*, and the lateral and vertical semantics of this model are worked out in the fabric of the *Symposium*. What the *Symposium* thematizes, one might say, is the character of intersubjective transformative passion in Socrates-Diotima's vertical ascent to the beautiful, something that is represented also by that little nugget of wisdom Socrates was apparently seeking in the porch on the way to Agathon's. The transformation of the individual by virtue of this ascent is also reflected in the divine images Alcibiades sees in Socrates.[28] At the same time, this vertical ascent is intersubjective at each level and with real consequences, as in Olympiodorus' adaptation of the *Alcibiades*' model to the political, kathartic, theoretic, and inspirational rungs of the ladder of virtue. This is the "right way of going ... of being led" or "guided" (210a4–7; e2; 211b5–6); at each level, the lover must give birth and rear the offspring, that is, "*logoi* that make the young better," "fitting thoughts in ungrudging philosophy," and, finally, "true excellence" (210c1–3; d1–2; 212a2–7). The emphasis upon giving birth at each level of the ascent only confirms that this is not a self-directed project because the whole context of the individual is transformed at every level and,

---

26. *Symposium*, 212d–214a.
27. See Corrigan and Glazov-Corrigan, *Plato's Dialectic at Play*, 163–79.
28. *Symposium* 211e–212a.

in a significant way, the ascent is not in the control of an isolated subject. In short, this is a shared, not a self-directed enterprise. But the irony is this: the vertical ascent to the beautiful-good is so characteristic of Platonism that we may forget that in the *Symposium* it is immediately punctured by the altogether physical entry of the dangerously alcoholic Alcibiades—presenting a very practical and perhaps fatal consequence of friendship that cannot be escaped. If Alcibiades was perhaps the most conspicuous pupil of Socrates, his subsequent behavior fatally affected the rest of Socrates' life.

The vertical axis of friendship in human life does not, in fact, exist without its individual counterpart, and this is developed first in the *Alcibiades*, whose closing words look directly to this scene in the *Symposium*. So fragility, vulnerability, and even the possibility of catastrophe are built into Plato's treatments of friendship and love: in the terms of Socrates' elenchus of Agathon and the first part of Socrates-Diotima's speech in the *Symposium*, to want x is not to seek to control x but to be in need of x; and in Socrates-Diotima's "greater mysteries," to want the beautiful to belong to one forever is a gift of the beautiful—not something that one can simply acquire oneself. Indeed, the possibility of failure is a feature of Plato's vision of philosophy, if the *Seventh Letter* is to be believed,[29] since what is clearly born in friendship must also be tested by "well-meaning refutations," and refutation, like birth and death, is a very risky business.

2.3 The ambiguities of ordinary experience

This provocation to refutation is also intrinsic to the participatory nature of the Platonic dialogue itself. The dialogue is an invitation to enter into the play of thought, images, speeches, and characters in order to test the mettle of each, to see which is more authentic or more counterfeit (to use Plato's language[30]) and to decide for ourselves, but in friendly participation, which image is closer to the model or what something *should* be, that is, to dimly perceive the "form" in a world of more or less adequate images. The *Symposium* is perhaps the most perfect representation of such participatory dialogue. How do we decide among all the layers of the text—speeches, glittering persons, genres—which is closest to any model worth following? Is it Aristodemus and Apollodorus, who love Socrates in an almost comically devoted but rather slavish way—and on whom, it must be emphasized, the

---

29. The authenticity of the *Seventh Letter* has recently been questioned (again). See Burnyeat and Frede, *The Pseudo-Platonic Seventh Letter*.

30. That is, counterfeit (*nothos*) versus true/authentic (*gnēsios*), as in *Republic* 5.461b; 535d. cf. 6.496a; *Timaeus* 52b.

story depends for its existence and transmission? Or is it Phaedrus, Pausanias, Eryximachus, Aristophanes, Agathon, Socrates, or Alcibiades? We find elements of compelling models in each speech—and yet ironically, Socrates' speech, in some respects the most unlikely, turns out to propose a fairly compelling model of ascent that nonetheless problematizes itself: it transposes monologue into a dialogue in which Socrates represents himself as the apprentice to a suspiciously mythical-looking woman, Diotima. It also looks to be the most fictitious, in the sense that it is initially represented as a single dialogue that turns out half way through to be a patchwork of different conversations at different times;[31] and its apparently spiritual ascent to the beautiful is immediately undercut by the drunken Alcibiades' very physical entry.[32] No one pulls the rug from under an apparently stable carpet better than Plato. The "suddenly" of mystical flights can just as easily become the "suddenly" of physical subversion.[33] Callicles in the *Gorgias*, Thrasymachus in the *Republic*, Alcibiades in the *Symposium*, and even Phaedrus in the dialogue of his name, may be ill or well-disposed to Socrates, but there is invariably some real or implied physical threat to his person in the background.[34]

For all of Plato's supposed devotion only to the perfect, part of the irony of Socrates-Diotima's speech is that Socrates' apprenticeship and lifelong pursuit of the beautiful-good is not only undercut by Alcibiades' physical knocking on the door—demanding entry—but simultaneously corroborated by Alcibiades testifying to the beautiful images within Socrates when he is "opened up."[35] At the same time, Plato presents a poignantly conflicted view of love: on his own admission,[36] Alcibiades both loves and hates Socrates, comes to praise him and yet also puts him on trial, however unconsciously or playfully he might do so in the language he uses.[37] And since we know the

31. *Symposium* 207a.

32. *Symposium* 212c–213a.

33. Compare *Symposium* 210e4 (the sudden vision of the beautiful); 212c6 (the sudden knocking at the door); 213c1 (the sudden, almost comical appearance of Socrates that so disturbs Alcibiades).

34. For Thrasymachus see *Republic* 1.336b–337a; and in fact the entire conversation of the *Republic* is initiated by a not-so-veiled threat, 1.327c; for Alcibiades see note 37 below; for Phaedrus, see *Phaedrus* 236b–d.

35. *Symposium* 215a6–b3; 216d6; e5–6; 222a1–6.

36. *Symposium* 213b–e; and see Corrigan and Glazov-Corrigan, *Plato's Dialectic at Play*, 166.

37. *Symposium* "punish" 214e; 216b1–c3 (Alcibiades is conflicted; even wishes Socrates non-existent); 219c–d ("O, gentlemen of the jury"); 227a–b8 (. . . praise . . . mixed with the faults I find in him . . . outrageous insult (*hybrisen*) to me . . . (don't) be deceived by him . . .); "charge," "penalty," "caution," "blame," "hybris,"

future exploits of Socrates' most famous pupil and lover, the "corroboration" is, in fact, bought at the expense of a failure that could not have been more conspicuous. Just as no one is immune to death or disgrace, so is no one, Socrates included, immune to refutation or safe from the casting of shadows. Arguably, Alcibiades is Socrates' biggest shadow—though the presence of Aristophanes in the *Symposium* also bears considerable latent menace.[38]

Thus, Plato depicts the imperfect everywhere and not simply as something to despise. The imperfect is, in fact, an integral part of the design of love itself. When Diotima describes the birth of eros, both elements, resource and poverty, are essential to the nature of love. Without poverty there would be no impulse, drive, or desire for the beautiful; and without resource there would be no possibility of attaining it. If we see the speeches of Aristophanes and Agathon as foreshadowing the birth of eros, we can see how much Plato emphasizes the need for poverty. Aristophanes introduces into the dialogue (especially after the good doctor Eryximachus has emphasized the need in his speech and earlier interventions for comprehensive order and harmony in life) the driving force of desire for the other and even for something nameless in that desire. Agathon, by contrast, presents a view of resource as the all-good perfection of love who trips over the heads of hard folk and visits only the soft parts of young people. Without the imperfection of both speeches, there would be no understanding of the need for both impulses—poverty and resource—in Diotima's speech, Without Agathon's speech we would have no ideal and no elenchus of the ideal. Without Aristophanes' speech, we would have only a bland perfection, a perfect mirror of the aristocratic boy who has everything. Balancing all of these conflicting elements, Plato refused to represent love without the chaotic world of human drives. Despite this, so much modern scholarship refuses to recognize the complexity of his approach both to the realities and often unsuspected ideals of ordinary life.

2.4 The *Symposium* and Pausanias' speech

Let me take one conspicuous example of this ambiguity of love in the *Symposium*: Pausanias, the boyfriend of Agathon. Plato plays upon the notion of the "good" in the *Symposium*, as we have seen;[39] he does this conspicuously

---

"arrogance"—213d–e; 217e; 219c5–6; 221e3–4; 222a8, b6–7; see also Corrigan and Glazov-Corrigan, *Plato's Dialectic at Play*, 163–81.

38. That is, Aristophanes, as the author of the *Clouds* (423 BCE) that ridiculed Socrates, who mentions him as one of the first accusers in the *Apology* 18c–d.

39. See above chapter 1.4.

with Agathon when he has Socrates first refute Agathon's speech, then get Agathon to admit that he didn't know what he was talking about, surely an admission of ignorance indispensable for the birth of philosophy: "I greatly fear, Socrates, I knew nothing of what I was talking about." "Ah, but you spoke beautifully, Agathon; but . . . you hold, do you not, that good things are beautiful?"[40] In other words, one may speak beautifully, but not necessarily truly or well! While good things might be beautiful, the beautiful is not necessarily or always good. So if Socrates can play or pun upon the "good" in Agathon's name, presumably Plato can play upon Pausanias as the "good's" boyfriend. I simply want to note this and leave it open-ended since if ever a speech had to be played out on a knife-edge, it is that of Pausanias: arguably Plato puts into the mouth of Pausanias a theory of love and friendship as improvement in virtue that looks rather like his own theory in the *Alcibiades I* and certainly one that we can find later in Proclus' *Commentary on the Alcibiades*.[41]

We can read Pausanias' speech in many ways: as the best of conventional sociological wisdom with a comparative sense of different customs; as a sincere plea for wisdom in love along with a genuine responsibility for educating the young; as a practical recognition of different forms of love; as a commitment to life-long rather than ephemeral relationships; as a commitment to the psyche in love rather than to simple bodily exchanges, etc. There is no doubt then that Pausanias' speech can be taken at face value— that Pausanias can be perfectly sincere in what he proposes: love of the soul rather than the body; life-long commitment rather than casual love; education and virtue rather than pleasure. And yet what he advocates, all the more so because he appears to be perfectly sincere, is also a consummate recipe for sexual exploitation; the younger beloved should be willing to do *anything* for the sake of improvement under the guidance of his teacher:

> And on the same principle he who gives himself to a lover because he is a good man, and in the hope that he will be improved by his company, shows himself to be virtuous, even though the object of his affection turn out to be a villain, and to have no virtue; and if he is deceived he has committed a noble error. For he has proved that for his part he will do anything for anybody with a view to virtue and improvement, than which there can be nothing nobler. Thus noble in every case is the acceptance of another for the sake of virtue. (*Symposium* 185a–b).

---

40. *Symposium* 201c.
41. See especially *in Alc.* 25, 19ff.

In the above passage, which effectively concludes Pausanias' speech, there is the tiniest "slippage" between the beloved giving his favors for the sake of wisdom and virtue, on the one hand, and the beloved being willing to "do anything for anybody" for the sake of virtue and improvement (ὅτι ἀρετῆς γ' ἕνεκα καὶ τοῦ βελτίων γενέσθαι πᾶν ἂν παντὶ προθυμηθείη). It is admittedly a tiny detail and slightly jingoistic in Greek (perhaps like one's impression of skipping over the small print, only to discover later that it contains really important details that may make or break one's future life); but it points nonetheless to unconscious amoral consequences hidden in what appear to be the best intentions. To be willing to exchange sexual favors for virtue is not the same as to be willing to do "anything for anybody" for the sake of virtue. Even Plato can scarcely refrain from editorial comment after Pausanias concludes his speech: "And Pausanias paused, for the sophists teach me to say such things in this way!" (Παυσανίου δὲ παυσαμένου, διδάσκουσι γάρ με ἴσα λέγειν οὑτωσὶ οἱ σοφοί) (185c). Pausanias' speech casts a big shadow—even for Plato, the author.

We should not, however, take this in a moralistic, mono-dimensional way. Like Agathon, we often have no idea of the real significance of the things we say or do. So it is not a case of censuring Pausanias because he can say things of whose broader significance he is unaware. Nonetheless, Pausanias' case poses a real dilemma. If we take him at his best, how do we avoid the worse and the worst nestling unconsciously, so it seems, in the garb of the best? How does Pausanias himself decide which is which? After all, the sexual predator will often blame the victim, will often think he acts in and for the best interests of his beloved. If we take Pausanias at his best, how do we recognize when the best is corrupted? And how do we avoid in any action that is apparently virtuous what Socrates clearly recognizes in the *Republic* Book 6, namely, that the corruption of the best is the worst,[42] if the best and the worst can inhabit the same action?

Furthermore, in such cases, it is not clear at all who the other, the beloved or lover, really is? Is the other an object to be directed or manipulated or a redeeming or exploiting subject? And what does it mean anyway to love individuals for their own sakes? Individuals don't come with signs or directions for assembly or use. Worse still, individuals, including ourselves, often have no idea of their best interests. Even when we get things right, we cannot control the consequences. Plato is profoundly aware of this. Even when we have the right mixture, indeed a perfect mixture, of gifts and circumstances, this is no guarantee that the gilded youth will not be corrupted by

---

42. *Republic* 6, 495a–e (*corruptio optimi pessima*).

adulation and countless other "good" things,[43] and no guarantee that what was just perfectly set up for the best governance will not end up in tyranny.[44] But if Pausanias' speech casts a big shadow, it nonetheless also bequeaths a positive model of education to posterity, namely, that it is possible for lovers to love each other genuinely with a higher purpose in mind (even if what Pausanias unconsciously advocates is actually immoral). How then did later antiquity read this issue in Pausanias' speech on both positive and negative sides of the issue?

2.5 Different models of erotic friendship in the *Symposium*, *Phaedrus*, and later Platonism

In Porphyry's *Life of Plotinus*, there is a contemporary third-century interpretation that Plotinus repudiates. This interpretation evidently read the case of Alcibiades from the *Symposium* and perhaps the *Alcibiades I* in the light of Pausanias' speech. Porphyry says: "The rhetorician Diophanes read a defence of Alcibiades in Plato's *Symposium* in which he asserted that a pupil for the sake of advancing in the study of virtue should submit himself to sexual intercourse with his master if the master desired it." (15, 7ff. trans. Armstrong, altered).[45] According to Porphyry, Plotinus made as if to get up and leave, but managed to restrain himself until after the end of the lecture when he asked Porphyry to write a refutation (which of course has not survived). Here then is one conspicuous example of a negative interpretation, which is plausibly dependent on the text of the *Symposium* and implicitly dependent on a broader interpretation of all the relevant dialogues, namely, the *Alcibiades I*, *Lysis*, *Symposium*, and the *Phaedrus*.

In the *Phaedrus*, by contrast, Socrates provides two positive models of erotic friendship, both of which involve sexual passion for the sake of higher wisdom (255e–256e)—and at least one of which, if not both, appears to involve sex.[46] In the first instance, the beloved is ready "for his part to grant favors to the lover," but the lover resists from shame; and "if the better elements of their thinking win out, they live a blessed life here and after death 'become winged and light'" (*Phaedrus* 255d–256b). In the second

43. See especially *Republic* 6, 494a–495a.

44. *Republic* Books 8–9 trace the devolution or genealogy (within the city and home) of city-type and individual from aristocracy, timocracy, oligarchy, through forms of democracy to tyrannocracy.

45. *Life of Plotinus*, 15, 1–17.

46. *Phaedrus* 255e2–256b3 (a7–8: "*if* the better elements of their thinking conquer . . ."); 256b7–c7.

instance, where they turn to a lesser way of life "without philosophy," they come to a "choice that is called blessed by the many and carry it through";[47] and so these two live their lives as friends, "believing that they have given and received the most binding pledges which it would be wrong to break by ever becoming enemies" (*Phaedrus* 256b7-d3).[48] This second instance, then, involves sexual intercourse, and is really a mixed, second-best option. Nonetheless, after death this pair "live in the light and are happy as they travel with one another, and acquire matching wings, whenever they acquire it, *because of their love*" (*Phaedrus* 256d8-e2). This passage demonstrates a love of the individual for the individual's own sake that is redeemed in and by love itself, an imperfect intimation of the highest form of love-friendship, and yet a fully positive view of ordinary love for all that.

These two models are colored by two further features in the *Phaedrus* myth: first, the cosmic-hypercosmic dyadic particularity or uniqueness of love, that is, two lovers in a unique love-relationship through a particular god; and second, the reflexive anterotic quality of love itself in which distinct individuality is in some sense dissolved. According to the first feature, the dyadic lovers follow in the train of "their own god" and together "take their habits and ways from him" (*Phaedrus* 252e-253a). In other words, horizontal or lateral love is pervaded by the vertical dimension of the soul's recollection of being or "what really is," waking up to a new way of living in a divine medium.[49] According to the second feature, love melts the physical barriers between lovers in an erotic, physical, yet irreducibly divine way:

---

47. *Phaedrus* 256b-c: "If however they live a life less noble and without philosophy, but yet ruled by the love of honour, probably, when they have been drinking, or in some other moment of carelessness, the two unruly horses, taking the souls off their guard, will bring them together and seize upon and accomplish that which is by the many accounted blissful; and when this has once been done, they continue the practice, but infrequently, since what they are doing is not approved by the whole mind" (trans. H. North Fowler, LCL) (ἐὰν δὲ δὴ διαίτῃ φορτικωτέρᾳ τε καὶ ἀφιλοσόφῳ, φιλοτίμῳ δὲ χρήσωνται, τάχ' ἄν που ἐν μέθαις ἤ τινι ἄλλῃ ἀμελείᾳ τὼ ἀκολάστω αὐτοῖν ὑποζυγίω λαβόντε τὰς ψυχὰς ἀφρούρους, ξυναγαγόντε εἰς ταὐτόν, τὴν ὑπὸ τῶν πολλῶν μακαριστὴν αἵρεσιν εἱλέσθην τε καὶ διεπράξαντο· καὶ διαπραξαμένω τὸ λοιπὸν ἤδη χρῶνται μὲν αὐτῇ, σπανίᾳ δέ, ἅτε οὐ πάσῃ δεδογμένα τῇ διανοίᾳ πράττοντες).

48. *Phaedrus* 256d2-4: πίστεις τὰς μεγίστας ἡγουμένω ἀλλήλοιν δεδωκέναι τε καὶ δεδέχθαι, ἃς οὐ θεμιτὸν εἶναι λύσαντας εἰς ἔχθραν ποτὲ ἐλθεῖν.

49. *Phaedrus* 252e: "And so those who are of Zeus seek that the one loved by them should be someone like Zeus in soul . . . and as they follow the scent from within themselves to the discovery of the nature of their own god . . ." 253a-c: "they take their habits and ways from him . . . those in turn who follow Hera seek someone royal in nature . . . those who are of Apollo and each of the other gods go in the same way in accordance with their god . . . ."

... the springs of that stream which Zeus as lover of Ganymede named "desire" flow in abundance upon the lover, some sinking within him, and some flowing off outside him as he brims over; and as a breath of wind or an echo rebounds from smooth hard surfaces and returns to the source from which it issued, so the stream of beauty passes back into its possessor through his eyes, which is its natural route to the soul; arriving there and setting him all of a flutter, it waters the passages of the feathers and causes the wings to grow, and fills the soul of the loved one in his turn with love. So he is in love, but with what he does not know. (*Phaedrus* 255c1–d3)

The powerful melting of boundaries and anterotic love or love-in-return that leads to a deeper identification of lover and beloved (namely, a wish on the part of the lover to "be of" or belong to the beloved[50])—so characteristic of Plato and yet difficult to explain away against interpretations such as those of Diophanes visiting the school of Plotinus—are important for later thought. And so the question becomes, for late antiquity and the Renaissance, how one might read Pausanias' speech in light of the *Alcibiades I*, the *Symposium* as a whole, and the *Phaedrus*. Here I shall sketch three different readings or cross-readings of Plato's dialogues from late antiquity and the Renaissance that seem to me to make perfectly good sense of important elements in the dialogues and that show together what love and friendship of individuals for their own sakes meant for the later Platonic tradition: first, a small example from Plotinus, against Raul Mortley's view that there is no lateral application in Plotinus' view of friendship; second, an example from Proclus, who shows how one might read the *Alcibiades I*, *Symposium*, and *Phaedrus* together; and, finally, a powerful example from Ficino's *Commentary on the Symposium* that shows how one might read Pausanias' speech in both positive and negative ways in the light of the *Phaedrus* myth, above all.

2.6 Plotinus: lateral attachment and reflexivity

First, a central question: does Plotinus eliminate lateral attachment in the ascent to the beautiful and the good? In *Ennead* I.6[1].9, 1ff., the soul, he says, must be trained to look at beautiful ways of life, the beautiful works, not of the arts, but of good people, and "then look at the souls of the people who produce those beautiful works." There is then a *direct* lateral relation involved in the initial stages. Just as in V.8[31].2, Plotinus reminds us to see *phronesis* in the face of the other and then see it first as one in ourselves

---

50. Compare Dionysius the Areopagite, *DN* 712a.

too.[51] Here it may seem that we move to a more self-directed focus, but the reality is more complex since it is already a reflexive focus. In I.6[1].9, for instance, in the very next words Plotinus says: "Go back *into yourself* and look . . . ." And there follows the image of the lover working not on his beloved's statue, as in *Phaedrus* 252d,[52] but upon himself: "*so you too* must cut away excess and straighten the crooked . . . ." This is not self-absorption or pure self-direction, but already reflexive. The "we" of Plotinus' discourse—a dialogue "among ourselves"[53] but open to "anyone"[54]—already pervades his whole approach to love and ascent: the self that one is asked to go back into is already a shared "you."

In other words, the "we" or "self-you" is not an ego or a solitary other, but an augmented being-with.[55] Yes, Plotinus is famous for the flight of the alone to the alone (VI.9[9].11) or for his "cut away everything" in front of the one (V.3[43].17),[56] but this does not and *cannot* mean that in the ascent to the one we simply abstract from everything, for the one is neither an abstraction nor a point, but a unity bigger and greater than the whole of existence.[57] So we have to think about the "alone" in a different way, not a point or individual or a void or empty place, but an immensity beyond immensity with or to which *love*—even crazy love—is the only possible response.[58] So in one of Plotinus' most famous thought experiments in V.8[31].9, in approaching intellect, we have to *keep* our thought of everything in "this sensible cosmos"[59] and *augment* it with our even-fuller psychic world, not diminishing or subtracting anything,[60] but taking away only "the bulk," "the places," and "the phantasm of matter in ourselves"[61] before we pray to the god "who made this of which you have the phantasm" to come and bring his even-larger intelligible world.[62] Augmentation occurs here on three levels: the sensible cosmos, the psychic world, and the intelligible universe. The

---

51. *Ennead* V.8[31].2, 38–46.

52. *Phaedrus* 252d5–e1: "So each selects his love . . . and fashions and adorns him like a statue, as if he were himself his god . . . ."

53. See, for example, *Ennead* III.8[30].1, 8–12.

54. See, for example, *Ennead* V.8[31].1, 5–6.

55. On Plotinus' "we," see O'Daly, *Plotinus' Philosophy of the Self*; Remes, *Plotinus on Self*; Mortley, *Plotinus*, 14–27.

56. On this see Corrigan, "'Solitary' Mysticism," 28–42.

57. *Ennead* VI.9[9].6, 12: "when you think him as intellect or soul, he is more."

58. As above *Ennead* VI. 7938].35.

59. *Ennead* V.8[31].9, 1–7.

60. *Ennead* V.8.9, 7-10

61. *Ennead* V. 8.9.

62. *Ennead* V. 8.9.

"we" of Plotinus' discourse generally or the self-you of this passage and of I.6[1].9 above is an augmented self who can only be seen as and for itself from an intelligible perspective.

2.7 Proclus: Pausanias' speech in light of the *Phaedrus*

If we look next at Proclus' *Commentary on the Alcibiades I*, we find that it sketches a positive interpretation of Pausanias' speech in the light of the *Phaedrus* myth and Socrates' love for, and education of, Alcibiades. Like Plotinus, Proclus finds a positive application for Pausanias' distinction between the heavenly and the pandemic loves. Commenting upon the lemma, *Alcibiades I* 103a (where Socrates says to Alcibiades, "O son of Leinias, I think you are astonished that although I was the first to become your lover, while the rest have ceased to be so, I alone do not depart"), Proclus distinguishes between the "divine" or "inspired" lover—that is, Socrates, who loves "the true Alcibiades" in an epistreptic or anagogic way—and the "vulgar" lover, who loves only the external image in an impassioned way.[63] Both lovers manifest enthusiasm about the beautiful, but in different ways. Socrates cares for the higher well-being of Alcibiades and for his conversion to the good and the beautiful, whereas vulgar lovers care only for the external image of beauty that they are happy to abandon, as in Pausanias' speech, after the early bloom fades.[64] It is easy from a modern perspective to read Proclus as a pedantic moralist who hides the real passion of love under a superficial overlay of distasteful allegory. But for him every image in a Platonic text is in search of what it represents and of what is its best model. "Everywhere something of the less perfect assumes the character of the more perfect, diverts to itself the souls that have not yet been set right and keeps them away from better things" (*in Alc.* 39, 7–9). The good, the not-so-good, and the bad occur in the same space—and so because we encounter an inspired Socrates or a heavenly love in Plato in the same space as we find other images of love does not mean that the heavenly inspired love is not real. For Proclus, these divine, epistreptic loves that are full of "forethought" for the beloved[65]—a kind of bodhisattva love who returns to incarnation out of compassion for others—"gather and unite with themselves the lives of their loved ones, and lead them up with themselves to intelligible beauty, 'pouring' as Socrates in the *Phaedrus* [253a] says 'into their souls' whatever they 'draw' from that source" (*in Alc.* 26, 16–27, 1). So Socratic love is an even more intimate way

---

63. *In Alc.* 34, 17ff.
64. *In Alc.* 35, 14–19.
65. *In Alc.* 26, 12–27, 12; 32.13ff.

of union simultaneously with the beloved, oneself, and the cosmos: all the orders above and in the cosmos are "woken, fired up, and warmed around 'the outflow of beauty' [*Phaedrus* 251b]; and the souls of human beings too receive a share of such inspiration and through intimacy with the god are moved around the beautiful and go down to the place of coming-to-be for the benefit of less perfect souls and because of forethought or providence for those in need of safety," without departing from their own natures.

This providential/epistreptic care for those in need, so characteristic of the *Phaedrus*' description of the care of "all soul" for that which is without soul,[66] is certainly an indication that this higher combination of friendship with erotic love is perhaps a higher value for Platonism than erotic love alone, as we have seen already in Alcinous' *Didaskalikos*.[67] However, it should not be construed as a kind of Freudian sublimation of erotic love, since for Plotinus earlier an intense *eros* most characterizes the highest aspect of intellect's being[68] and for Proclus this does not mean that one loves only the higher being, and not the individual in front of us. Proclus makes it clear that in the chain of love that binds everything, individuals really do love individuals: "For all that is good and makes for safety in souls has its cause determined from the gods; and for this reason, Plato [perhaps *Laws* 1.631b-c] says that the paradigms of all the virtues and the bodily goods pre-exist in the divine world, such as health, strength, justice, moderation. How much more shall we suppose that the primary cause of love lies among the gods . . . given by a divine gift [*Phaedrus* 244a]? *So gods too love gods, the superiors their inferiors providentially, and the inferiors their superiors reflexively*" (*in Alc.* 55, 17–56, 3).[69]

Here we can see how Proclus reads Pausanias' speech, positively and negatively in the same space, together with the *Alcibiades I* and the *Phaedrus* myth. However quaint this may appear to most modern readers of Plato, Proclus deals with a real problem: how to determine in any speech or dialogue how images are to be distinguished from one another and yet related to a reasonable model or models? Perhaps the inevitable impression of the modern reader, nonetheless, is that the higher love is just a desiccated version of real down-to-earth passion. When Proclus argues, for instance, that Socrates loves the "true Alcibiades" not the image, this only confirms a typical modern reading of the *Alcibiades* that in loving only the "soul"—and

---

66. *Phaedrus* 246b6.
67. Alcinous, *Didaskalikos* 33.3–4.
68. *Ennead* VI.7[38].21, 12; 34, 3.
69. *In Alc.* 56, 2–4: καὶ θεοὶ τοίνυν θεῶν ἐρῶσιν, οἱ πρεσβύτεροι τῶν καταδεεστέρων, ἀλλὰ προνοητικῶς, καὶ οἱ καταδεέστεροι τῶν ὑπερτέρων, ἀλλ' ἐπιστρεπτικῶς.

not "what belongs" to Alcibiades or "what belongs to the belongings" of Alcibiades[70]—we love only some impossible disembodied phantom, not the real thing. But this is plainly not Proclus' interpretation of the "soul," for the soul is richer in reference than the "body" alone, since Proclus makes it clear that "bodily goods preexist in the divine world."[71] And, indeed, in Plato's *Alcibiades I*, Socrates makes it plain that reflexive seeing of what is best in the soul provides a panoptic vision of the soul, the divine, and is the wellspring of all intelligent action in the world.[72] In short, Proclus *means* that Socrates' love for Alcibiades in Alcibiades' love-in-return is a fully erotic experience (even if Proclus, from his own ascetic viewpoint, sees this rather differently from us).

2.8 Marsilio Ficino: Pausanias' speech and the *Symposium* as a whole

Before I look at Ficino's reading of Pausanias' speech, let me first say a few things about dialectic in the *Republic* and *Phaedrus* that will help to situate this speech in Ficino's commentary. The dialectician in *Republic* Book 7 is the one who knows how to look at all things together in order to see their kinship—he or she is *synoptikos*.[73] This synoptic vision first appears in Book 5, when Socrates argues two things: first, the lover of wisdom is in love with the whole of wisdom, not just a part;[74] and second, a corollary, the lover of wisdom is the one able to see clearly both "the itself" (that is, the form) and the participants, and who does not think "the participants are it or it the participants" (476d1–3).[75] This is to say that the dialectician recognizes images as images because he or she sees the whole source and the parts in the light of that whole.[76] The person who does not believe in the existence of the

---

70. For this language of the *Alcibiades I*, see 2.9.1 below.

71. *In Alc.* 55, 18–21: διὸ καὶ τῶν ἀρετῶν πασῶν καὶ τῶν σωματικῶν ἀγαθῶν ἐκεῖ πρ οὔπάρχειν τὰ παραδείγματά φησιν ὁ Πλάτων, οἷον ὑγείας ἰσχύος δικαιοσύνης σωφροσύνη ς. πόσῳ δὴ μᾶλλον τῆς ἐρωτικῆς ἐν θεοῖς εἶναι τὴν πρωτουργὸν αἰτίαν ὑποθησόμεθα.

72. *Alcibiades* I.133c–134d.

73. *Republic* 7.537c.

74. *Republic* 5.474c–475c.

75. *Republic* 5.476d1–3.

76. Later in *Republic* Book 7, this ability to see both form and participants together will become the upward synoptic view of dialectic (533b–534d—the person who can give a reasoned account of the being of each thing and distinguish the form of the good from "all the others," 534b8–10); the one who can distinguish the genuine article from the counterfeit (535c–536a), who is "sound of limb and mind" (536a-b: ἀρτιμελεῖς τε καὶ ἀρτίφρονας), is the dialectician: "for the person who sees things as a whole is a

form, by contrast, has opinion only, directed solely to the part (cf. 493e: the "many" are like this). In a famous statement in the *Phaedrus*, Socrates puts this as follows: "the person who knows the truth knows best how to discover the resemblances" (273d4–6: τὰς δὲ ὁμοιότητας . . . πανταχοῦ ὁ τὴν ἀλήθειαν εἰδὼς κάλλιστα ἐπίσταται εὑρίσκειν).

All of the above, I suggest, is a model for interpretation not only in Plato, but especially in the later Platonic tradition, including Plotinus and Ficino; the whole form is prior to the part; it is that by which the part can be known properly, and this involves the "way" of dialectic, namely, the ascent to an unhypothesized beginning and a descent through forms (*Republic* 6 *ad fin.*).[77] What sort of person is it who will be led upward, Plotinus asks in his little work on dialectic (I.3[20])? And he answers adapting a phrase from *Phaedrus* 248d1–4, "Surely, one who has seen all or most things." In Ficino's Commentary on the *Symposium*, it is invariably "from the top down," so to speak, that is, from the whole of Plato's thought and beyond, that each speech is generated. This can seem to be a whitewashing device: Phaedrus knows just too much theology for modern readers. At the beginning of the equivalent of Phaedrus' speech in Ficino's Commentary, for instance, we read a text that on the face of things bears no relation whatsoever to Plato's *Symposium*: "In the beginning, God created the substance of the angelic Mind, which we also call essence. This, in the first moment of its creation, was formless and dark; but since it was born from God, it turned toward God . . . with a certain innate desire. . . . In the glow of [God's] radiance, its passion was set alight" (*Oratio Prima*, cap. 3, 39; trans. S. Reynolds Jayne, 127).

Not only does Ficino's approach bear no textual correspondence to anything in Plato; it also seems to eliminate some of the psychological complexity of Plato's portraits: as we have seen above, Pausanias in Plato proposes, presumably in all innocence, that the beloved pupil should gratify the lover for the sake of virtue and wisdom—in fact, that he should be prepared to do anything for anyone for the sake of virtue, whereas with Guido Cavalcanti in Ficino, after mention of Pseudo-Dionysius and Pseudo-Plato's *Second Letter*, we discover the unlikely hypothesis that Pausanias disapproves of too much copulation with women or of unnatural consorting with men (*Oratio Secunda*, cap. 7).

Plotinus, as we have seen from Porphyry's *Life*, and maybe even Plato himself,[78] would have approved, but we might not be too impressed with Ficino's exegetical acuity at this point. However, this would be unfortunate,

---

dialectician" (537c: ὁ μὲν γὰρ συνοπτικὸς διαλεκτικός, ὁ δὲ μὴ οὔ).

77. *Republic* 6.511a–c.
78. *Phaedrus* 251a; *Laws* 636a–637b.

because Ficino goes on to interpret the phenomenon of Pausanias' *eros* implicitly in the light of Socrates' second speech in the *Phaedrus* (namely, the famous myth)[79] in which lover and beloved find themselves, through the erotic outflow of love, in and through each other and are thereby lifted into contemplation; and I suggest that, for the great translator of Plato and Plotinus, this is not a silly idea, namely, to read the reflexive phenomenon of love in the *Symposium* through the *Phaedrus*, *Lysis*, and *Alcibiades I*. Through the persona of Cavalcanti, Ficino puts this as follows:

> The truth must be that each has himself and has the other too . . . A has himself, but in B; and B also has himself, but in A. When you love me you contemplate me, and as I love you, I find myself in your contemplation of me; I recover myself, lost in the first place by my own neglect of myself, in you who preserve me. . . . And then this too is remarkable: that after I have lost myself, if I recover myself through you, I have myself through you, and if I have myself through you, I have you sooner and to a greater degree than I have myself. I am therefore closer to you than I am to myself . . . . (*Oratio Secunda*, cap. 8, 144–45, trans. S. Reynolds Jayne).

Such passages have surely throughout the centuries attracted readers to Ficino and through him to Plato. In contrast to my somewhat negative interpretation of Pausanias above, I cite this passage to show that Ficino speaks from the perspective of an interpretation of love on the basis of all the relevant dialogues, and yet he remains true in an important way to Pausanias' level of thinking: Ficino/Cavalcanti makes no mention of god, no linking of such contemplation to any divinity other than Cupid, and no attempt to relate this reflexive phenomenon to intelligible reality; this remains a gap in the speech; it is not made explicit. Ficino understands the positive possibility of striving for something better in Pausanias' speech and he encapsulates this in the erotic contemplative stream of love from the *Phaedrus* through which normal boundaries are erased in an intimate fusion of horizons. Yet at the same time he doesn't make Pausanias into some proto-Christian missionary. He lets him be Pausanias, just as he is. This doubleness of understanding lies at the core of Plato's dialogues: in the *Phaedo*, as we have seen, Socrates argues that sensible things are like something else, but they fall short; they "desire of it," but they are defective (74d–75a).

At the conclusion of Ficino's *Commentary* there is a striking example of this perspective from the whole or from the primary designation from which subsequent resemblances and gaps or deficiencies might be espied—a model I cited from the *Phaedrus* above (273d4–6: τὰς δὲ ὁμοιότητας . . . πανταχοῦ

---

79. *Phaedrus* 243e–257b.

ὁ τὴν ἀλήθειαν εἰδὼς κάλλιστα ἐπίσταται εὑρίσκειν) and one that Plato uses frequently (*Republic* Books 8–9 provide well-known examples and the hunt for the sophist in the dialogue of that name is part of the family of such examples). Here Ficino has Christophoro Marsuppini assume the role of Alcibiades to praise Socrates as the practical model right before our eyes: "Put the figure of Socrates before your eyes." He then enumerates the positive qualities in Socrates that we should keep in mind (clever hunter, trickster, lover of wisdom, sorcerer, halfway between wisdom and ignorance) and indicates the practical inner content of his wisdom: 'in what way Socrates loved, anyone can understand if he remembers the teachings of Diotima. For Socrates loved exactly as Diotima taught above" (*Oratio Septima*, cap. 2). He then asks: what is the opposite of Socrates (cap. 3)? And after an analysis of the negative kinds of divine madness, he concludes: "Adulterous passions seem to imitate these four madnesses falsely in just as many ways: the poetic, that vulgar music . . . ; the mysteries, the vain superstitions . . . ; the prophetic, the fallacious conjecturing of human knowledge; the amatory, the impulses of lust . . ." (cap. 15). This is exactly one of the principles of the *Phaedrus*: the one who knows the true can best discover the resemblances. Or in the *Sophist* 260c: if falsity exists, then deceit is possible and "all things everywhere are full of phantoms, likenesses and images" (Καὶ μὴν ἀπάτης οὔσης εἰδώλων τε καὶ εἰκόνων ἤδη καὶ φαντασίας πάντα ἀνάγκη μεστὰ εἶναι). So in the final pages of his *Commentary*, Ficino points to Socrates as the practical guide or primary model Plato represented: "only one way of saving the youth remains, the companionship of Socrates. . . . So the true lover, like a shepherd keeps his flock of lambs safe from false lovers as from the ravage of wolves and disease" (cap. 16, 234). He then concludes by returning to the proper form of the whole enquiry: ". . . we seem to have learned what love is, who the true lover, and what the utility of love. . . . But remember also that without a doubt *the cause and teacher of this most fortunate discovery was the very same Love who has been discovered . . . so that we must be thankful to Him equally for the question and its answer*" (cap. 17, 235, trans. S. Reynolds Jayne).

The "form"—if I might put it in this way—is the cause and the goal of all enquiry. Ficino thus returns explicitly in the concluding words of the *Commentary* to the perspective of the whole that I sketched above from *Republic* Book 5: "Therefore, my friends, let us worship this Love . . . so that, under Love's leadership, we may possess, so to speak, the *whole God*, and, loving the *whole* with the glow of love, we may enjoy the *whole God* with perpetual love" (cap. 17, 235).[80] The motive force of the whole God of

---

80. In this, Ficino follows Plato and Plotinus. In the *Phaedrus eros* is a god and in

love, refracted in the many different speeches and characters of the drama, turns out to be the attractive force that draws the many different faces into wholeness.

This then is what reading a Platonic dialogue like the *Symposium* appears to mean for Ficino; to see the whole refracted in the many different participants, to distinguish the form of the whole from the participants, and to gather all back into the whole by virtue of the motive and attractive force of "the whole God" who provoked the entire journey in the first place and who is, thus, the real Master of the Feast. Love of the individual for the individual's sake requires the larger frame of a cosmic and hypercosmic drama, but this drama does not annul the individual; rather, it provides different models of such love, but at the same time brings the individual into sharper focus.

2.9 Conclusions

Plato does not (and neither in my view does Aristotle) make friendship simply an extension of self-direction or self-love. Nor again is what one gives to the other simply a measure of how one is related to oneself. Self-relatedness and other-relatedness are not simple states but fundamental questions to be engaged or dynamic transcendental tendencies that cannot easily be determined, managed, controlled, or persuaded.[81] The whole purpose of scientific insight *(episteme, theoria*, or *nous)* and of Platonic friendship and love is to see the individual *from the perspective of the whole*, for this is to see or love the individual *as individual*, faults and all. That is, to recognize deficiencies and yet, in light of desire, to see what something can be: all sensible objects strive after the ideal and yet fall short of it (*Phaedo* 74d–75b). In the *Phaedrus*, in particular, Plato provides at least two different models for understanding the love of individuals, but these and other models can also be seen in the *Alcibiades I* and the *Symposium*.

---

the *Symposium* a daimon; Plotinus builds both into his treatment of *eros*: the *eros* of the higher soul is a god, that of the mixed soul a daimon (*Ennead* III.5[50].4, 24–25).

81. If the individual x or y is an image or reflection of the form, then it is plain that the individual as such or as object only is an abstraction. As for Plato and Plotinus, so too for Dionysius the Areopagite, "there is no such thing as an individual being conceived as a closed, self-contained unit which extrinsically enters into relations with other beings." Perl, *Theophany*, 80–81.

2.9.1 Three models for seeing the individual (*Republic*)

In order to see something of the profound value accorded to friendship by the Platonic tradition, we should look briefly at two striking examples of what it means to be *without* friendship in Plato, and then one further model for understanding friendship in a somewhat different positive key. Let me take two negative models first. The *Republic* gives us (at least) two striking examples of different approaches to the individual in negative contexts, one unsuccessful, purely external, and the other successful, penetrating, but profoundly sad.

There is, first, the sophistic, political model that Socrates sketches in Book 6. According to his analogy between the mob and some powerful beast, Socrates says that it is as if the keeper of a mighty, powerful beast studied its

> moods and desires, . . . how to approach, how to handle it, how it becomes most difficult and most gentle and what makes it so, what sounds it utters on each occasion, and what sounds addressed to it soothe or anger it. Having learned all this by tending the brute over a period of time he calls this wisdom, gathers his information together as if it were an art, and starts to teach it. The truth is that he knows nothing about these beliefs and desires . . . but he gives them names in accordance with the brute's reactions: what it enjoys he calls good, what angers it he calls bad, and he can give no other account of them. (*Republic* 6.493a–c)

To the modern eye, such an approach is close to hard behaviorism, that is, the view that there is no inner dimension, but simply observation of behavior on the basis of which one determines, on purely conventional, pragmatic grounds, what works or what doesn't, and what is therefore "good" or "bad." Evidently, there is a place for such observation in any diagnostic approach, but it is plainly unable to account for every instance since the "goodness" or "badness" of x cannot be determined exclusively by observation of behavior. The beast is merely an object and the observer remains external to any understanding. In fact, the entire model implicitly says that no understanding is possible since the beast is assumed to be *outside* understanding from the beginning. But the result of such observation is nonetheless given a value in the marketplace of education as the highest understanding, in a gigantic implicit contradiction of its own assumptions. "Wisdom" thus becomes marketable. There is, in other words, no friendship, no properly human dimension—merely, dispassionate observation of an *object*.

By contrast in Socrates' view in *Republic* 9, a different model is required even to deal with the ultimate beast, the tyrant. This cannot involve only external observation with the requisite dispassionate, professional distance; one actually *lives with* the beast "in the same house," as Socrates puts it in Book 9.[82] One therefore has to enter into the beast's life and character in order to see its behavior as a *subject*, as far as this is possible, "through and through." On Thrasymachus' account of justice in *Republic* Book 1,[83] the most unjust behavior is proclaimed to be perfect justice simply because the tyrant, from the perspective of power, says it *is* so. But though the tyrant's life *looks* glittering, it is, on Socrates' account from the perspective of the *Republic* as a whole, really a nightmare.[84] The meaning of any individual cannot be given simply because the individual says so; it cannot be gauged only from itself. Rather, the meaning of something can only be seen more fully from the perspective of the whole, that is, from other perspectives that include some understanding of what it is like to be seen through someone else's eyes: you, me, or the *polis* as a whole.

To participate only in the life of desire and spirit or only in a money-loving life is like living in one or two dimensions: such a life is "real," but not fully so, whereas to participate in all dimensions is genuinely a fuller existence.[85] Moreover, such a fuller existence is not a life removed or abstracted from things; it does not abandon lower levels but sees them more fully for what they are. In the case of the tyrannical city, for instance, Socrates says we have "to go into the city and observe *the whole of it*" (*Republic* 9.576d9–e2); and in the case of the tyrant (with whom we live in the same house),[86] we must "enter in thought into a person's character and look at it though and through (δύναται τῇ διανοίᾳ εἰς ἀνδρὸς ἦθος ἐνδὺς διιδεῖν), not like a child peeping in from outside" (*Republic* 9.577a).

In other words, after following the arguments of Books 1–8 and entering into the concluding force of Book 9 of the *Republic*, we already know that we cannot make the beast into our own understanding simply, for we cannot pretend that we stand outside all other processes in the cosmos, as though we alone possessed the necessary dispassionate rationality. Both of these examples are negative—the hard behaviorist approach to the object of study without any understanding, and the penetrating gaze that attempts to

---

82. *Republic* 9.576e–577b.
83. *Republic* 1.378cff.
84. *Republic* 9.574e–575a; 576b.
85. Against such language, Vlastos, "Degrees of Reality," 1–19 and for taking it more seriously Guthrie, *Greek Philosophy*, IV, 497.
86. *Republic* 9.577a–b.

understand as a subject what the tyrant really looks like, the tyrant who will dominate everyone, including himself. However, the point is that they present two examples of seeing someone or something directly, either purely externally with no real understanding of anything, just pure guesswork in the case of the beast, or seeing someone with understanding and experience only to discover the absolute poverty of an existence that had looked so full. This latter is, in fact, the discovery of the tyrant's complete friendlessness: the tyrant may have appeared to be master of himself and everyone else, but his mastery is a form of enslavement to others and to himself, for the worst tyrant is also tyrant of himself.[87] Tyrants, for instance, "live their whole lives without being friends with anyone; their relations with other human beings are either those of a master or a slave, and the tyrannical nature never has a taste of freedom and true friendship" (*Republic* 9.576a).

True friendship, in other words, does not enslave oneself or the other, nor does it look at the other as an object only. Instead, it frees someone to be himself or herself even in the midst of the ambiguities of ordinary experience, that is, it frees one to be an individual in a meaningful or authentic way.

This is surely what is at stake in the famous definition of the just human being in *Republic* Book 4. Conspicuously, such a person is friend to himself or herself and, because of this, can be just to others. Here instead of observation of an object or understanding of a subject, we find a *subject-object* interrelational model or definition. It is possible to see in this definition a focus upon an inner self to the exclusion of the outer world, but this is not the case for several reasons: First, the entire definition of the just person, some eighteen lines, is, in fact, a single, unified but fully articulated sentence in Greek that includes both the inner and the outer dimensions of just action. In other words, it is a fully articulated whole within a single comprehensive thought. Second, Plato compares the self-relation of the just person to a musical attunement and, thus, he portrays the inner musical disposition or self-relatedness of the just person as a precondition for just action in the city. This is explicitly said to be where the individual, the city, and "justice" meet (*Republic* 4.444a3–5). I translate the sentence below as literally as possible in order to show how it articulates a complex but complete, unified thought.

> And the truth at any rate was something like this: Justice is not about external action of the things of oneself, but about inner action, truly about himself and the things of himself, not allowing each element in him to do alien things or the kinds in the

---

87. *Republic* 9.577cff; 588b–c.

soul to meddle with one another, but disposing well what are truly his own things and himself ruling himself and ordering himself, having become friend to himself, harmonizing what are three parts, like three delimiting notes of a harmony straightforwardly, high, low, and middle, and any others that happen to be in between, having bound all of them together, and from many having become altogether one, wisely temperate and attuned, so then already to perform any action at all, whether about the acquisition of money or care for the body, whether some public action or private contract, in all of them thinking and naming the just and beautiful action to be that which keeps this disposition and works to achieve it, wisdom as the knowledge that stands over this action, and an unjust action to be that which always loosens this, and ignorance the belief that in turn stands over this. (*Republic* 4.443c9–444a2)

This single sentence is always rendered into English by means of several sentences—which makes perfect sense in a polished translation that aims to convey an accessible meaning. However, Plato clearly intended this definition to be captured in a unified comprehensive thought, exactly as in any real definition in Plato and Aristotle. This definition integrates a principle, fundamental to the *Republic*, that each power, function, or part should do its own work, not that of something else. It also expresses the principle that self-related friendship or the inner music of one's own being is a priority or precondition for just action in the world. Only by putting oneself in order can one hope to work justly with others or bring just order to the city.[88] As Socrates will finally express this priority in Book 9, the person of good sense "will cultivate harmony in the body for the sake of symphony in the soul" (591d). This is not to disregard the individual, as if one were to move from the concrete individual to some ghostly counterpart, but to bring the individual self, the other, and the city into focused alignment.

In fact, this definition of the just person as one who cultivates inner harmony as a precondition for proper action employs elements of the epistemological framework that is already found in the *Alcibiades I*. We should not concern ourselves with the outer "things of oneself"; we should look to the inner disposition of our being: "really about ourself and the things of ourselves" from this perspective. Once we order this inner reflexive medium, then action flows from *within* it. This priority is not temporal but rather logical and existential. Of course, one needs many things and much

---

88. By contrast with the tyrant, at 9.579c, who "badly governed within himself... is compelled by some chance to be a tyrant and, while not in charge of himself, to attempt to rule over others."

practice to be just, and this plainly involves a lot of time, but the definition makes manifest what is already an expression of one's being in action. This is clearly a precursor of Aristotle's notion of activity, that is, it is or it aims to be complete in itself at any given moment, and Aristotle sees some actions, like seeing, thinking, virtuous activity, and happiness as having precisely this character.[89]

The *Alcibiades* places a similar priority upon the "self," rather than upon the things or belongings of oneself, or at an even further remove, upon the belongings of the belongings. From this perspective of the self, everything else flows. This is the way Socrates puts it in the *Alcibiades I*: in looking into the best part of the soul, as by looking into the pupil of the eye of the other, one will find the real wisdom of the soul and so "know all the divine . . . and gain the best knowledge of oneself" (133c). The result will be that, in seeing clearly who you are, you can also know what belongs to you (τὰ ἡμέτερα) and what belongs to your belongings (τὰ τῶν ἡμετέρων) (133d–134b). And the consequence of this, precisely as in *Republic* 4, is that with your eyes focused on what is divine and bright, "you will act" (134d: πράξετε); "you will act in the right way and well" (134d: ὀρθῶς τε καὶ εὖ πράξετε). Self-knowledge is the precondition of truly just action in the city.

There is, then, not only a pronounced affinity between the *Alcibiades I* and *Republic* 4, but also the epistemology in both works is undoubtedly that of Plato.

So one's relatedness to the best flourishing of oneself with respect to what is best or most fine in the whole is a model, or precondition, for love of the other. But, in the *Republic,* this is not the imposition of an ideal upon someone else, but rather an experience of mutuality in one's own relations with oneself and with the other. This relational mutuality is a kind of recalling of oneself or, rather, of both selves in each other,[90] in relation to an intimate hypercosmic/cosmic paradigm (Zeus, Aphrodite, etc.) on different levels: a lower more mundane level or a higher form of life, in accordance with the unlikely paradigm of Pausanias' speech in the *Symposium* and its sequel in Socrates' second speech or "myth" in the *Phaedrus*. What Vlastos or Dover consider to be the obvious facts of ordinary experience—namely, that we love others for themselves only—involves for Plato the much more complex, dangerous inscrutabilities of ordinary experience in which success and failure may look fatally alike each other at different points. Vlastos and Dover appear to live in a steady state universe where present identifica-

---

89. In all of these activities, unlike learning, walking, building, we say that each simultaneously "is" and "has been" (*Metaphysics* 1048b23).

90. Cf. *Phaedrus* 252c–253c.

tions are not particularly problematic. Plato inhabits a dynamic, constantly changing universe where it is possible to love others for themselves, but not at the expense—for long—of the well-being of the other, ourselves, or the cosmos. Nonetheless, Plato is more practical than his critics suppose: some lovers *do* live on a very recognizable ordinary plane.

From this broader perspective, I think, we can see why friendship in later Neoplatonism includes so many aspects ranging from the hypercosmic and cosmic to the intrapersonal and personal, individual relationships, so characteristic of the Pythagorean tradition. We need as many good models as we can find in all our experience of the cosmos. From the bottom up, we find these aspects fragmented, whereas from the top down we experience an expansion of spirit. The healthy functioning of the universe and its inhabitants gives us a reasonable model for understanding friendship and love. As Iamblichus puts this in the *De Mysteriis*, "friendship is an activity in the whole" that "augments divine love" (*DM* 5.26); but it can be simply passion in the fragmented parts (*DM* 4.9. 192, 14-193,1). Prayer, then, for Iamblichus, establishes, on the one hand, links of friendship between us and the gods (*DM* 5.26.238,6-8; 5.26.239. 5) and, on the other, "one single bond of friendship embracing all things" (*DM* 5.10.211,12-13). We shall come to this in chapter 3. For Iamblichus in his *Life of Pythagoras*, in fact, friendship exists at every level of being, links the divine to the human, is interpersonal, intrapersonal (i.e., body and soul), and links all living beings, both animals and plants.[91]

So, in bringing *Alcibiades I*, as we saw above, into the broader picture of the major Platonic dialogues on love and friendship, and in insisting that love of the individual for the individual's own sake has a proper, nuanced place in Platonism, we have uncovered a more well-rounded view of love and friendship, one that can be seen in all of these dialogues and also in the later tradition. The position that Platonism, whether that of Plato, Aristotle, or the later tradition, simply ignores the ambiguities and realities of ordinary experience or eliminates love of individuals for their own sakes in favor of the givine or, as Grube put it, "the eternal preservation of the soul in the cold storage of eternally frozen absolute Forms," is demonstrably false. Let us now turn our attention from human love and friendship to the other side of this issue in chapter 3, namely, the "cold storage" side of the question, or the nature of divine loving.

---

91. Iamblichus *Life of Pythagoras,* 229–30. So too in Proclus' *Commentary on the Alcibiades*, the god of friendship is a unifying, binding power in souls (233, 5–7), so that the divine speaks in them and they speak divine things.

3

The Problem of Divine Love

3.1 Pleasure, pre-inclusion, joy, and vulnerability

WE MAY LOVE AND honor the gods, but do they love us back? In many of the ancient myths, the gods roam the earth to discover good-living, honest people, such as Baucis and Philemon, and then reward them for their piety. An ancient story is relayed by Porphyry in late antiquity to illustrate the thesis that the gods "take more pleasure in" humble, inexpensive things than great wealth. Such things are "dear to the gods" who estimate the quality of the sacrificers rather than the quantity of the sacrifice, *ēthos* or character rather than *plēthos* or abundance. Porphyry tells the story of a wealthy man from Magnesia in Asia who came to Delphi, wanting to please the gods because of his major donations and piety, and asked the Pythia, the priestess of Apollo, which human being honored the divine power in the best ways. To his surprise, the priestess named a total unknown living in an obscure village, a certain Clearchos from Methydrion in Arcadia. So the wealthy man went up to Methydrion and asked Clearchos for his secret. There was no secret. Clearchos said his prayers at the right times, giving the first fruits of his crops to the gods and in public sacrifices, never killing animals (an important feature of Porphyry's case against violence to animals) but "offering what he had available." This story, however apocryphal, catches something of the Greek respect for moderation and self-restraint.[1]

The Delphic maxim "Know Thyself" is not an intellectual injunction so much as the recognition that human life is as nothing by comparison with divine life, as we see in the case of Socrates in the *Apology*. Proper humility, justice to all, respect for the holy, and, in Socrates' case, an examined life—these are some of the hallmarks of real excellence, of what it means to be loved by the gods. We find in Plato's *Republic* the after-image from an earlier age of the practically good person beloved of the gods. When

---

1. Porphyry, *On Abstinence*, 2.16.

in Book 10 the much-enduring and crooked-thinking Odysseus makes his free choice of the lowliest herdsman's life on the Plain of Truth,[2] something decidedly both old and new takes place. Odysseus, in a sense, completes the question "what is justice" that began with Cephalus in Book 1,[3] but turns the expectations of the world upside down. He has come through much experience to know the good and so he gladly, joyfully embraces its lowliest part.[4]

In all of this, do the gods love human beings in return or do they simply return favors or show favoritism, as in the Homeric world? We know in the *Apology* that "the god," presumably Apollo, is moved by "care" for his Athenian people,[5] but how far does this extend and what does such care involve? What happens when the familiar city and household deities who have lived with the people for thousands of years give way to the forms, to the beautiful and the good, to the demiurge or craftsman, or to the unmover mover? In this chapter, I shall tell my own version of a pagan story of divine love that unfolded over a period of more than one thousand years, a period that ranged from the Presocratics in the sixth to the fifth centuries BCE to Dionysius the Areopagite who lived somewhere between the late fifth and early sixth century CE. It is a story that led to the passing of all the ancient gods, but also to the discovery of a new, yet very old mode of divine being that deserves to be better known than it has been. I start with the unmoved mover's self-relatedness and its life as the purest pleasure.

3.2 Self-relatedness, inclusion, pre-inclusion?

If self-relatedness is the best and most inclusive expression of what we give to others, and if god-belovedness appears to be the highest expression of self-relatedness, can this most inclusive relation in human life actually be a two-way relation, namely, a relation of human being to god and of god to human being? In the *Symposium*, *eros-daimon* is an expression of something divine self-communicating in ordinary converse that links god to humanity, resource to poverty.[6] In Proclus' *Commentary on the Alcibiades*, the god of friendship is a unifying, binding power in souls (233, 5–7), so that the divine speaks in them and they speak divine things. Even in Aristotle, it must be emphasized, there are, at least, two different views on this question:

2. *Republic* 10.620c–d.
3. *Republic* 1.328c–331d.
4. *Republic* 10.620d: καὶ εἰπεῖν ἰδοῦσαν ὅτι τὰ αὐτὰ ἂν ἔπραξεν καὶ πρώτη λαχοῦσα, καὶ ἀσμένην ἑλέσθαι . . . .
5. *Apology* 31a.
6. *Symposium* 202d–204c.

on the one hand, friendship requires human exchange of affection; indeed, "it would be strange if one were to say that one loved Zeus" (*EN* 1159a5–8; *MM* 1208b26–31). On the other hand, there is also suggested a pre-eminent friendship of human beings to god and of god to the human being, as of father to son[7] (*EN* 1162a4–5; 1160b25–26; *EE* 1242a31–35; cf. *EE* 1239a1–24). In addition, the wise person who acts in accordance with intellect is, on Aristotle's view, θεοφιλέστατος, because he shares most in the unity of god's activity.[8] For Philo later, Moses "became god-beloved and god-loving" and because of this he was also "human-loving."[9]

On the one hand, then, there is obviously no possibility of a loving, caring unmoved mover in Aristotle's *Metaphysics*, partly because it is precisely the anthropomorphic and external character of causality in Plato (e.g., the divine craftsman of the *Timaeus*) that Aristotle is concerned to combat—and there is also a precise economy in Aristotle's procedure, that is, in so far as he implicitly develops Plato's notions of final causality in the *Symposium* and *Republic* to undermine and erase Plato's anthropomorphic causality in the *Timaeus* and elsewhere. Nonetheless, the context in both Plato and Aristotle, in my view, shows that the notion of care or love is not entirely foreign. In Plato, particularly, there is a care of the higher for the lower, not only at every level of ascent[10] (just as in the *Phaedrus* all-soul cares for that which is without soul),[11] but also in so far as immortality and god-belovedness[12] are *gifts* of the beautiful-good.[13] Nothing quite like this appears in Aristotle,[14]

---

7. This is the relation that Proclus thematizes between Socrates and Alcibiades (*in Alc.* 26ff.).

8. *EN* 1179a22–24: ὁ δὲ κατὰ νοῦν ἐνεργῶν καὶ τοῦτον θεραπεύων καὶ διακείμενος ἄριστα καὶ θεοφιλέστατος ἔοικεν.

9. Philo, *Life of Moses* II.67 and 163: . . . φιλόθεός τε καὶ θεοφιλὴς ἐγένετο, καταπνευσθεὶς ὑπ' ἔρωτος.

10. *Symposium* 210c1–6; d5–6; 212a3–6.

11. *Phaedrus* 246b–c.

12. In the Platonic tradition, the question of divine love is decidedly ambiguous. Is it our own love of the divine or is it a divine love for, and in, us? Cf. *Laws* 4, 716c–e. For an interesting clarification in a different, but related context, see Philo, *Life of Moses* II 67 (τοιγαροῦν μετ' ὀλίγων ἄλλων φιλόθεός τε καὶ θεοφιλὴς ἐγένετο, καταπνευσθεὶς ὑπ' ἔρωτος οὐρανίου καὶ διαφερόντως τιμήσας τὸν ἡγεμόνα τοῦ παντὸς καὶ ἀντὶ τιμηθεὶς ὑπ' αὐτοῦ); cf. *Life of Moses* II.163.

13. *Symposium* 212a.

14. However, we should note that while the disproportion between the divine and the human is so great as to change the nature of any relation of *philia* between the two, nonetheless Aristotle is prepared to suggest and *think* such a unique relation, even if he does so *en passant*: "reciprocal love is possible without its being the love of friends" (*EE* 1239a20–21; cf. a18–19; and see Bodéüs, *Aristotle*, 151). Compare Eijk, *Medicine and Philosophy*, 243 and note 20: on the question of "divine concern" (*epimeleia*), at

but there is something equally significant that should not be overlooked. While a loving unmoved mover might be entirely beyond the pale, the question of how the unmoved mover is related to itself and how it is related to the world is very much a part of Aristotle's treatment.[15] (Picking up in a different mode, we might suggest, Aristotle's treatment of friendship in the *Ethics*: that is, the quality of one's relation to oneself is an integral precondition of how one is related to one's friend or of what one gives to another.)[16]

But is the unmoved mover's self-relatedness (its thinking of thinking) a precondition or pre-containment, as it were, of the world's relatedness to the unmoved mover, that is, the world's relatedness as love, desire, and thought? It does not follow that, in thinking itself, the unmoved mover bears no relation to the world or that its thinking is empty or non-creative, for it makes more sense to suppose that in thinking itself it includes the whole world, not, as we experience it, piecemeal and extended in time and space, but rather as indivisibly *whole*: "intellect does not have the good in this bit or in that bit, but *the best is in a certain whole, being something different*" (*Metaphysics* 12.9.1075a7–9).[17] In other words, god's self-thinking is richer than the contemplation of the universe because god's life is both himself and all the energy of the world, but in a divine mode; and if this is so, then god's self-relatedness pre-includes our relatedness to god.

My thesis here is not that Aristotle implicitly describes the unmoved mover as somehow self-loving or as loving the world. He does not. One can fully understand, when one looks at anthropomorphic representations of

---

EN 1179a23ff. and 1099b10ff. "Aristotle neither accepts nor rejects the conception of 'divine concern' (*theia epimeleia*) or 'divine dispensation' (*theia moira*); it seems that he did not want to go so far as to draw the conclusion, which in the light of his theology in the strictest form was inescapable, that there is no room for such divine concern."

15. *Metaphysics* 12.9–10.

16. *Nicomachean Ethics* (*EN*) Books 8–9, especially Book 8.10 and Book 9.4.8–9. And in Aristotle, it must be emphasized that there are different views on the complex question of friendship: on the one hand, friendship requires human exchange of affection; indeed, "it would be strange if one were to say that one loved Zeus" (*EN* 1159a5–8; *Magna Moralia* 1208b26–31). On the other hand, there is a pre-eminent friendship of human beings to gods and of god to the human being, as of father to son, also suggested. Thus, *EN* 1162a4–5 ("the friendship of children to parents, and of men to gods, is a relation of them as to something good and superior . . ."); 1160b25–26; *Eudemian Ethics* (*EE*) 1242a31–35 (the friendship "of father and son is the same as that of god to man, benefactor to beneficiary"); cf. *EE* 1239a17–19 (when there is an excessive difference between friends, then "not even the respective parties themselves seek that they be loved in return or loved equally in return, for example, if someone were to make the claim of god").

17. *Metaphysics* 12.9.1075a7–9: οὐ γὰρ ἔχει τὸ εὖ ἐν τῳδὶ ἢ ἐν τῳδί, ἀλλ' ἐν ὅλῳ τινὶ τὸ ἄριστον, ὂν ἄλλο τι.

the demiurge in Plato's *Timaeus* and *Politicus,* why Aristotle should rigorously avoid such tendencies and not make god either "love" (in the mode of Agathon's speech)[18] or a lover (in the sense of earlier mythological depictions or even of any favoritism attached to the meaning of god-belovedness) or a principle that cares for everything (in the role of "all soul" according to the myth of the *Phaedrus*).[19] What Aristotle does instead, on my account, is bequeath a problem to the later tradition, namely, how the self-relatedness of the unmoved mover precontains or prefigures the *best* of the world as a whole.[20]

3.3 Pleasure and indivisible wholeness

However, there is a deeper and somewhat problematic connection here between Plato, Aristotle, Plotinus, and the later tradition on the question of pleasure, indivisibility, and the divine life. This needs further analysis because it has perhaps escaped the attention it merits. First, Aristotle does something that Plato could not have done: he identifies god's life with the purest pleasure, but he articulates his theory of pleasure in a compelling Platonic way that no one after Epicurus could accept and yet that everyone somehow had to deal with. Second, an important part of Aristotle's theory of time and space is compressed into his statement in *Metaphysics* 12.9, cited just above, about the indivisible wholeness of god's best life that we experience piecemeal. This, in fact, provided a template for understanding how ordinary human experience might be related to god's life. I shall examine each of these in turn, starting with Aristotle's radical identification of god's way of life as pleasure and then linking this up with the important question of indivisibility and "wholeness."

Aristotle's description of god's life as the purest pleasure is in one way a radical break with Plato, but since he also builds into his own theory of pleasure a framework that is deeply in tune with other elements from Plato's dialogues, the overall result is somewhat ambiguous. First, why did Aristotle break with the theory of pleasure outlined in the *Philebus*, namely, that pleasure is a movement, something indefinite, to be given a lowly place in any hierarchical ranking in the column of goods? If we follow what Aristotle actually does in *Ethica Nicomachea* 7.1152b1–1154b34 and

---

18. *Symposium* 195aff: "Love . . . is the loveliest and the best," that visits only the young, soft, and dainty!

19. *Phaedrus* 246b–d.

20. This is also a problem for Plato too. See, for example, *Laws* 900d–901b: God must be characterized by self-love, not self-hate.

10.1172a19–1176a29, we see that he rejects the *Philebus'* low estimation of pleasure for two principal reasons: First, because Socrates sees pleasure as a movement, however complex, that has to be classified as "indefinite" or unlimited and that is, therefore, subordinate to "limit," form, measure, etc. (*Philebus* 24e; 27e; 31a; 53c–54d; cf. Aristotle *EN* 1173a29–1173b7). Second, because Socrates' language in both the *Philebus* and *Republic* 9 about pleasure and pain being respectively a "restoration" or a "lack" of a natural condition is based on bodily functions such as nutrition and does not properly capture the nature of some pleasures that do not presuppose pain, such as the pleasures of "learning . . . smells . . . sounds, sights, memories, and hopes. Of what will these be the coming-into-being? There has been no lack of which there might be a replenishment?" (compare *Philebus* 31e–32b; 42c–d; and *EN* 1173b7–20). In other words, in the *Philebus* we have a division of *pleasures as pleasures*, that is, of movements or qualities, not of *substance*; so, despite the pure or true pleasures ranked by Socrates with experiences unmixed with pain and ranged primarily with the soul, pure pleasures are only ranked fifth in order (*Philebus* 67b). The best Socrates can say about pure pleasures in the *Philebus* is that they are not simply *genesis* or coming-to-be but on their way to *ousia* or the order of being; in other words, a pure pleasure is a pathway or *hodos* in relation to an end-state, a *telos*, but it remains a *kinēsis* or movement.[21] This is also true in some measure of Socrates' earlier treatment of pleasure in *Republic* 9. "What is sweet in the soul or painful is a movement (κίνησίς τις)" (9.583e9–10)—and an ambiguous movement; in fact, "a form of bewitchment" (9.584a10: γοητεία τις), since pleasure and pain are so often mixed together in different ways that what seems pleasant is pleasant, but only by contrast with a previous pain or vice versa.

However, in the broader context of the *Republic*, there is, first, an implicit positive view of pleasure. Socrates argues that there are pleasures that do not presuppose pain or involve some exchange of pleasure for pain or vice versa, and he gives smell as an example (9.584a–b), as in Aristotle (*EN* 1173b7–20), but there is only a fleeting glimpse at this point of what such pure pleasures might be. To be fair to Aristotle, Plato points out elsewhere the need to think positively about pleasure. At the beginning of the *Phaedo*, for instance, Socrates' opening remarks problematize the "astonishing relation [pleasure] has with its opposite, pain" (*Phaedo* 60b–c);[22] as Socrates

---

21. *Philebus* 32b: . . . τὴν δ' εἰς τὴν αὐτῶν οὐσίαν ὁδόν, ταύτην δ' αὖ πάλιν τὴν ἀναχώρησιν πάντων ἡδονήν.

22. This is already anticipated in the frame of the dialogue when Phaedo observes to Echechrates concerning his own feelings that day alongside Socrates that he had no feeling of pity, or of pleasure, but a strange mixture of simultaneous pleasure and pain

rubs his leg, the pain caused by his fetters seems to give way to pleasure. And this apparently casual detail surely foreshadows one of the dialogue's principal concerns, namely, how is it possible to overcome the cyclical exchange of pleasure and pains in order to articulate a proper view of formal, as opposed to material, causality. If then the *Phaedo* is about causality; and if one should not be brave out of cowardice, but rather because of wisdom, as Socrates argues early in the dialogue (68b–69d); and if further, as Socrates will later argue, Anaxagoras' theory of mind is not to be reduced to physical or material explanations, as if one were to say that Socrates is in prison because of his bones and sinews but not because he thinks it just and *best* to be there (96a–100a), then surely a proper theory of pleasure should not link it only to pain or to bodily functions or, again, to an oscillating movement between pleasure and pain, but rather to the integral functioning of the good and wise person. The *Phaedo*, therefore, strongly implies the need for a positive treatment of pleasure, beyond the cyclical exchange of opposites, whereas the *Philebus* sees pleasure as a movement fairly low down on any hierarchical ranking of goods. So there are grounds in Plato for Aristotle wanting to develop a more positive view of pleasure than he found in the *Philebus*.

But second, and most important, in the *Republic* Socrates argues for a ranking of substantive *ways of life*—not qualitative movements—in which pleasure appears to be integral, that is, proper or *oikeia* to the kind of life to which it is attached, as Aristotle also argues (*EN* 1175a30–31). It may well be that pleasure *as such* is subordinate to wisdom or to intellect *as such* (and Aristotle worries about this throughout his analysis—e.g., *EN* 1175a18–19; 1175b31–33), but it is not clear that in a particular way of life the pleasure that is proper to this life is really subordinate, since love of wisdom as a way of life is pleasurable intrinsically. In other words, if in *Republic* 9 the highest form of life participates in and is filled by what is "most real," as opposed to lower forms that are filled by "less real things,"[23] and if the highest form of participation is by loving, touching upon, and giving birth to truth (as in both the *Republic* and *Symposium*),[24] then the highest way of life in Plato is surely a receiving and having or touching upon a life of the purest pleasure that is love of wisdom.

My general thesis then is this: Aristotle develops his own theory of pleasure, not from the *Philebus*—which for him is a division of *pleasure as a quality or movement*—but from the *Phaedo, Republic, Symposium*, and other

---

(*Phaedo* 58d–59a).

23. *Republic* 9.585d–e.
24. *Symposium* 209e5–212a7; *Republic* 6.490a–b.

dialogues in which there is a division of *substances,* i.e., concrete *ways of life* in the *Republic,* or particular ways of approaching the question of love through *individual substances.*[25] Consider, for instance, individuals in the *Symposium* who find themselves in a position of pain, after the heavy drinking of the night before and, therefore, in need of finding a way out of the pleasure-pain cycle by virtue of love-discourse in the *Symposium* (that is, the participants: Phaedrus, Pausanias, Eryximachus, Aristophanes etc.). They fail, of course, all of them—except Socrates, who is "equal to both"[26]—but the entire *Symposium* is the attempt to rise above such opposites. So Aristotle picks a problem in Plato's dialogues that is *not* resolved in the *Philebus.*

What then does it mean to speak of pure pleasure, not as a qualitative movement, or as a restoration of a natural condition, or as a mixed condition with measure, form, intellect, etc., but as an integral feature of the lives of *individual substances*? Why, for Aristotle, is pleasure not a coming-to-be or a movement that needs to be complete?

Possibly against Eudoxus, who held that pleasure is the good, and against Speusippus and Xenocrates, who held that pleasure is bad,[27] Aristotle argues that there are many things we would choose even if they brought no pleasure (such as seeing, remembering, knowing, healthy flourishing)[28] and, conversely, while movements admit of quickness and slowness, and while we can *become* pleased or angry quickly, we cannot *be* pleased quickly or slowly.[29] Therefore, pleasure is neither the good nor a process of change.

What then does Aristotle mean by a process of change—that is, *"becoming* pleased" versus *"being* pleased"—and what is the alternative to change? For Aristotle, all change involves transition or development from potentiality (*dynamis*) to capacity or state (*hexis*); however, the "change" from *hexis* (capacity) to *energeia* (full actualization or activity) is not a physical transition or change but an instantaneous manifestation of what the activity or thing already is. Activity in this sense—seeing, thinking, or contemplating—has its *telos* or goal inside itself. My seeing you obviously *depends upon* highly complex developmental processes, on the one hand, but I see or think you *instantaneously* as a complete expression of my being, on the other. Or as Aristotle puts it: "seeing seems to be at any moment complete, for there is no lack of anything which coming into being later will

25. *Symposium* 176a–d.
26. *Symposium* 176c.
27. *EN* 1173a18–1173b7.
28. *EN* 1174a4–6.
29. *EN* 1173a34–1173b1: "ἡσθῆναι μὲν γὰρ ἔστι ταχέως ὥσπερ ὀργισθῆναι, ἥδεσθαι δ' οὔ."

complete its form" (*EN* 1174a15–16). And he goes on to argue that pleasure is like this: "for it is a whole, and at no time could anyone take a pleasure whose form will be completed if the pleasure lasts longer' (*EN* 1174a17–19: ὅλον γάρ τί ἐστι, καὶ κατ' οὐδένα χρόνον λάβοι τις ἂν ἡδονὴν ἧς ἐπὶ πλείω χρόνον γινομένης τελειωθήσεται τὸ εἶδος.).

In what sense, then, is pleasure a "whole"? We can perhaps see what Aristotle means if we contrast activities and movements. Movements or processes, like house-building, take time and they occur for the sake of an end, and they are only complete "in the whole time" it takes to complete them or "at the final point" (*EN* 1174a21: ἐν ἅπαντι δὴ τῷ χρόνῳ ἢ τούτῳ.). Activities like seeing and pleasure are complete "at any and every time" (*EN* 1174b5–6: τῆς ἡδονῆς δ' ἐν ὁτῳοῦν χρόνῳ τέλειον τὸ εἶδος), "for what occurs in the now is a whole" (*EN* 1174b9: τὸ γὰρ ἐν τῷ νῦν ὅλον τι).

This seems even more problematic on the face of things: surely the "now" is an abstract limit: and time, for Aristotle, is not composed of "nows" any more than a line is composed of points. This is why time, for Aristotle, is a *measure* of motion and a line is a *line*,[30] that is, a reality different from an assembly of abstract points or units. Here we have to think outside of our customary frameworks. We tend to talk about intelligible reality *and* sensible reality, mind *and* feeling, mind *and* body, or the body-mind *relation*. But Aristotle does not think of "reality" in the same way we do.

Activities that are complete in themselves are "whole" at any given moment we care to pick. In Aristotle's language, they are "indivisible" or "without parts" and anything without parts cannot come to be. Coming-to-be applies only to things "that are divisible, things that are not wholes; there is no coming-to-be of seeing or of a point or of a unit" (1174b11–13).[31] In other words, while we can distinguish activity and potentiality, activity and movement, and the distinction is real, nonetheless, the potentiality and the movement are not distinct from activity as though they could be added up and expressed as x *and* y, for the activity is the indivisible timeless expression of what the process or potentiality manifests in a developmental form.[32]

30. See *Physics* 6.231a20–b6; 5.227a10–12; for time as a measure of motion, 4.220b32–221a1;221b7; 221b22–3; 221b25–6.

31. *EN* 1174b11–13: ἐκ τούτων δὲ δῆλον καὶ ὅτι οὐ καλῶς λέγουσι κίνησιν ἢ γένεσιν εἶναι τῆς ἡδονῆς. οὐ γὰρ πάντων ταῦτα λέγεται, ἀλλὰ τῶν μεριστῶν καὶ μὴ ὅλων· οὐδὲ γὰρ ὁράσεώς ἐστι γένεσις οὐδὲ στιγμῆς οὐδὲ μονάδος (οὐδὲ τούτων οὐθὲν κίνησις οὐδὲ γένεσις)· οὐδὲ δὴ ἡδονῆς· ὅλον γάρ τι.

32. Cf. *Metaphysics* Z.17.1041b19: "And flesh is not simply fire and earth or the hot and cold, but also something else . . . but this 'something else' would seem not to be an element but it is a cause that this matter is flesh and that matter is a syllable; and similarly in the other cases; and the substance of each is this; for this is a primary cause of the being" (καὶ ἡ σὰρξ οὐ μόνον πῦρ καὶ γῆ ἢ τὸ θερμὸν καὶ ψυχρόν, ἀλλὰ καὶ ἕτερόν τι

There is no process without activity. So for Aristotle, of course, there is no need for two worlds, a sensible world *and* an intelligible world. Intelligible reality is not only the perfection of this world; it *is* what this world strives to be. Of course, unlike god, we are never entirely "partless" or "indivisible." But we know what indivisibility is "like" from our experience of individual substance, of mathematical entities, and of our active faculties. As an individual substance, I am divisible in many different ways, but my experience is in some measure indivisible since I am an *archē*—an originative principle,[33] an agent-center of experience; and my faculties act as indivisible centres for the ordering and reception of divisible stimuli, organs, and data. Alexander of Aphrodisias, for instance, will later describe the "common sense"—that which synthesizes individual sense perceptions—as an indivisible center for the radii of the *propria sensa*. In other words, it is a fundamental part of our ordinary experience of time and space to be able to recognize how what is indivisible grasps as a whole what we also experience in a developmental way over a lengthy period of time. In other words, when Aristotle describes god's way of life as perhaps including indivisibly what we experience piecemeal, he points to a range of indivisible "wholes" that run right through our experience (*Metaphysics* 12.9). What we experience as piecemeal, from a developmental viewpoint, we can also experience indivisibly as a whole from another, even if this latter experience is always imperfect, by comparison with what we imagine god's experience to be.

Before we follow Aristotle's analysis of pleasure to its conclusion, let me briefly turn to Plato. Aristotle finds Plato's proposition of two worlds unnecessary, as involving "poetic metaphors," and as solving nothing unless the source of movement is actually *"in"* things. This does *not* mean that he rejects Plato's vision completely, for he thinks that his own theory is what Plato really should have meant, namely, a view of reality based not on duplication of entities but on the opening up *within substances* of an ascent or natural hierarchy that points ultimately to the primary substance or paradigm of everything, namely, the unmoved mover. This primary substance is the true form—separate, unmixed, etc. Equally, while Plato posits two worlds, he cannot mean two things or an episodic aggregate, that is, a sensible *and* an intelligible world, for the reality of sensible things is derived wholly from the intelligible form. For Aristotle, then, the divided line of Plato's thought is really a continuous line of activities that culminates in indivisible thinking or contemplation, ranging from the activities and proper

---

... δόξειε δ' ἂν εἶναί τι τοῦτο καὶ οὐ στοιχεῖον, καὶ αἴτιόν γε τοῦ εἶναι τοδὶ μὲν σάρκα, τοδὶ δὲ συλλαβήν. ὁμοίως δὲ καὶ ἐπὶ τῶν ἄλλων. οὐσία δὲ ἑκάστου μὲν τοῦτο· τοῦτο γὰρ αἴτιον πρῶτον τοῦ εἶναι).

33. *EN* 1139b5.

pleasures appropriate to different animals and finally those appropriate to the complete and supremely happy human being (*EN* 1176a3–29).

Aristotle's view here is, therefore, not without reference to Plato's view of activities in *Republic* 6. In *Republic* 6–7, Socrates defines the power/capacity/nature of agency as any *activity* at all: seeing, hearing, thinking, understanding, or contemplating (cf. 479e) are *dynameis*, actualized by the *power* of the sun in the sensible world or implicitly by the *power* of the good in the intelligible world. Perception is not just the lowest section of a divided line but the actualizing confluence of three (or four) powers in a single reality: the perceiving power (507c8); the object perceived; light as an efflux from the sun (508b6–7); and the power of the sun itself (507b–508d), together with its integral counterpart in the intelligible realm. That is, contemplation, thought, or understanding, with the proviso that in the intelligible realm this is, in addition, the creation or production of a new reality (508d–509d),[34] for the good not only *makes* substance and being, it also makes us *think* and, ultimately, *see*. Each activity, therefore, has not only a psychological and social/political dimension, but also a cosmic dimension. Perception does not require thought, but it depends on thought for its being; and the activity of thought requires, in addition, an intelligible dimension, that is, the soul must turn itself back to being and to the light that makes being visible from the supreme power of all: the form of the good that is "beyond substance in dignity and surpassing power" (509b).

When Aristotle comes to define the role of pleasure in relation to "both the intelligible or sensible object" (*EN* 1174b34), then, he thinks, first, of the healthy or best relation between subject perceiving and object perceived (i.e., its good condition, its relation to the most beautiful of its objects, etc., 1174b14ff), as a range from perception through discursive reason and contemplation to "the worthiest of objects" (*EN* 1174b20–23). Also, second, he thinks of the precise way that pleasure perfects such activities as at least analogous to the role that light, on the one hand, or truth and being, on the other, play in relation to perception and thought in Socrates' account in *Republic* Book 6. He formulates the function of pleasure in the following way: "Pleasure completes the activity, not as the indwelling state does, but as a supervenient end, as the bloom of youth supervenes upon those in the prime of youth" (EN 1174b31–33: τελειοῖ δὲ τὴν ἐνέργειαν ἡ ἡδονὴ οὐχ ὡς ἡ ἕξις ἐνυπάρχουσα, ἀλλ' ὡς ἐπιγιγνόμενόν τι τέλος, οἷον τοῖς ἀκμαίοις ἡ ὥρα.). So the appropriate pleasure of being human does not merely perfect the activity of contemplation, as a healthy relationship between subject contemplating

---

34. The "demiurge of our senses" at *Republic* 507c probably includes both sensible and intelligible.

and object contemplated; it *adds* something beyond that dyadic relation, something that is not entirely "of" the relation.

Commenting on this passage in order to explain this "addition" or "supervenient end," J. A. Stewart introduces implicitly the light analogy: "[*hēdonē*] is not the organic source of [*energeia*]; it is rather a sort of end— the beauty of [*energeia*] itself, when once it has 'risen up into the borders of light.' As such, it sustains and strengthens [*energeia*] . . . in some such way as the [first mover] moves the universe . . . ."[35] The light analogy with *Republic* 6 may seem partly appropriate, and one could add the state or *hexis* like light that Aristotle attributes to the making intellect in *De Anima* 3.[36] However, the image Aristotle uses is *not* that of light but more like the phrase used by the later tradition of the height of intellect—the *anthos* or bloom of intellect.[37] Moreover, Aristotle never speaks of light in this passage; light does not *belong to* contemplative activity; instead, for Aristotle, pleasure and activity seem to be "inseparably united; for without activity there is no pleasure, and pleasure perfects every activity" (1175a19–21: συνεζεῦχθαι μὲν γὰρ ταῦτα φαίνεται καὶ χωρισμὸν οὐ δέχεσθαι· ἄνευ τε γὰρ ἐνεργείας οὐ γίνεται ἡδονή, πᾶσάν τε ἐνέργειαν τελειοῖ ἡ ἡδονή). Indeed, this "bloom" of Aristotle's analogy seems to have a remarkable second-order capacity: it makes contemplative activity *belong to itself*; but it also *intensifies, augments* activity: "each of the pleasures is *made akin* to the activity it perfects; for an activity is intensified by its proper pleasure" (1175a29–31: φανείη δ' ἂν τοῦτο καὶ ἐκ τοῦ συνῳκειῶσθαι τῶν ἡδονῶν ἑκάστην τῇ ἐνεργείᾳ ἣν τελειοῖ. συναύξει γὰρ τὴν ἐνέργειαν ἡ οἰκεία ἡδονή). What Aristotle seems to mean is that a contemplative activity such as geometry, music, building, or any form of scholarship has a kind of self-increasing power in it (if the activity is healthy), a power that goes beyond the activity and yet also makes the activity more intimately itself. "Kinship," "affinity," or "adaptation" (three possible translations) do not really convey the meaning of *synoikeisthai* in this instance, though Aristotle is plainly thinking of the kinship between disciplines that Socrates emphasizes in *Republic* 7 and the *Symposium*.[38] Pleasure-activity "dwells together," as it were, lives (or is lived) in one home; and Aristotle concludes

35. Stewart, *Notes on the Nicomachean Ethics*, 429.

36. *De Anima* 3.430a15.

37. Compare the *Chaldean Oracles*, fragment 1.3: "For there exists an intelligible object which you must think by the power of intellect" (cf. fr.49); and applied to fire, the highest faculty of soul and akin to the fiery essence of the first god: fragments 34, 4; 35, 5; 37,15; 42; Majercik, *Chaldean Oracles*, 130, 1989. The oracles were said to have been "handed down by the gods" to a certain Julian the Chaldean and/or his son, Julian the Theurgist. For date and transmission, see Majercik, *Chaldean Oracles*, 1–5.

38. See *Republic* 7.531d; *Symposium* 210a–212a.

(with a rhetorical flourish in Greek): "so the pleasures *intensify* the activities and what *intensifies* a thing is proper to it" (1175a35–36: συναύξουσι δὴ αἱ ἡδοναί, τὰ δὲ συναύξοντα οἰκεῖα).

Nonetheless, Stewart rightly catches the connection between pleasure and the action of the unmoved mover here, since at this point of the *Ethica Nicomachea* Book 10, we are also very close to some of Socrates' views of light and pleasure in *Republic* Books 6–9: "it [the sun] causes our sight to see *as beautifully as possible*" (*Republic* 6.508a). Moreover, when Socrates says, "It [the good] provides knowledge and truth, and is itself superior to them" (*Republic* 6.509a), Glaucon immediately connects this with pleasure: "You surely do not mean this to be pleasure." Here in Book 6, just as at the beginning and end of the *Philebus*, it would seem that pleasure could neither be the good nor even close to the good, even if Glaucon has just apparently *thought* that pleasure *might* be that in us which is closest to the light of the "good!" However, when we reach *Republic* 9, pleasure is not the lowest part of the soul; it characterizes all the different kinds of life, from the profit-loving to the wisdom-loving. In fact, the best life of wisdom is the sweetest, and so even "the desires of the profit-loving and honor-loving parts, which follow knowledge, will attain the truest pleasures possible for them, since they are following the truth. These pleasures are, in fact, *their own* [i.e., not alien—as also in *EN* 1175b8–23], if *what is best for each is most fully its own.*" The pleasure that is best for each is what most belongs to each, or in other words, most completely expresses what the activity is as a form of "belongingness" or "ownness." In choosing the good we are choosing what belongs to us, not something alien. So the highest pleasurable way of life, for Socrates, is not only the truest but the *most intimate* good, that which expresses most *who we are*. And it also serves to lead every other pleasure into its *own* proper nature: if the whole soul follows the wisdom-loving part, then "each part will reap *its own pleasures*, the best and the truest as far as possible" (9.586d–587a). It is precisely this thought that we see so clearly in one of the most famous passages in Aristotle that concludes his treatment of pleasure and happiness: for the highest activity, he says, "would seem, too, *to be each himself*, since it is the ruling and better part. So it would be absurd if one were to choose *not his own life but the life of something else . . . that which is proper to each thing* is by nature *most powerful and best . . .*" (*EN* 1178a2–8).[39]

---

39. *EN* 1178a2–8: δόξειε δ' ἂν καὶ εἶναι ἕκαστος τοῦτο, εἴπερ τὸ κύριον καὶ ἄμεινον· ἄτοπον οὖν γίνοιτ' ἄν, εἰ μὴ τὸν αὑτοῦ βίον αἱροῖτο ἀλλά τινος ἄλλου. ὁ λεχθέν τε πρότερον ἁρμόσει καὶ νῦν· τὸ γὰρ οἰκεῖον5 ἑκάστῳ τῇ φύσει κράτιστον καὶ ἥδιστόν ἐστιν ἑκάστῳ. Here Aristotle is clearly thinking of that striking phrase in *Republic* 9.586e–587a: truest pleasures "are their own, if what is best for each is most fully its own."

Let me sum up some of our findings here. *First*, in disagreement and yet in dialogue with Plato, Aristotle rejects Plato's theory of pleasure in the *Philebus* in favor of an integral, positive view of pleasure that is surely implicit in the *Phaedo, Symposium*, and *Republic* 9. Aristotle bases his own view not on pleasure as pleasure, that is, on pleasure as movement or qualitative change, but on pleasure as a substantial way of life that intensifies activity. *Second*, Aristotle's positive view links the pleasure of god's activity in *Metaphysics* 12.7–10 to the pleasures of all living things, but especially to the life of contemplation, which is, from one viewpoint, a "life too high for a human being," and yet the "most pleasant" of all experience, from another. *Third*, Aristotle provides a practical template for understanding how time and space are related to god's life. In the world of motion, houses can only be built *bit by bit* over lengthy periods of time, and they are understood *as a whole* only by including the whole building process together with the purpose or end of house-building. What happens piecemeal is grasped as a whole by the indivisibility of thought. So we have a model for understanding how what seems unpacked or loosely related in our successive experiences can nonetheless be grasped simultaneously in our ordinary thought that points beyond itself to the indivisible perfection of god's activity. *Fourth*, Aristotle also shows us something to which Plato was also committed. The so-called spiritual world is not utterly removed from our experience but what our experience really and concretely *is*. *Finally*, Aristotle develops or rather suggests a curious model for understanding the intimate co-dwelling of pleasure in activity and activity in pleasure. Pleasure is not "light"; yet neither is it an indwelling state or formal character of a substrate or compound activity. By "compound" activity, I mean the unity of subject and object in any activity such as contemplation. Instead, it is an epigenetic feature, like growth, that intensifies or augments a natural state and brings it into the best state of itself or makes the subject who she or he really is. Pleasure in this intensity is a curious feature; it is as natural as the fullness of spring reaching into summer or as the glow of the beautiful in a good person's face and eyes; and yet it doesn't entirely belong to the good person either; or rather, it makes the good person belong both to herself and to the divine life of active pleasure promised in this increase or outgrowth. Pleasure is somehow connected not only to our being but to our *becoming* better or best, and this is no longer a movement, but a second-order *telos* of our being, implicitly a higher perfection that does not belong to the compound state. This is the sort of good we are looking "to participate in," as Aristotle had promised at the beginning of his analysis of pleasure in *Nicomachean Ethics* Book 10 (1172b34–35).

For Aristotle, of course, the world is not created, crafted, or recovered from some pre-cosmic chaos, as it is so depicted as being by Plato. Secondary intellects and intellects do not come-to-be by an outpouring of light from the one, as they do for Plotinus. However, if pleasure intensifies active contemplation as a second-order, epigenetic feature of its being, we do have in this special case a kind of coming-to-be in intellect, a *coming into being* of its best active state that is not a physical movement, but a coming into being that must somehow resonate with the *causal* activity of the unmoved mover, for it is "because" of the pleasure of god's activity that all timeless activities are "most pleasant" (according to *Metaphysics* 12.7, as we saw above), that is, are activities that are "whole" in themselves and that involve no temporal transition. So this curious epigenetic character of pleasure must also have a genetic or causally generative power in intellect and soul. This thought is not developed in Aristotle, of course, but it does become a major feature of later thought in Plotinus and the Neoplatonic tradition. And this is why in later thought, pleasure and pain are intimately connected not simply with well-being and disease respectively but with substantial life and death processes: the generative strengthening of the soul-body relation, on the one hand, and the dissolution of that relation, on the other.[40]

3.4 Plotinus: the joy of existence

Following Plato, and after Epicurus, Plotinus could not have spoken of the good or intellect as pleasure. But it is fascinating to see how in one of his treatments of pleasure, he finds a way between Plato and Aristotle on the question of pleasure and so develops some of the most striking chapters to

40. See, for example, Plotinus, *Ennead* IV.4[28].19, 1–5: "This is what is said to be pleasure and pain: pain is the knowledge of withdrawal of a body in process of being deprived of an image of soul, and pleasure is the knowledge of a living creature that an image of soul is again being entuned back in the body" (trans. Armstrong, altered). In his treatise on the Resurrection (*Summa Theologica*, Tertia Pars, Supplement, Q. 84, article 1), Thomas Aquinas asks about the agility of bodies of the blessed in the resurrection. In one of his replies (Reply to Objection 2), he argues that since the connection of soul and body will be closer and more perfect, the labor will be less, their movements more agile and, therefore, implicitly their beings more happy and pleasurable: "The more the power of the moving soul dominates over the body, the less is the labor of movement, even though it be counter to the body's nature. Hence, those in whom the moving power is stronger, and those who through exercise have the body more adapted to obey the moving spirit, labor less in being moved. And, since after the resurrection, the soul will perfectly dominate the body, both on the account of the perfection of its own power, and on account of the glorified body's aptitude resulting from the outflow of glory which it receives from the soul, there will be no labor in the movements of the blessed, and thus it may be said that their bodies will be more agile."

be found in the *Enneads* on the primary shapelessness of intellect, on the super-beauty of the one that links intellect's beauty to it,[41] and on the two erotic power-activities of intellect, that we saw in chapter 1. Here I shall, first, summarize Plotinus' approach to the question of pleasure, draw relevant conclusions about the joy of existence, and then go on to show how Plotinus conceives the relation between Intellect/intellect and the sensible world, not as the indivisible versus time-space succession, but as the implicate and the explicate, enfolded and unfolded, orders of being.

One of the most important passages in which Plotinus treats of pleasure is VI.7[38], chapters 23–31 and, indeed, it is reasonable to suppose that this colors the subsequent development of thought in chapters 32–42 of the same work. Plotinus first represents some cantankerous person objecting to any supposedly good life that is pleasure-less or friend-less: why would we choose the good if it has no pleasure, except perhaps if we are deceiving ourselves? He then goes on to tackle Plato's reluctance in the *Philebus* (21d–22a; 61b–d) "to put the good altogether in the sweet or pleasant" (25, 1ff), and he defends the mixed life of pleasure and intellect in both Plato and Aristotle. Plato in the *Philebus* does not deal with the good as such, he says, but with "the good for us." The *ultimate* good cannot be a deception or a passion, a *pathos*, because we choose the good not for some qualitative movement or feeling; equally, desire cannot be the determining feature of the good: something is desirable because it is good, not good because it is desirable. Equally, the good for something cannot simply be what is akin to it; and so Aristotle had argued that we choose some things not for pleasure but for the good (*EN* 1174a6–8). Given the cantankerous objection that prompted the enquiry in the first place, Plotinus recognizes that it is difficult enough for anyone to think about intellect and good, and even harder to get some inkling of a good beyond intellect, but if anyone can, it will be someone of a "more self-controlled nature" who doesn't have immoderate needs. "This is why," Plotinus argues, " the first [i.e., the good] has no pleasure, not only because it is simple, but because the acquisition of something needed is sweet" (29, 9–10). As he will argue later, the good is not in need; intellect is the one in need, the one who must, as it were, go in search of its own substantiality, namely, its vision of the good that it breaks up and articulates as itself.[42]

How then can "intellect be mixed with pleasure into one composite perfection of nature" (30, 14–15)? Plotinus dismisses bodily pleasure and argues that Plato (and Aristotle presumably) talked in this way because they

---

41. From the suggestion of Socrates in *Republic* 6.508e–509a, that the good is "more beautiful" than knowledge and truth—an "amazing beauty," as Glaucon replies.

42. Cf. *Ennead* VI.7[38].15, 20–22.

could not find an appropriate way of speaking about it and so used metaphors like "drunk with nectar" (*Symposium* 203b5) and "feasting and entertainment" (*Phaedrus* 247a8). Plotinus concludes, however, that intellect is not so much the place of pleasure as the place of delight, joy, longing: "For there in the realm of Intellect is true delight and the greatest satisfaction, the most loved and longed for, which is not in process of becoming nor in movement ..." (30, 30–32; trans. Armstrong; ἔστι γὰρ καὶ τὸ ἄσμενον ὄντως ἐκεῖ καὶ τὸ ἀγαπητότατον καὶ τὸ ποθεινότατον, οὐ γινόμενον οὐδ᾽ ἐν κινήσει).[43] Here evidently Plotinus combines the delight and longing that come from Plato with the insight that such delight or pleasure is not a movement or qualitative change, but an instantaneous manifestation of being that comes from Aristotle.

I sketch this argument for several reasons: First, I want to emphasize the centrality of delight, longing, and grace in Plotinus' view of intellect and its relation to the good. Earlier in VI.7[38].22, 10ff, even the beauty of intellect is "boring," "inactive," before it takes light of the good or grace from the good; the soul falls flat on its back, numbed with boredom. But when the light is there, it gains strength, wakes up, and though moved with passion for what "lies close alongside it, it is lifted up to another ... by the giver of love" (22, 16; cf. *Phaedrus* 246aff). Here in chapter 30, he uses the word *agapētaton*, "most loved," to describe intellect, but later in VI.7, as in VI.8[39], he also employs *eros* and cognates, to illustrate the intensity of feeling at this level. He is evidently talking inclusively: not simply to intimates of his own circle but also to gnostic, perhaps Christian, friends known to frequent this circle.[44] *Agapē*, *erōs*, and cognates are not rigidly demarcated terms employed by two opposed camps of thought, but a shared heritage.[45]

---

43. In the following chapter, Plotinus emphasizes the delight of intellect in the one, even to the extent of linking it to the experience of lovers in this world, and in this case to the second best lovers of the *Phaedrus* myth (256c–e), See VI.7.31: " So Intellect was raised to that height and stayed there, happy in being around that Good; but the soul also which was able turned to it and, when it knew and saw, *rejoiced* in the vision and, in so far as it was able to see, was *utterly amazed* (ἥσθη τε τῇ θέᾳ καὶ ὅσον οἷά τε ἦν ἰδεῖν ἐξεπλάγη). It saw, as if in *utter amazement*, and, since it held something of it in itself, it had an intimate awareness of it and came into a *state of longing* (καὶ ἐν αὐτῇ ἔχουσά τι αὐτοῦ συνῄσθετο καὶ διατεθεῖσα ἐγένετο ἐν πόθῳ), like those who are moved by an image of the loved one to wish to see that same beloved. And just as here below those who are in love shape themselves to the likeness of the beloved, and make their bodies handsomer and bring their souls into likeness, since as far as they can they do not want to fall short of the integrity and all the other excellence of the loved one—if they did they would be rejected by loved ones like these—and *these are the lovers who are able to have intercourse*. [cf. *Phaedrus* 256b–e]" (trans. Armstrong, altered).

44. Porphyry, *Life of Plotinus* 16; *Ennead* II.9[33].10, 8.

45. On this see Corrigan and Glazov-Corrigan, *Plato's Dialectic at Play*, 44–46.

Second, I want to suggest another important, but rather unsuspected, line of thought that comes out of these chapters. The good for us may not be what is "akin" to us, as Plotinus has just argued. Nonetheless, in this mixed life of intellect, "what is truly desirable is ourselves, leading *ourselves* up *for ourselves* to *the best of ourselves*" (30, 34–36). This is, Plotinus says immediately following, "the form which is not part of the composite, and the clear, intelligent, beautiful life" (37–38). As in *Republic* 9, and in *Nicomachean Ethics* 10, what is best is what most truly belongs to us, that is, something that completes our natures. However, there is another layer of our being that does not "belong" entirely to our composite nature. This is a unique kind of self-dependence or a coming into our selves of ourselves, on the one hand, and yet a need and intense love that drives intellect, or us in and through intellect, to mingle with the good (a daring metaphor), in which neither "soul" nor "human being," neither "living creature" nor "intellect" really "moves or lives" any more: "nor could you still make a distinction while it is present; lovers here below and their beloveds imitate this in their will to be united[;] . . . it . . . looks at that instead of itself; who the soul is that looks, it hasn't even the leisure to see" (34, 14–22, trans. Armstrong). In the ascent of these chapters in VI.7.32 and following, boundaries disappear so that infinite love speaks directly to infinite love, as it were: "love is not limited here, because neither is the beloved, but the love of this would be unbounded" (32, 24–28). Furthermore, the bloom of youth is no longer the bloom of pleasurable activity in Aristotle or even the bloom of intellect in the *Chaldean Oracles*, but "the productive power of all is the bloom of beauty, a beauty which makes beauty . . . and makes it beautiful not in shape. But makes the very beauty which comes to be from it to be shapeless, but in shape in another way; for what is said to be this itself is shape in another, but, in respect of itself, shapeless. Therefore, what participates in beauty is shaped, not the beauty" (32, 24–38; trans. Armstrong). There is then at the heart of intellect, and in us too, a kind of ambiguous meeting ground where lover and beloved are no longer distinct, an ambiguity of infinite beauty that is self-standing or "of itself." This is shapeless in respect of itself—Plotinus so often asks of this: is it me or something other? As he puts this elsewhere, "is it myself or another" (V.5[32].7)? Where there is otherness and sameness, there are intellect and substance, Plotinus argues in chapter 39, but where there is no "distance or difference" what can there be except itself (*auto*) (39, 3–5)?

So I want to draw two conclusions, one about the epigenetic nature of intellect and the other, a little more complex, about the genetic nature of intellect and its double existence-substance structure.

First, Plotinus articulates the nature of intellect as a double activity that shows how something that has its own distinct nature on one level is simultaneously enfolded into its cause on a higher level by virtue of love, where its highest activity and the power of the good by which it acts coincide.

Second, we find in one of the last chapters of VI.7[38].40 the articulation of a double structure of thought: a power of existence and an act of substance proper. Thought is a single activity that articulates within itself power, form, and potentiality. As in seeing, so there are two moments in the generation of thinking, one described as "self-dependent generative power" and the other as the "completion" of the substrate that is "potentially" the fully formed thinking of intellect proper. In his great commentary on VI.7, Pierre Hadot sees these two moments as referring to the different character of thought in intellect and soul respectively,[46] but even though Plotinus speaks in terms of persuasion here (that is, a persuasion that characterizes an address to soul), the two moments characterize *all* thinking; they also parallel the two powers of intellect in relation to its mystical ascent that Plotinus has argued for a few chapters earlier (VI.7.35, 19–23: the power by which intellect/soul thinks/loves its source and the power by which it thinks itself),[47] and, furthermore, they explain how something purely *self-dependent* or self-standing, such as unrestricted beauty, can be the first moment of intellect's being, as Plotinus had argued in VI.7, chapter 33, 34–39.

Plotinus writes:

> ... all thinking is from something and of something; and one thinking, *being together with that from which it is, has as its substrate* that of which it is the thought (καὶ ἡ μὲν συνοῦσα τῷ ἐξ οὗ ἐστιν ὑποκείμενον μὲν ἔχει τὸ οὗ ἐστι νόησις) and itself *becomes so to speak overlying, being its substrate's activity and filling what is potentially [in power] but does not itself generate* (οἷον δὲ ἐπικείμενον αὐτὴ γίνεται ἐνέργεια αὐτοῦ οὖσα καὶ πληροῦσα τὸ δυνάμει ἐκεῖνο οὐδὲν αὐτὴ γεννῶσα), for it is only a perfection, as it were, of that of which it is. But *the thinking that accompanies substance* and has brought substance into being could not be in that from which it came to be (ἡ δὲ οὖσα νόησις μετ' οὐσίας καὶ ὑποστήσασα τὴν οὐσίαν οὐκ ἂν δύναιτο ἐν ἐκείνῳ εἶναι, ἀφ' οὗ ἐγένετο); for it would not have generated anything if it were in that. But *being a power of self-dependent generation it generated* (ἀλλ' οὖσα δύναμις τοῦ γεννᾶν ἐφ' ἑαυτῆς ἐγέννα) and its activity is substance, and is *together with it too in the substance* (καὶ σύνεστι καὶ ἐν τῇ οὐσίᾳ) (40, 5–18).

---

46. Hadot, *Plotin: Traité 38*, 360–64.
47. Cf. *Ennead* VI.7[38].35, 19–23.

Although there are two notionally different dimensions to thinking, Plotinus emphasizes that both powers—the second and the first self-dependent power—are "together with that from which it came" and "together in the substance." The two aspects articulate a single reality: self-dependent power (like light) and a compound of form and intelligible matter as a single substance. Both together make a *synhypostasis* at 40, 46–49 (cf. VI.7.2, 37). While the filling of the ground or substrate makes thinking concrete—"of something" or, in modern terms "intentional"—there remains in thought a purely self-dependent, non-intentional generative power. It cannot be *in* the good (and, therefore, must be distinguished from the good's power) or else it would not have generated anything. This moment then is a kind of ambiguity in the heart of self-dependence, that is suggested elsewhere when Plotinus makes the otherwise unfathomable statements that "thinking does not think" (VI.9[9].6, 53–54; V.6[24].6, 9–10)[48] or where he speaks of *perinoesis* (VI.9[9]), *hypernoesis* (VI.8[39]) or simply *blepsis* (VI.2[43].8, 14–15: *hē men gar energeia hē eis auton ouk ousia, eis ho kai aph' hou, to on; to gar blepomenon to on, ouch hē blepsis*).[49]

Pure unrestricted power, as for instance in the highest power of thought in the above passage, is where activity and power coincide. If the activity that is thought or perception has to "lean on something"[50] in order to think or see any object or even light, then purely self-directed activity must be unrestricted power for existence, distinguished from the one only because such power is ultimately a creative act *in* the thing caused.[51] What is worth emphasizing here is that this double structure is a function of *all* thought—in fact, of everything, since thought for Plotinus is not what it seems to be for us, namely, a human achievement. A horse is a "thought" in its own way, for Plotinus. Thought includes everything. How this is to be conceived is, of course, problematic, but it provides a window for us to understand the fluidity between levels of being in both ascent and descent, on the one hand, and to see how one level of being can be unpacked, as it

48. *Ennead* VI.9[9].6, 53–54: *Noēsis de ou noeu, all' aitia tou noein tōi allōi·* Thus, we can reconcile the idea that a power at one level possesses pre-eminently what the effect has derivatively with the idea that the higher power does not have what it gives to the effect: the cause does not *have* x; it *is* x supremely; the effect has x in its own way (V.6[24].6, 8–10).

49. *Ennead* VI.9[9].11, 22–5: "another mode of seeing . . . *perinoēsis pros epharmogēn;*" VI.8[39].16, 32: ("waking up and hyper-thinking" are the act of the good [as it were]).

50. *Ennead* V.5[32].7, 9–10.

51. On this passage, see Corrigan, *Plotinus' Theory of Matter-Evil*, 285–89. Compare *synaesthesis* in *Ennead* V.1[10].7; VI.7[38].16, 19 (cf. 41, 27), and Plotinus' de-spatializing experiments, with hand and light-sphere, to experience pure power in VI.4[22].7.

were, out of a higher level, on the other, or to see how indivisible reality can in some sense pre-contain what is divided in time and space.

One last feature of the above passage should be noted. The "power of self-dependent generation" in the above passage is obviously a principal if unnoticed part of Plotinus' philosophy. But it is also implicitly an analogue to the highest unique function of thought in Aristotle's unmoved mover. In other words, it is analogous to the "thinking of thinking" that is Aristotle's definition of the unmoved mover's activity, that is, this thinking is not the thinking of an object, but the highest self-reflexive power there can be. Plotinus, in the course of his argument with Peripatetics over these chapters culminating in chapter 40, implicitly concludes that there cannot strictly speaking be a "thinking of thinking"; however, there is in intellect a purely reflexive activity that does not belong to the compound, but that must nonetheless be linked to the compound and cannot be self-standing in a primary sense. Here then in VI.7.40, we effectively have Plotinus' answer to Aristotle's unmoved mover. The self-dependence of the good that is beyond intellect is the first self-dependent power of intellect's own being, which must be other than the good only because it leads generatively within intellect to the coming-to-be of intellect itself.

3.5 Implicate and explicate orders in Plotinus: Divine love?

Let us go back to one of my conclusions above, namely, that Plotinus' thought provides a window for us to understand how one level of being can be unpacked out of a higher level or to see how indivisible reality can in some sense pre-contain what is divided in time and space. To illustrate briefly what this means in practice for Plotinus, I shall pick out two further features of his thought.

The first relates to the intelligible world. In the *Timaeus*, Plato has Timaeus represent the demiurge as taking thought, deliberating, and doing a lot of things, none of which is possible for a divine being, on Plotinus' account, if the intelligible living creature is complete or perfect before deliberation or any discursive reasoning.[52] Reason is an achievement, from one perspective, but a defect, from another. A divine craftsman will not have to work out how to go about making the world since such a being must have complete total understanding, not piecemeal reasoning.[53] Intelligibility or beautiful design is not the result of reason, but *prior* to reason.[54] Conse-

---

52. *Ennead* VI.7[38].1, 1–48; cf. V.8[31].5–7; VI.2[44].21, 24–25, 50–52.
53. *Ennead* VI.7[38].1, 45–58.
54. *Ennead* VI.7[38].1, 21–35.

quently, Plotinus argues that what is unfolded or explicate in our experience as beings subject to the time-space continuum is "earlier" enfolded or implicate in the complete activity of the divine intellect,[55] just as even in our present discursive experience of forms in nature, "if you unfold the form to itself, you will find the reason why."[56] Even in the sensible world the mutual implicative causality of all things that we can work out by discursive reasoning manifests the total simultaneous implicate nature of divine activity in the explicate order.[57] Here then at the intelligible level, and from our experience of discursive reason in the sensible world, there is a model for understanding how one order of apparent being can in reality be woven out of a higher and simpler order of complexity, so that in the language of Aristotle "the best is indivisibly whole, but as something different"[58] from the way we experience succession in time and space, namely, as a "this after this."[59]

A second feature of Plotinus' thought follows from this, but only deepens the problem bequeathed by Aristotle. To some extent, Aristotle inhabits a steady-state universe, and yet his thought, like that of Plato, is inherently dynamic. Plotinus goes further than Aristotle. Aristotle's unmoved movers move and preside in stately serenity over a thoroughly dynamic world. Plotinus argues for a very different and conflicted picture. On the one hand, the divine intellect is no less stately and serene;[60] on the other, every intellect is part and whole of every other intellect, pervaded by teeming life, otherness, stability, motion, and rest;[61] and even more so, everything is pervaded by love and desire since intellect as a whole, just like soul and everything in the sensible universe, eternally emerges out of the one and eternally returns into loving, intimate contact and vision of the one.[62] Just as there is something like the one in us, so in a daring analogy Plotinus says there is

---

55. *Ennead* VI.7[38].1, 45–58. By "earlier" Plotinus means not in time, but logically earlier, that is, what is enfolded in the intelligible world "can show this after this, but as all together it is entirely this; and this means having its cause also in itself" (1, 56–58).

56. *Ennead* VI.7[38].2, 18–19.

57. *Ennead* VI.7[38].2, 1–37; Cf. also VI.8[39].14, 16–31.

58. Cf. Aristotle: "intellect does not have the good in this bit or in that bit, but *the best is in a certain whole, being something different*" (*Metaphysics* 12.9.1075a7–9)

59. *Ennead* VI.7[38].1, 56–57.

60. *Ennead* V.4[7].2, and for difficulties in and interpretation of this passage see Corrigan, "Plotinus, 'Enneads' 5, 4 [7], 2," 195–203.

61. *Ennead* V.8[30].4; VI.7[38].12–16; cf. Plato, *Sophist* 254d.

62. *Ennead* V.4[7].2, 27–33; VI.9[9].3, 32–36; VI[10].6; VI.7[38].16, 16–22 and VI.7, 34–35 (of soul and the intellect of soul).

"a kind of intellect in unity."⁶³ So even if we do not really know what this means—since it is an experience beyond knowing, if it is an experience at all, we have some intimation that just as unfolding time-space experience emerges from enfolded intelligible being as its real ground, so the implicate intelligible world must emerge out of the most intense enfoldedness of all: the one or good. We are not soul in the sense of being universal or every soul; instead, we *have* souls; soul is not intellect; soul *has* intellect. Might not the experience of intellect or the intellects of our souls be a little like having and being? Intellect is not the one, but it could perhaps be said "to have" the one—at least as its own unity, a unity that is in any case not entirely its own but porous, since unity and goodness are always gifts.

So like unity and goodness, the "intense love" that intellect and the intellects of our souls "have" for the one is at the same time an intensity of love given by the one. We know that the one does not "have" what it "gives,"⁶⁴ but that it is what it is beyond even any being what it is. In this light, when Plotinus argues, as have seen above, that the good is infinite and formless and that there is correspondingly an infinite love in the soul for the one, "so great a degree of happiness has it reached" (VI.7[38].34, 35–38; cf. VI.9[9].9, 44–45); or when in *Ennead* VI.7[38].35, 3–28 he can speak of a loving, drunken intellect that, by virtue of the continuity of its contemplation, no longer sees a sight, but *mingles its seeing with what it contemplates*, there is more than a suggestion that such dynamic love of itself must include or pre-include everything that is valuable or loveable in the intelligible world and even in the sensible world. This might still seem to be a stretch; but when in VI.8[39]—probably because of the questions of his colleagues, his students, and the influence of the Valentinian gnostic *Tripartite Tractate* and other works⁶⁵—he speaks of the good's *love of itself*,⁶⁶ then, if soul or intellect can be "mingled" with the good, and the good loves itself, then anything "mingled" with the good *must love and be loved by the good*.⁶⁷

---

63. *Ennead* VI.8[39].18, 20–21.

64. *Ennead* VI.7[38].41–42; V.3[49].13–17, especially 14 and 20ff. ("he gives us these, but he is not these himself. . . . But how does give them? By having them or not having them? But how did he give what he did not have?" trans. Armstrong).

65. *Tripartite Tractate*, 56, 1–4; *Trimorphic Protennoia*, NHC XIII 45, 2–6. See Corrigan and Turner, *Plotinus, Ennead VI 8*, 313–14.

66. *Ennead* VI.8[39].15. For the gnostic background see Corrigan and Turner, *Plotinus, Ennead VI 8*, 308–14.

67. For different views of the significance of this see Rist, *Eros and Psyche*, 82, 104; Rist, *Plotinus*, 224, 227–28, 230 and Bussanich, *The One*, 209–10. And for evaluation see Corrigan and Turner, *Plotinus, Ennead VI 8*, 332–34.

Here, as J. Bussanich has argued, Plotinus speaks from within an experience that cannot be translated into any other language[68] since it has already been carried out of itself "by a swelling wave"[69] from any identity it might have had or will have, and yet it is an experience that nonetheless seems to announce[70] or to hover on the brink of announcing a new reality of divine love.[71] And yet, at the same time, Plotinus' view is not possible without Aristotle's *Metaphysics*, *Nicomachean Ethics*, and the notion of divine care in Plato.

3.6 Later Neoplatonism: Iamblichus and Proclus

This "new" view of divine love is, of course, not an explicit step that Plotinus himself will take, but it will be developed later by Iamblichus, Proclus, and Pseudo-Dionysius in different ways. Here I can only give a brief sketch of a much larger picture. With Iamblichus and Proclus, we find a new sensibility about divine love. As we have seen above, Proclus distinguishes two forms of love: first, an ascending love (*eros epistreptikos*) that urges lower principles to aspire towards their superiors, and, second, a descending or providential love (*eros pronoetikos*) that obligates the superiors to care for their products and to transmit divine grace (*In Alcib.* 54–56). Divine love reaches intimately down into all lower things and brings them back into its care. Prayer, for example, wakes up a unity that is already always responded to in the active, unitary divine energy that pre-comprehends everything. If we say that the gods "hear" such prayer, we don't mean that they have ears, but that this divine unity is supremely responsive; and for Iamblichus it is

---

68. See Bussanich, *The One*, 70–71.

69. This is the image Plotinus uses in *Ennead* VI.7[38].36, 17 (15–21): "There one lets go all learning, and up to here one has been led along (παιδαγωγηθείς, cf. *Symposium* 210e3; cf 210a6–7) and settled in beauty, and up to this point one thinks that in which one is, but having been carried out of it by *the wave*, so to speak, of intellect itself, and lifted on high *by a kind of swell*, he saw suddenly not seeing how, but the vision filled his eyes with light and has not made him see another through it, but the light itself was what he saw."

70. It is worthwhile emphasizing that the self so situated still appears in Plotinus' thought to have a dialectical, civic, or cosmic responsibility, that is, a responsibility "to announce" what it experiences—just as in the *Symposium* each step of the ascent begets "beautiful discourses." See, for example, *Ennead* V.8[31].12, 3.

71 For this later development, see also Corrigan, "Unmoved Mover," 82–115. Theurgy is particularly important for the question of *eros* and ascent since, in Iamblichus especially, theurgy is based upon divine love and involves a continuum of ritual action, from material to immaterial practices (as in the *Chaldean Oracles* already). On this, see most recently, Addey, *Divination*; for the *Chaldean Oracles* see fragments 97, 110, 115, 121 on the ascent of the soul, and fragments 39, 42, 44 on *eros* or divine love.

responsive not only to, and through, the actuality of words, but in the actuality of good holy action, namely, theurgy or god-work (see *De Mysteriis* 1.13, 46–47).[72] As in Plotinus implicitly, so explicitly in Iamblichus, divine activity pre-includes all that is best in our own activities.

There is a sense here in which Iamblichus' view goes beyond not only philosophy but also religion in any conventional organized way, since prayer plainly starts to break down any normal separation between two heterogenous beings and seems to suggest what Henry Corbin calls—in relation to the Sufi tradition and Ibn 'Arabi—a bi-unity, a one being encountering itself, the divine in the human and the human in the divine.[73] Just as "seeing" in the Platonic tradition is a function of the activity of the good *in my perception*, so more intimately my desire of god is also god's desire manifested in me. For Aristotle too, as we have seen above, just as teaching and learning are a single activity that nonetheless involve two subjects and result in qualitative change in the learner, so even ordinary actions, such as scientific enquiry, perception, waking up, doing the right thing to the right persons at the right time, etc., are *our* actions, yet they are also one with the purest single activity that is god's life. Such yearning unity resonates because it is part of its implicate, unified, or enfolded structure, as it were, that becomes unfolded in my individual experience and needs, on the human side, to be developed or woken up.

The awakening of such unities "establishes links of friendship between us and the gods" (*DM* 5.26.238, 6–7), as we have seen above, and is an integral part of divine love in a somewhat perplexing way. Why, Iamblichus asks, should we pray to the gods, if they are, as Porphyry claims, "unbending and unmixed with sensible things?" Iamblichus' answer is interesting and complex, though it looks thoroughly foreign to many modern sensibilities at first sight. Prayer is not a form of ordinary address, as of one person addressing another, but a kind of waking up something in us that wants to be united with the divine itself and that produces a response or "hearing" from the gods not insofar as they have organs or ears, but rather, as we have seen above, in so far as it resonates with a unity that is already responded to in the active, unitary divine energy that pre-comprehends everything: "For that element in us which is divine and intellectual and one . . . is aroused (ἐγείρεται) then clearly in prayer and, when aroused, strives (ἐφίεται) primarily towards what is like to itself and joins itself to essential perfection.

---

72. Especially *DM* 47, 5–9: the gods "embrace in themselves the activities of the words of good people, and above all of those [the antecedent could be 'words' or 'people' or both] who through the sacred liturgy are seated in the gods and united with them; for in this case the divine is simply united with itself."

73. See Corbin, *Alone with the Alone*, 147.

... So then, it is neither through faculties nor through organs that the gods receive into themselves our prayers, but rather they embrace within themselves the actualities (ἐνεργείας) of the words of good people and in particular of those [words] which, by virtue of the sacred liturgy, are seated in the gods and united to them; for in that case the divine is literally united with itself" (*DM* 1.15, 46–47).

Our implicate pre-inclusion in the life of the gods is, to put it mildly, still hard to understand. On the one hand, it is not a temporal relation as of "before" in the divine and "after" in our experience, but integral to our entire experience of ascent or of life lived according to the higher axis of our being. On the other hand, does it mean that in some sense our best aspirations and hopes are prearranged or that we are not real actors in our own lives—that the gods really do the work, not us? However obscure the subject and however difficult it might be to understand Iamblichus, I think that this is why he emphasizes the importance of our actually *doing* concrete actions, *asking* for things, *lifting* up ourselves and ordinary things into the proper medium of divine love and friendship. Yes, it is not difficult to imagine a struggle for power and authority over the issues of divine love, prayer, and sacramentality among Christians, gnostics of various stripes, and these latter-day pagans. And arguably we can see this in Iamblichus' emphasis on theurgy, Proclus' triad of trust/faith, truth, and love,[74] which comes close to the Christian triad of faith, hope and love, though its application is different,[75] and this central emphasis on prayer in both Iamblichus and Proclus (especially in Proclus' famous statement—from Theodore of Asine: "All things pray except the First" *in Tim.* I.213, 2–3).

At the same time, it is out of the Platonic-Aristotelian tradition that Iamblichus articulates three levels of prayer: first, introductory prayer or gathering together; second, conjunctive prayer (*syndetikon*, binding together, as in Plato's *Symposium* in Diotima-Socrates' description of *eros-daimon*);[76] and finally, perfective or unificatory prayer. But against Porphyry, and perhaps with Plotinus,[77] Iamblichus insists that *we have to ask*: "no sacred work occurs without the supplications contained in prayers" (*DM* 5.26.238, 11–12). Extended prayer apparently not only wakes up, but opens up and increases on its own account the capacity of divine unity in the soul to the degree that—in a striking and otherwise philosophically

---

74. The triad first appears long before Proclus in the *Chaldean Oracles*, fragment 46, Majercik.

75. See *in Tim.* I.212, p. 48n44 (Runia/Share); also *PT* 1.25.110, 6; *in Alc.* 51, 16–53, 2. Wallis (Gerson), *Neoplatonism*, 153–55.

76. *Symposium* 202e–203a.

77. Compare *Ennead* V.8[32].9, 1–18.

perplexing phrase—it "co-increases divine love" (*ton theion erota synauxei*) (*DM* 5.26.2). This is a remarkable passage that deserves some analysis and I cite the prolonged *single* sentence that encapsulates the entire sequence of the activity and effects of prayer from Iamblichus as follows:

> Extended practice of prayer nurtures our intellect, makes our soul's capacity to be a receptacle of the gods much broader, opens up divine things to human beings, provides a co-habituation to the brightness of light, little by little perfects the capacities in us for contact with the gods, until it leads up to the very highest level, draws up gently the habits/dispositions of our thinking, and gives to us the habits/dispositions of the gods, wakes up persuasion, communion, and indissoluble friendship, co-increases divine love, fires up the divine element in the soul, purges all that is opposite to it, casts out from the aetherial and luminous vehicle around the soul everything that tends to physical generation, perfects good hope and faith concerning the light and, in a word, makes those who employ prayers familiar consorts of the gods, if we may put it in this way. (*DM* 5.238, 12–239, 10)[78]

The way Iamblichus puts this, prayer is an in-between reality initiated in time by us but completed eternally by the gods in and through us that makes us genuine partners with the divine. If we think of this as something successive or already perfected by the gods, then it is impossible to see how we could contribute anything to what is already always perfected in the divine world. But if we see it as an integral function of all experience that is significantly in our power—not only to initiate, but also to enact and perfect—then we can see the function of divine love as so authentically operative in us that our actions can contribute to its perfection.

The language Iamblichus employs also reflects significant words in the Platonic tradition from the *Symposium* and *Republic*, for example. In Diotima's higher mysteries, the apprentice is "increased and strengthened" at a higher rung of the ladder of ascent (*Symposium* 210d6–7); again, Alcibiades "opens up" the divine statues in Socrates (*Symposium* 215a6–b3; 216d6;

---

78. DM V.26.238, 12–239, 10: Ἡ δ' ἐν αὐταῖς ἐγχρονίζουσα διατριβὴ τρέφει μὲν τὸν ἡμέτερον νοῦν, τὴν δὲ τῆς ψυχῆς ὑποδοχὴν τῶν θεῶν ποιεῖ λίαν εὐρυτέραν, ἀνοίγει δὲ τοῖς ἀνθρώποις τὰ τῶν θεῶν, συνήθειαν δὲ παρέχει πρὸς τὰς τοῦ φωτὸς μαρμαρυγάς κατὰ βραχὺ δὲ τελειοῖ τὰ ἐν ἡμῖν πρὸς τὰς τῶν θεῶν συναφάς, ἕως ἂν ἐπὶ τὸ ἀκρότατον ἡμᾶς ἐπαναγάγῃ, καὶ τὰ μὲν ἡμέτερα τῆς διανοίας ἤθη ἠρέμα ἀνέλκει, τὰ δὲ τῶν θεῶν ἡμῖν ἐκδίδωσι, πειθὼ δὲ καὶ κοινωνίαν καὶ φιλίαν ἀδιάλυτον ἐγείρει, τόν τε θεῖον ἔρωτα συναύξει καὶ τὸ θεῖον τῆς ψυχῆς ἀνάπτει, ἀποκαθαίρει τε πᾶν τὸ ἐναντίον τῆς ψυχῆς, καὶ ἀπορρίπτει τοῦ αἰθερώδους καὶ αὐγοειδοῦς πνεύματος περὶ αὐτὴν ὅσον ἐστὶ γενεσιουργόν, ἐλπίδα τε ἀγαθὴν καὶ τὴν περὶ τὸ φῶς πίστιν τελειοῖ, καὶ τὸ ὅλον εἰπεῖν, ὁμιλητὰς τῶν θεῶν, ἵνα οὕτως εἴπωμεν, τοὺς χρωμένους αὐταῖς ἀπεργάζεται.

e5–6; 222a1–6); here, analogously, prayer "opens up" divine things to us and "co-increases" divine love. In the *Republic*, the mark of power is its ability to make or experience something. In each case, Socrates argues (477d), we look to what a power *does*—in the sense of what it *produces* or *effects* (*ho apergazetai*), and in this way define the power or capacity in relation to its object. Here in Iamblichus prayer is a natural power that fashions or makes (*apergazetai*) us into familiar consorts of the gods. Above all, however, Iamblichus adapts Aristotle's language about pleasure: prayer, Iamblichus argues, co-increases, intensifies, augments divine love; as we have seen above, the verb *synauxein* is conspicuously applied to pleasure as a complete activity by Aristotle (*EN* 1175a30–36; 1177b21). Pleasure cannot be a synapse between the divine life and our ordinary experience for Iamblichus—at least after Epicurus—as it was for Aristotle, but prayer can appropriately perform a similar dynamic function.

There is also a precise and down-to-earth logic to the entire sentence. The ascent is an extended practice of *habituation*; it *feeds* the mind; makes the soul *broader* as a receptacle or *material holder* for the gods; *opens up* divine reality for us *as composite human beings*; allows for a *synaptic fusion of different habits/dispositions, divine and human*—just as in any relationship we *"little by little" grow accustomed* to the beloved other; it makes a bond of persuasion, community, and friendship—in other words, there is no compulsion, no law is necessary; where friendship and love prevail, we have no need of external justice, as Aristotle puts it;[79] a different manner of co-being has become established in us, so that, in such a way of being, divine love co-increases, that is, in becoming familiar with the beloved we become more than the simple sum of any parts; *love answers to and increases love*; and so the divine in the soul is *kindled*, with the result that the axis of one's being is no longer directed to generation or succession, that is, no longer body-based, but light-focused in divine friendship and intimacy. In a single sentence, Iamblichus articulates the dynamic unity of divine love initiated by us and perfected by the divine in us, a unity that augments our co-being and that even appears to contribute something to the divine to such a degree that we can almost speak of a mutual love—we can almost say that in our love of the divine, the divine loves us.

But is this only divine love on a lesser level, not at the level of the first principle? Since love is the principle that not only binds everything together, but also dissolves boundaries between god and beings, love is, so to speak, the love of god running through everything at every level. We can see this

---

79. *EN* 8, 1155a26–27: "for when people are friends they have no need of justice, but when they are just they need friendship too."

clearly in a parallel passage from Proclus' *Commentary on the Timaeus*, Book 2, 212: the person who has undertaken the practice of prayer, Proclus argues,

> ... should preserve unshaken the right order of his acts towards the gods and set before himself virtues that purify him from the realm of generation and cause him to ascend, and also trust and truth and love, that renowned triad,[80] as well as hope of good things and unchanging receptivity to the divine light and ecstasy separating him from all other preoccupations so that he is *united alone with god alone* and does not attempt to join himself to unity while in the company of plurality. (*In Tim.* 212, 19ff.).

The language of the "alone to the alone," I have argued elsewhere, is not evidence of narcissism or of solitary self-absorbed mysticism, but of a union more intimate and larger than anything in our entire experience.[81] It is also evidence that Proclus is speaking of union at the highest level of the first principle.

With Iamblichus and Proclus then we encounter the unfolding of a remarkable view of divine love that is implicit in earlier Platonism, especially in Plato and Aristotle, and not simply a reaction, I suggest, to Christian influence, namely, the view that god's love involves a kind of radical intimacy, that pierces and already includes the activities or real energies of all created life.

3.7 Dionysius and Divine loving

However, it is only in Dionysius or Pseudo-Dionysius (as he has come to be known),[82] in a famous passage from the *Divine Names*,[83] that this new sensibility reaches its conclusion and where the unmoved god is simultane-

---

80. Cf. *Chaldean Oracles*, fragment 46.

81. Corrigan, "'Solitary' Mysticism," 28–42.

82. Dionysius' identity was doubted already in the sixth century by Hypatius of Ephesus and later by Nicholas of Cusa, was first seriously called into question by Lorenzo Valla in 1457 and John Grocyn in 1501, a critical viewpoint later accepted and publicized by Erasmus from 1504 onward. It has only become accepted in modern times that instead of being the disciple of St. Paul, Dionysius must have lived in the time of Proclus, most probably being a pupil of Proclus, perhaps of Syrian origin, who knew enough of Platonism and the Christian tradition to create a new hybrid form of both.

83. For Greek text, see Suchla, ed., *Corpus Dionysiacum I* (*Divine Names*); Heil and Ritter, eds., *Corpus Dionysiacum II* (*Celestial Hierarchy, Ecclesiastical Hierarchy, Mystical Theology, Letters*); and for translation, Luibheid and Rorem, trans., *Pseudo-Dionysius*; see also Corrigan and Harrison, "Pseudo-Dionysius."

ously moved to care for everything. Of course, this is no longer Aristotle's unmoved mover, but it is the culmination of a long pagan tradition starting with Plato and Aristotle. This tradition runs through the Neoplatonists and culminates in Pseudo-Dionysius, probably a pupil of Proclus, who brings about the instantaneous conversion of the pagan tradition into a daring Christian form of thought that remains faithful to its best pagan wellsprings. Dionysius thus retains the word *eros*, together with *agape*, despite the former word's potentially dangerous pagan heritage (see *DN* 713a–b).[84]

As in Proclus, divine providential love is at root a love that recalls everything to itself, an *eros pronoētikos/epistreptikos*, that is also a function of our love for each other. However, Pseudo-Dionysius no longer views this simply as a kind of structural relation between cause and effect or as a ritualistic relation between god and worshipper; it is instead an intimate paradoxical coincidence of opposites—transcendence and immanence—in which the divine longing for created things is manifested:

> And we must dare to say even this on behalf of the truth that the very cause of all things, by virtue of the beautiful and good yearning love for everything through superabundance of loving goodness is also carried outside of himself in the loving care he has for everything. He is, as it were, enchanted by goodness, by love, and by yearning love and is led away from his transcendent dwelling place and comes to abide within all things, and he does so by virtue of his supernatural and ecstatic capacity to remain, nevertheless, inseparable from himself. (*Divine Names* 712a–b; trans. Luibheid and Rorem)[85]

---

84. *DN* 713a–b: "When we talk of yearning (*eros*), whether this be in god or an angel, in the mind or in the spirit or in nature, we should think of a unifying and commingling power which moves the superior to provide for the subordinate, peer to be in communion with peer, and subordinate to return to the superior . . . (Τὸν ἔρωτα, εἴτε θεῖον εἴτε ἀγγελικὸν εἴτε νοερὸν εἴτε ψυχικὸν εἴτε φυσικὸν εἴποιμεν, ἑνωτικήν τινα καὶ συγκρατικὴν ἐννοήσωμεν δύναμιν τὰ μὲν ὑπέρτερα κινοῦσαν ἐπὶ πρόνοιαν τῶν καταδεεστέρων, τὰ δεὁμόστοιχα πάλιν εἰς κοινωνικὴν ἀλληλουχίαν καὶ ἐπ' ἐσχάτων τὰ ὑφειμένα πρὸς τὴν τῶν κρειττόνων καὶ ὑπερκειμένων ἐπιστροφήν.)

85. *DN* 712a–b: Τολμητέον δὲ καὶ τοῦτο ὑπὲρ ἀληθείας εἰπεῖν, ὅτι καὶ αὐτὸς ὁ πάντων αἴτιος τῷ καλῷ καὶ ἀγαθῷ τῶν πάντων ἔρωτι δι' ὑπερβολὴν τῆς ἐρωτικῆς ἀγαθότητος ἔξω ἑαυτοῦ γίνεται ταῖς εἰς τὰ ὄντα πάντα προνοίαις καὶ οἷον ἀγαθότητι καὶ ἀγαπήσει καὶ ἔρωτι θέλγεται καὶ ἐκ τοῦ ὑπὲρ πάντα καὶ πάντων ἐξῃρημένου πρὸς τὸ ἐν πᾶσι κατάγεται κατ' ἐκστατικὴν ὑπερούσιον δύναμιν ἀνεκφοίτητον ἑαυτοῦ. Compare *DN* 949c–952b: in perfect peace, all are "*unified indivisibly*" (ἀδιαιρέτως τε συνεχομένη) (949c; Suchla, 219, 13); "it unites all things, binding the extremes together with the extremes by means of intermediaries in accordance with a single homogeneous yoke of *friendship*" (952b16–17; Suchla, 219, 16–17) . . . "For the divine Peace is indivisible and is revealing of all in a single act and it permeates the whole world without ever departing from its own identity. It goes out to all things. It gives of itself to all things in the way they can receive it and it overflows

This is one of the most remarkable passages in the whole of ancient thought. God is, by the end of antiquity, primarily the beloved who remains unmoved *but also simultaneously* the loving one (transcendentally and paradigmatically the unity of all the causes deployed by Aristotle). Against Agathon's conception of love as completely beautiful and as "enchanting the thought of all gods and human beings" (*Symposium* 207e), Diotima-Socrates had pointed out the needy, vulnerable side of love: "What you thought love to be is not surprising. You supposed, if I take what you said as evidence, that the beloved and not the loving was love. That is why, I think, *eros* seemed completely beautiful to you. In fact, it is the beloved that is really beautiful . . . and blessed; but loving has this other character" (204b8–c6). Dionysius brings both aspects together as integral to the Divine—in god's self-abiding beloved nature there is also vulnerability, even a passivity beyond all passivity: God is "led down" to dwell in all. God does not merely enchant, as Agathon had supposed, but is simultaneously *enchanted* by goodness, love and longing for all by virtue of "his ecstatic, hyper-substantial power that does not stop visiting itself" (ἀνεκφοίτητον ἑαυτοῦ).

Iamblichus had insisted in the *De Mysteriis* that the gods cannot be beguiled or enchanted by human prayers; they cannot be lured down somehow into our power.[86] The *Chaldean Oracles*—a second-century-CE collection of sacred sayings, and the closest thing that the Neoplatonists had to the Christian Scriptures—warn the initiate against a certain group of demons, because "they enchant souls and lead them away from the sacred rites."[87] Dionysius turns the whole of pagan thought on its head, while simultaneously remaining faithful to its wellsprings in Plato and Aristotle. The care of the divine for all things is so much a measure of its majesty that the godhead itself becomes vulnerable, and the whole universe is turned upside

---

in a surplus of its peaceful fecundity. And yet because it is transcendently one it remains in its own complete and utter unity" (Suchla 219, 19–24: ταῖς συναγωγαῖς ἀδιαιρέτως δηλαδὴ τῆς θείας εἰρήνης ἑστώσης καὶ ἐν ἑνὶ πάντα δεικνυούσης καὶ διὰ πάντων φοιτώσης καὶ τῆς οἰκείας ταὐτότητος οὐκ ἐξισταμένης, πρόεισι γὰρ ἐπὶ πάντα καὶ μεταδίδωσι πᾶσιν οἰκείως αὐτοῖς ἑαυτῆς καὶ ὑπερβλύζει περιουσίᾳ τῆς εἰρηνικῆς γονιμότητος καὶ μένει δι' ὑπεροχὴν ἑνώσεως ὅλη πρὸς ὅλην καὶ καθ' ὅλην ἑαυτὴν ὑπερηνωμένη). As perfect peace, god is "indivisible" and yet "visits" everything and everyone in a way that is appropriate to them—in a way that belongs to them (οἰκείως). Here we find a culmination of the themes of "indivisibility" that was crucial in Aristotle's thought about god and the world of time and space, of "belongingness," so much a part of the thought of Plato and Aristotle, and of friendship that has been our concern throughout this book—the vertical dimension permeating the horizontal and vice versa, like someone "visiting."

86. *DM* 12.40, 12–41, 3; especially 45, 4–5: "the divine is exempt from external bewitchment or affection or forceful constraint" (trans. Clarke, Dillon, Hershbell, slightly modified).

87. *Chaldean Oracles*, fragment 135, 6.

down. Where there was virtually nothing to notice, god is already there. To be god-beloved takes on new and yet old meaning: to love and to be loved by god is a form of enchantment, no less.[88] The ancient pagan myths that Plato and Aristotle had fought so hard to overcome, in their own different ways, become no longer the obstacle they once had been. Paganism and Christianity, before the advent of Islam, helped to fulfill some of the strongest intimations of the pagan philosophical tradition, in the strange hybrid person of Dionysius, and also to give new life to the hybrid traditions that would become known as the Abrahamic religions—Judaism, Christianity, and Islam.[89]

88. No one in the pagan tradition, before Dionysius, could have said such a thing. Plato emphasized the care of the divine. Aristotle implied the intimate connection between the activity of the unmoved mover and every activity in the cosmos. Numenius, following the "alone to the alone" formula that can be traced back to Alexander of Tralles, emphasized the intimacy of meeting the good (see fragment 2, Petty), an intimacy that is deepened in the thought of Plotinus (on this see Corrigan, "Solitary Mysticism," 28–42). The *Chaldean Oracles* at some point in the second century had come even closer to suggesting an active divine love (fragment 42: *eros* is the first to leap from the paternal intellect); for assessmentWallis (Gerson), *Neoplatonism*, 154; Majercik, *Chaldean Oracles*, 16.

89. On these various traditions and particularly on the translation from Syriac to Arabic, from 750 on, of the works of (some) Plato, (more) Aristotle, Alexander of Aphrodisias, Galen, Plotinus, Proclus, and Dionysius, etc., first, by the father-and-son team of Syriac Christians Hunayn ibn Ishaq and Ishaq ibn Hunayn, the father specializing in Galen and the son a brilliant translator of Greek philosophical texts into Arabic; and then the work of Al Kindi and his circle, see Adamson, *Philosophy in the Islamic World*, 19–32; D'Ancona, *Origins of Islamic Philosophy*, 869–94; Pessin, "Jewish and Islamic Neoplatonisms," 541–58; see also Pessin, *Ibn Gabirol*. On the difficulty of determining the end of "late antiquity" see G. Fowden, who wants to include the period of Islamic maturation up to the end of the first millennium or just into the second (*Before and After Mohammed*). For a recent different view, see Cameron, *The Mediterranean World in Late Antiquity*.

Conclusion

THE THREE STRANDS OF Plato and Aristotle's thought I have examined in this book, ascent to the beautiful-good, love of individuals, and divine love, have to be seen together: there is no immanence without transcendence for Plato, no real love of an individual without the vertical dimension that makes this possible, no genuine human understanding that is devoid of loving, and no real thought without feeling. As Plotinus puts it, the real desire of the soul is for that which is greater than itself (*Ennead* I.4[46].6). At the heart of this mystery there is the mystical ascent to the beautiful and the good, on the one hand, and the divine life that makes ascent possible and empowers it, on the other. This is true not only of Plato and Aristotle, but also of the many other figures in later antiquity and up to the Renaissance that we have examined as part of a much broader tradition. So unfamiliar has this picture become in the postmodern world that it will strike many readers as strange.

As we noted at the beginning of this book, Plato and the Platonic tradition are often—even predominantly—characterized in our post-metaphysical times as espousing essentialism, universalism, abstract idealism, and intellectualism over the much more obvious desires and needs of individuals. Plato can apparently love abstract, cold forms but not individuals or sensible realities. And even if Aristotle reconnects Platonism with ordinary reality, he ends up creating an even more frigid god, the unmoved mover. Plotinus and the later tradition are even worse, fabricating a "Plato" that no one in his or her right mind from the nineteenth century on could recognize and weaving a tissue of mystical nonsense. Platonism, as we noted above, has long been identified with "the determination to identify the universal spirit which informs matter and, having identified it, to disengage it from the bewildering variety, the inert machinery, the practical compromises in which, in practice, it is trapped and buried." And the ascents of the soul to the beautiful and the good, likewise, have been thought to leave any recognizable existence far behind, namely, to leave out of account, "and therefore out of love, everything about the person that is not good and fine, . . . the flaws and the faults, the neutral discrepancies, the bodily history, . . . the very fact of difference." So for Rorty, truth "is not a goal of inquiry," and for postmodernism generally, all truth and ideas are constructed, subject only to the "truth" of discursive analysis. Plato, Aristotle, and the ancient tradition are therefore largely excluded on the postmodern axiom that they do not fit the postmodern constructivist, embodied model.

This book has argued for a different picture. It would seem necessary if we are to understand something, that we try first to understand it on its own terms and, as far as possible, from the major texts we have inherited. Against the view of Platonism as intellectualism privileging mind and reason over feeling, we have found even in the hardest test case of the *Phaedo* that purified feeling is an intrinsic part of the life of soul/mind. The whole point of the practical life is not to be driven by blind impulses and passions but to awaken a different axis of one's being that is open to everyone, namely, to awaken a more integrated, subject-initiated focus of reason and desire, a life, in other words, that is not only self-directed, but focused upon a wisdom bigger than itself. This for Plato is to become "like to god." For Aristotle too, the convergent point at which the human being becomes a genuine agent is the point at which reason becomes desiring and desire becomes reasoning: real agency therefore awakens a new axis of being. Furthermore, love and desire must also be true of the human intellect and all secondary intellects in Aristotle's thought if the primary intellect moves everything by being loved. Certainly later, in Plotinus, some impressions to the contrary, love, impulse, and even desire as *epithymia*, are fundamental to the life and generation of intellect, soul, and body.

In contrast to the view of Platonism as abstract idealism, essentialism, and universalism, and equally in contrast to the impression of Aristotle's unmoved mover as even more frigid a supreme reality than the Platonic form, we have found the *opposite* to be the case. If Aristotle's god is an "essence," then it is certainly not like any essence posited by postmodernism, since in the major passage in his *Metaphysics* on god's nature Aristotle weaves into the fabric of god's life the significance not only of human life at its highest but of *all* experience at whatever level of existence. god's way or mode of life (διαγωγὴ) is the purest pleasure, something we experience only intermittently. Furthermore, all animal activities throughout the cosmos—rational and non-rational, both intellect *and* feelings—are not only dependent on god's life; they are in a sense transfixed at the core by that life.

We went on to argue that Aristotle's theology and physics involving a hierarchy of forms, immaterial and enmattered, and final causality through desire and love were implicitly developed from the "lesser" and "greater" mysteries of Diotima-Socrates' speech in Plato's *Symposium*. As in Diotima-Socrates' speech, Aristotle's physics includes all movement in the cosmos for all living creatures, rational and irrational. And as in Diotima's greater mysteries, Aristotle's theology represents the culmination of all desire in the supreme participation in and touching upon god's life, the "beautiful" and the "good." Here, features of Aristotle's presentation of participation in the divine life resonate demonstrably with Socrates' treatment in the *Republic* of a range of activities or powers, from thought, through perception, to memory and hope that characterize the life of wisdom; and indeed, Aristotle's famous statement that "the heaven and nature *hang from* such a principle" must surely be a deliberate reference to the *Ion*'s image of divine creativity from which a long chain of iron rings "hangs." In other words, Aristotle presents his theology consciously in the after-image of Plato's dialogues in order to highlight both the differences and the continuities.

More precisely still, both the *Symposium* and *Metaphysics* 12.7–10 present the ascent to god as a movement, first, to the beautiful of final causality and, finally, to the good. This has escaped attention in both texts. In Aristotle, demonstrably, the language of the beautiful, τὸ καλόν (1072a28, b34, 11; 1074b24), in chapter 7 gives way to the language of the good and the best in chapters 7–10.[1] The *Symposium* is a more difficult case, since the good of the *Republic* seems almost entirely absent. However, at the conclusion of Socrates-Diotima's speech, something unsuspected in modern scholarship actually happens. Diotima's words "*that by which the beautiful is visible*" and that "*by which it is necessary to contemplate it*" can only have one ultimate referent: the beautiful is evidently visible or able to be contemplated (not only by itself but) by the ultimate source of light and intelligibility, namely, the good. Consequently, even if we should be cautious about making chronological claims about these dialogues, the *Symposium* demonstrably has to be read in the light of the *Republic*, just as Aristotle's theology and physics have to be read in the light of both Platonic dialogues.

Finally, as in Aristotle, so in Plato, the ascent through the beautiful to the good is not a disembodied search for abstract truth—even if it leads in both to the "grasp" or "touch" of immaterial forms or the ultimate immaterial object of thought; it is instead an embodied, inter-subjective search with practical consequences at every level. In the *Symposium*, the apprentice travels with a guide together with whom he or she gives birth at every level to the children of such labor, and cares for and rears this offspring at different layers of life (bodily, psychic, ethical, epistemic, and mystical). Even at the highest level, the revelation is not given to a soul or mind or to a science but "to a human being."

---

1. *Metaphysics* 7.1072a35–1072b1, 12, 15, 24, 28, 29, 32; 9.1074b20, 33; 1075a8–9; 10.1075a12, 14, 36–38; 1075b, 2.8, 11; 1076a4.

Some modern scholarship has viewed the beautiful and the good of the *Symposium* as coincident classes, that is, as generic universals or essences. We have argued that this is not a plausible or possible interpretation of the transcendent Platonic form.

The forms of the good and the beautiful cannot be conceived as abstract in the sense of essences, genera, or universal concepts since while the form informs everything, it is simultaneously separated from everything and is the only truly singular, unique, or individual reality that can be conceived in the Platonic dialogues. If the form were generic, then, by contrast, it would not be fully real, but something abstracted and empty without the species and the things in which it finds itself instantiated. Therefore, a form cannot be a universal or a class in this sense. The form intimates a different order of experience than anything purely discursive, namely, not only understanding but also the direct mystical grasp of something so supremely real that it changes everything. The form is, indeed, the "what it is" in each case—goodness, beauty, justice, wisdom, holiness, etc.—namely, "the itself to itself/in itself" (*auto kath' auto*) or even "itself itself" (*auto t'auto*), that is, some entity so unique that it cannot be coordinated with anything else, and yet so much "itself" that it gives rise to everything—genera, species, particular things—and the uniqueness that makes them themselves.

The word "essence," by contrast, is a much later term, derived from the Latin infinitive *esse*—"to be," from which is formed the participial substantive or noun *essentia*. There is no term for essence as such in Greek. Substance or *ousia*, later mistranslated into Latin as *substantia* (something "standing under"), means simply "stuff" in texts earlier than Plato's time, and comes to mean in Plato "the real stuff" or "what is really real" (*to ontōs on*), or in Aristotle, individual things with their specific and generic natures, from dogs and cats to souls and unmoved movers. The only word resembling "essence" in Aristotle, apart from phrases like *to anthropoi einai* or "what it means to be a human being," is the strange phrase "the what it was to be" (*to ti ēn einai*), whose meanings it is difficult to unpack. So we have no direct word for "essence" in any real sense before at least Aristotle—and not really even then, since the term is a later Latin neologism.

Even if it is true that forms, essential in some other sense, bestow natures on things, this still ignores the dynamic quality of Plato's thought, namely, that the forms have to be understood against the background of what appear to be two chief forms for Plato, that is, the forms of the beautiful and the good in the *Symposium* and *Republic*. Neither of these forms is a determinate essence, but in the case of the beautiful in the *Symposium*, an ocean of beauty or a force-field and, in the case of the *Republic*, a power that makes everything possible (beauty included), something that is dimly intuited from the beginning of experience, but something that is, in fact, not a "something" at all: The good is "beyond being," "beyond thought." However we are to understand it then, the form of the good is neither entity nor essence, but for Plato (as later for Plotinus and Boethius) more like pure existence, that is, unrestricted, infinitival "to-be," prior to any form of essentiality, nature, or thingy-ness.

We then went on to show that not only is this the most reasonable interpretation of these famous texts in Plato and Aristotle, but that this is clearly the way that the later tradition understood them, not only a "Middle Platonist" like Alcinous, but the later Neoplatonic tradition, from Plotinus through Porphyry and Proclus, and even up to Marsilio Ficino in the Renaissance. This is not "reconciliation" of Plato and Aristotle, I suggest, but the recognition that while their texts do, in fact, say very different things, they can also speak simultaneously in, to, and through each other. All of this suggests that Neoplatonic interpretations of Plato and Aristotle can be much more compelling than they have so often been made out to be since the nineteenth century. It also shows that what I have called the Romantic identification of beauty and truth in Keats' *Ode on a Grecian Urn* may be true of the Neoplatonic intelligible world, but it is not true that this is all we need to know on earth. Every qualification—true, beautiful, or good—can wander or admit of opposites, as Socrates puts it in the *Republic*. Only when the beautiful and the true are configured in and by the highest good do we have an ascent we can hold to in the shifting fortunes and appearances of ordinary life. Nowhere do Plato and Aristotle say exactly this, But this is their clear practice, a practice confirmed by the interpretations of later antiquity.

We next examined the shifting fortunes and wandering appearances of ordinary life in chapter 2. Despite the remarkable Platonic-Pythagorean tradition of friendship at every level of reality, Platonism has been criticized for proposing not love of the whole person but only one's preferred ideal state and for its refusal to see imperfection and the ambiguities of ordinary experience in favor of a sanitized version of reality. No real genuine friendship or love of the other, therefore, is possible. This could not be further from the truth—it is, in fact, a complete misunderstanding of the complexity of Plato's thought.

Chapter 2 argues for a much more balanced view of Plato's treatments of friendship and love of individuals. It suggests the need to include the *Alcibiades I* in the series of dialogues that examine this crucial human issue, namely, the *Lysis, Symposium, Phaedrus,* and to a lesser extent, the *Republic*, for many reasons. First, *Alcibiades I* fits thematically into this series of dialogues, adding a crucial element to the treatment of love and friendship. A successful performance of how one should love an individual in the appropriate way intimated in the *Lysis* occurs, in fact, only in the *Alcibiades I*. Second, not only was the authenticity of the *Alcibiades I* never questioned until Schleiermacher in the nineteenth century, but it was long held to be the first dialogue that anyone should read. There is therefore no good reason to doubt its authenticity. Indeed, stylometric analysis seems to support the view that it is close to the *Phaedo*, that is, an "early" middle dialogue. Third, the *Alcibiades I* fits the series of these dialogues, not because it presents a less self-directed or egoistic view of love than they do, but because these dialogues develop some of its principal themes and bring them into a sharper reflexive, inter-subjective, and vertical focus. Finally, the epistemological model of inter-subjective self-knowledge in the pupil of the eye/soul of the other that Socrates develops in the famous final section of the *Alcibiades I* is precisely the model Socrates also articulates in the famous sentence that defines justice in *Republic* 4.443c9–444a2 (a single sentence of eighteen lines).

We therefore argued that Vlastos' distinction between loving the person for his or her sake or loving only the excellence in the person is simply superficial and that, far from wanting to avoid the ambiguities of ordinary experience in favor of some bland spiritual universality, Plato actually foregrounds and explores those complexities. In the eye/soul analogy of the *Alcibiades I*, for example, one sees oneself and the god not in a purely external way but in and through another human being. Here self-realization clearly depends on the presence and mutuality of friendship. The images Socrates employs—conversation, love, looking into the eye of the other, one's beloved friend—indicate the personal, individual, and inter-subjective. And so the appropriate love of the individual is what the *Lysis* aspires to but the *Alcibiades* actually performs: "I alone was a lover of *you*, Alcibiades, whereas the rest were lovers of *what belongs to you*" (131e).

So a model of individual love and friendship is articulated, first, in the *Alcibiades I*, and the lateral and vertical semantics of this model are worked out in the *Symposium*, where the vertical ascent is embodied and inter-subjective at each level, and with real consequences, as in Olympiodorus' later adaptation of the *Alcibiades'* model to the political, kathartic, theoretic, and inspirational rungs of the ladder of virtue. This is the "right way of going . . . of being led" or "guided" (210a4–7; e2; 211b5–6); at each level, the lover must give birth and rear the offspring, that is, "*logoi* that make the young better," "fitting thoughts in ungrudging philosophy" and, finally, "true excellence" (210c1–3; d1–2; 212a2–7). In the *Phaedrus*, again, love of the individual, through the conscious or unconscious medium of the cosmic gods, is given emphatic individual application, for Socrates provides two positive models of erotic friendship, both of which involve sexual passion for the sake of higher wisdom (255e–256e)—and at least one of them, if not both, appears to involve sex. The second model, in fact, demonstrates an imperfect love of the individual for the individual's own sake that is redeemed only by love itself. We have effectively, then, in this series of dialogues on friendship and love, a cartography of friendship that can sustain one through life, in short, an art of love, a phrase first coined in the *Phaedrus* and later mentioned by Ovid, as John Dillon has noted.

There is, however, another important side to this: the possibility of failure. Throughout the dialogues, Plato depicts the imperfect everywhere and not simply as something to despise. The imperfect is, in fact, an integral part of the dialogue form itself that provokes us to enter into all the layers of the text to decide for ourselves which among all the images, persons, arguments, speeches, etc., comes closest to any model worth following. In the *Symposium*, for instance, the potential fragility of the ascent to the ideal beautiful-good is emphasized immediately by the violent entry of an alcoholic Alcibiades who is certainly brilliant but may also be strong evidence that Socrates does corrupt the youth. Moreover, the imperfect is a conspicuous part of the design of love itself in the *Symposium*. When Diotima describes the birth of eros, both elements, resource and poverty, are essential to the nature of love. Without poverty there would be no impulse, drive, or desire for the beautiful; and without resource there would be no possibility of attaining it. If we see the speeches of Aristophanes and Agathon as foreshadowing the birth of eros, we can see how Plato emphasizes the need for both imperfection and perfection—the necessity of imperfection and the fragility of perfection. Aristophanes introduces the driving force of desire for the other. Agathon, by contrast, presents an all-good perfection of love who trips over the heads of hard, old folk and visits only the soft parts of young people. Without the imperfection of both speeches, there would be no understanding of the need for both impulses, poverty and resource, in Diotima's famous myth of the birth of eros. Without Agathon's speech we would have no ideal and no *elenchus* of the ideal. Without Aristophanes' speech, we would have only a bland perfection, a perfect mirror of the aristocratic "good" boy who has everything. Balancing all of these conflicting elements, Plato refuses to represent love without the chaotic world of human drives and imperfect visions of individuals. To overlook this side of Plato and to ignore the subtle balance he is able to maintain between the philosophical and the dramatic is to show the limitations of one's own approach rather than the multifaceted face of Plato.

In the rest of chapter 2, we examined the depth and freedom of interpretation with which ancient and later figures approached the Platonic dialogues and argued for three major features of this tradition. First, against the view that Plotinus eliminates lateral attachment in the ascent to the beautiful and the good, we argued that the self that Plotinus often asks the reader to go back into is already a *shared* "you"—the "we" of Plotinus' discourse itself—a dialogue "among ourselves," as he often says, but open to anyone, a reflexive image of the intelligible world. Second, we showed through the prism of Pausanias' speech on *eros* and friendship in the *Symposium* that the multi-edged way of reading Plato across different dialogues, articulated above, was how such figures as Proclus and Ficino interpreted Plato—albeit in their own ways.

Third, we outlined three models of individuality in the *Republic* itself that do not seem to have received the attention they deserve. First, a behaviorist model that observes the beast from outside as an object, a scrutiny, by definition, friendless—by contrast with the Platonic-Pythagorean tradition that stresses the possibility even of interspecies friendship. Second, a model based upon a different kind of beast, the tyrant, seen as a subject from a holistic, internal-external perspective through long association, observation, and contemplation; in this case, the scrutiny is holistic, but the subject is shown to be utterly friendless. Finally, a subject-in-object and object-in-subject model of friendship with oneself and others that forms the basis both for personal and for civic justice and provides, in tune with the *Alcibiades I* and *Symposium*, an inter-subjective epistemology for friendship in action that is distinctively Platonic.

In chapter 3 we examined a major problem bequeathed to later antiquity by Plato and Aristotle. If everything loves god, does god love everything back? In Plato there are hints that this may be so—on the model of the care of "all soul" for that which is without soul, or the care of "the god" for the people of Athens, or, again, simply from the ambiguity of what is involved in being "god-beloved." But then is one god-beloved because one loves the god through a virtuous way of life? Surely, one cannot be god-beloved if one is evil? Furthermore, in the intelligible living creature of the *Timaeus*, all species are included, but surely not all individuals? So is divine love selective or does it really take account of individuals?

This set of problems remains in Aristotle's works, which envisage the possibility of a genuine two-way relation between gods and human beings that is other than any normal friendship and which present common opinions about the gods caring for human beings but fall short of endorsing them. And so even in the case of the cosmic gods, the idea of a god loving a human being seems doubtful, and the only case where Aristotle seems seriously to contemplate the possibility is that of the morally good person who is "most god-beloved." What, however, of "the god"—the unmoved mover? This seems altogether unlikely, as it did to many later thinkers and to most modern scholarship. But what if god's "most pleasant way of life" reaches right down into everything in the cosmos and forms one activity with everything, in however attenuated a fashion this might turn out to be the case in the lives of frogs, dolphins, and human beings? If god actually moves within everything, does this movement tell us anything about love and ordinary experience? As we pointed out, Aristotle seems to suggest in the *Metaphysics* that god's self-thinking is richer than the contemplation of the universe because god's life is both himself and all the energy of the world but in a divine mode—"in some whole"; and if this is so, then god's self-relatedness must pre-include our relatedness to god. But what can this really mean if one of Aristotle's most famous interpreters, Alexander of Aphrodisias, held the view that providence does not extend to the sublunary world? Plato's forms and Aristotle's unmoved mover are far removed from the God of Abraham, Isaac, and Jacob, and perhaps even more so from Jesus Christ.

So chapter 3 explores this problematic Platonic-Aristotelian legacy with the object of discovering from within this heritage (as far as such a thing is possible) if god can love us back, and not only "us" but everything. We therefore started by tracing an important line of thought in Aristotle about pleasure and indivisible wholeness in order to suggest that when Aristotle describes god's way of life as perhaps including indivisibly what we experience piecemeal, he points to a range of indivisible "wholes" that run right through our ordinary experience (*Metaphysics* 12.9). What we experience as piecemeal, from a developmental viewpoint, we can also experience indivisibly as a whole from another viewpoint, even if this latter experience is always imperfect, by comparison with what we imagine god's experience to be. So Aristotle provides a model for understanding how what seems unpacked or loosely related in our successive experiences can nonetheless be grasped simultaneously in ordinary thought that points beyond itself to the indivisible perfection of god's activity. And in his positive view of pleasure at its most intense (that I argued Aristotle developed against the *Philebus*, but in tune with the *Republic*, *Symposium*, and *Phaedo*), I suggested that this pleasure is neither an indwelling state or formal character of a substrate or compound activity, such as a seeing or contemplating person, but rather an epigenetic feature, like growth, that intensifies or augments a natural state and brings it into the best state of itself or makes the subject *become* who she or he really is. Pleasure is as natural as the fullness of spring reaching into summer; and yet it doesn't entirely belong to the good person either; instead, it makes one belong both to oneself and to the divine life of active pleasure promised in this increase or outgrowth. There is, in other words, a synapse, so to speak, in Aristotle's thought between the pleasure of loving that moves us as an epigenetic feature of our being and the indivisible whole pleasure that characterizes god's life, according to *Metaphysics* 12.9.

So if pleasure intensifies active contemplation as a second-order, epigenetic feature of its being, I argued that we do have in this special case a kind of coming-to-be in intellect, a *coming into being* of its best active state that is not a physical movement, but a coming into being that must somehow resonate with the *causal* activity of the unmoved mover, for it is "because" of the pleasure of god's activity that all timeless activities are "most pleasant" (according to *Metaphysics* 12.7), that is, activities that are "whole" in themselves and that involve no temporal transition. So this curious epigenetic character of pleasure must also have a genetic or causally generative power in intellect and soul. This thought is not developed in Aristotle, of course, but it does become a major feature of later thought in Plotinus and the Neoplatonic tradition, though after Epicurus, naturally, the emphasis on pleasure disappears, and becomes, instead, the joy, longing, and grace of existence with Plotinus.

So in developing important strands in the thought of Plato and Aristotle, Plotinus articulates the nature of intellect as a double activity that shows how something that has its own distinct nature on one level is simultaneously enfolded into its cause on a higher level by virtue of love, where its highest activity and the power of the good by which it acts coincide. This higher level is epigenetic in the sense that it doesn't belong to the compound but is a purely self-dependent power that is not the one only because it generates intellect *in* intellect.

This view Plotinus develops above all in one of his greatest works. God does not deliberate or reason about making, as Plato represents this in the *Timaeus*. Instead, unfolding time-space experience emerges freely and spontaneously from enfolded intelligible being as its real ground without any planning; we therefore encounter everywhere design and meaningfulness without prior reason. Similarly, the explicate intelligible world emerges out of the most intense enfoldedness of all: the one or the good. As in Aristotle if in a very different way, this emergence and return are prompted by an intense love in intellect and in the intellects of our souls that is a love given by the one. Just as the good is infinite and formless, there is correspondingly an infinite formless love in the soul for the Good (VI.7[38].34, 35–38; cf. VI.9[9].9, 44–45); and so in *Ennead* VI.7[38].35, 3–28 Plotinus speaks of a loving, drunken intellect that, by virtue of the continuity of its contemplation, no longer sees a sight, but *mingles its seeing with what it contemplates*. Such dynamic love must then include or pre-include everything that is valuable or loveable in the intelligible world and even in the sensible world, though in its own way. But if the soul or intellect can be "mingled" with the good, and if, in the next work in Porphyry's chronological order, VI.8[39], Plotinus can apply the gnostic divine love of itself to the Good so that the Good loves itself, then anything "mingled" with the Good *must love and be loved by the Good*. Plotinus stops short of speaking of a "divine loving" but this is what he is really arguing, even if he cannot say it outright; and his new view emerges out of Plato and Aristotle, but clearly against the background of Jewish and Christian thinking mediated through his contact with the gnostics, and this new vision, in turn, helps to reshape the later development of these traditions.

In the latter part of chapter 3, we charted out a new sensibility about divine love that we find in later thinkers. We find this in Proclus' converting love (*eros epistreptikos*), which urges lower principles to aspire towards their superiors, and a descending or providential love (*eros pronoetikos*), which obligates superiors to care for their products and to transmit divine grace. In Iamblichus' (and Proclus') complex view of prayer, we (and all physical things) are pre-included in the life and love of the gods—so much so that love answers to, and increases, divine love. As we argued, Iamblichus articulates the dynamic unity of divine love initiated by us in prayer and perfected by the divine in us, a unity that augments our co-being and that even appears to contribute something to the divine to such a degree that we can almost speak of a mutual love—we can almost say that in our love of the divine, the divine loves us. Here I suggested that we already encounter what Henry Corbin calls—in relation to the Sufi tradition and Ibn 'Arabi—a bi-unity, a one being encountering itself, the divine in the human and the human in the divine. Just as "seeing" in the Platonic tradition is a function of the activity of the good *in my perception*, and in Aristotle the activity of god is together with and in my every real action, so with Iamblichus even more intimately my desire of god is also god's desire manifested in me.

However, in Dionysius, I have argued, there is something genuinely new that goes beyond anything in the previous tradition. For Dionysius, divine love is no longer a structural relation between cause and effect or even a ritualistic relation between god and worshipper. Such love is, instead, an intimate paradoxical coincidence of opposites—transcendence and immanence—in which the divine longing for all created things is manifested. In god's self-abiding, transcendent, beloved nature there is a remarkable vulnerability, even a passivity beyond all passivity: God is "led down" to dwell in all. God does not merely enchant, as Agathon had supposed in the *Symposium*. God is simultaneously *enchanted* by goodness, love, and longing for all by virtue of "his ecstatic, hyper-substantial power that does not stop visiting itself."

It is easy to see this as a Christian conclusion to a failed pagan story, but this would be to underestimate the power of both the pagan and the Christian traditions: namely, I suggest, to recognize the very best of each other in each other—through something more powerful than both, divine love itself, that can simultaneously overturn expectation and yet fulfill aspiration in unexpected ways. Plotinus could never have spoken about any passivity in the good, and yet he can say that the good "is gentle, kindly, gracious, and open to anyone when anyone wishes," which implies not only a radical democratization of mystical aspiration but also paradoxically that the supreme will of the good is somehow in our power. For Plato earlier, festival, feasting, charms to enchant our souls and charm-songs are parts of the music of philosophy through which we aspire to divine-human community, to live the life of the god by becoming like to the god. Even in the somewhat darker vision of the *Laws*, such songs of self-enchantment are what the citizens of Magnesia should sing. Surely something of this aspiration is part of Aristotle's ethics and theology if the wise person who acts in accordance with intellect is most god-beloved, because he or she shares most in the unity of god's activity.

To be enchanted by something is also to be magnetized by it, to hang upon it, as in Plato's *Ion* and Aristotle's *Metaphysics*; it is also to hold to something and to be held by it—to be possessed or inspired by it, as in Plato's *Phaedo*, *Republic*, and *Phaedrus*. Without mentioning the Christian heritage in this passage of the *Divine Names*, Dionysius draws out the deepest implications of the entire pagan tradition and transforms them for their later co-existence in Jewish, Christian, and Islamic thought.

Select Bibliography

Adamson, Peter. *Philosophy in the Islamic World*. Oxford: Oxford University Press, 2016.
Addey, Crystal. *Divination and Theurgy in Neoplatonism: Oracles of the Gods*. Farnham UK: Ashgate, 2014.
Allen, Reginald, E. "Participation and Predication in Plato's Middle Dialogues." In *Studies in Plato's Metaphysics*, edited by R. E. Allen, 43–60. London: Routledge and Kegan Paul, 1965.
Annas, Julia. "Self-Knowledge in Early Plato." In *Platonic Investigations*, edited by D. O'Meara, 11–138. Studies in Philosophy and the History of Philosophy, 13. Washington, DC: Catholic University of America, 1985.
Armstrong, Arthur Hilary, ed. *The Cambridge History of Later Greek and Early Medieval Philosophy*. Cambridge: Cambridge University Press, 1967.
———. "Eternity, Life and Movement in Plotinus' Accounts of Nous." In *Le Néoplatonisme*, edited by P. Hadot and P. M. Schuhl, 67–74. Paris: C.R.N.S., 1971.
———, trans. *Plotinus*. 7 vols. Loeb Classical Library. Cambridge: Harvard University Press, 1966–88.
Ast, D. Fredericus. *Lexicon Platonicum*. 3 vols. 1835. Reprint. New York: Franklin, 1969.
Baltès, Matthias. "Idee (Ideenlehre)." *Reallexikon für Antike und Christentum* 17 (1994) 213–46.
Barnes, Jonathan. *Porphyry. Introduction*. Translated with an introduction and commentary. Oxford: Clarendon, 1993.
Bodéüs, Richard. *Aristotle and the Theology of the Living Immortals*. Translated by Jan Garrett. New York: SUNY, 2000.
Bonitz, Herman. *Index Aristotelicus*. 2nd ed. 1870. Reprint. Graz, Austria: Akademische Druck-U. Verlagsanstalt, 1955.
Brandwood, Leonard. *The Chronology of Plato's Dialogues*. Cambridge: Cambridge University Press, 1990.
Bréhier, Emile. *Plotin: Ennéades*. 7 vols. Paris: Vrin, 1924–38.
Brisson, Luc. "Comment rendre compte de la participation du sensible à l'intelligible chez Platon." In *Platon. Les Formes Intelligibles*, edited by Jean-François Pradeau, 55–86. Paris: Presses Universitaires de France, 2001.
Brisson, Luc, and Jean-François Pradeau. *Plotin Ennéades, Traités 1-6, 7-21, 22-26, 27-29, 30-37, 38-41, 42-44, 45-50, 51-54*. Paris: Flammarion 2003–10.
Brunschwig, Jacques. "La deconstruction du 'connais-toi toi-même' dans *l'Alcibiade Majeur*." *Recherches sur la Philosophie et le Langage* 18 (1996) 61–84.
Burnet, John. *The Ethics of Aristotle*. London: Methuen, 1900.
Burnyeat, Myles, and Michael Frede. *The Pseudo-Platonic Seventh Letter*. Edited by Dominic Scott. Oxford: Oxford University Press, 2015.

Bussanich, John. *The One and Its Relation to Intellect in Plotinus' Enneads*. Brill: Leiden, 1988.
Cameron, Averil. *The Mediterranean World in Late Antiquity: AD 395-700*. The Routledge History of the Ancient World. 2nd ed. London: Routledge, 2011.
Chang, K-C. "Plato's Form of the Beautiful in the *Symposium* versus Aristotle's Unmoved Mover in the *Metaphysics* (12)." *Classical Quarterly* 52.2 (2000) 431-46.
Clark, Stephen R. L. "Animals in Classical and Late Antique Philosophy." In *The Oxford Handbook of Animal Ethics*, edited by Tom L. Beauchamp and R. G. Frey, 35-60. Oxford: Oxford University Press, 2011.
Clarke, Elizabeth C., John M. Dillon, and Jackson P. Hershbell, trans. and notes. *Iamblichus, De Mysteriis*. Atlanta: Society of Biblical Literature, 2003.
Cooper, John. M., ed. *Plato: Complete Works*. Indianapolis: Hackett, 1997.
Corbin, Henry. *Alone with the Alone: Creative Imagination in the Sufism of Ibn 'Arabi*. Translated by Ralph Manheim. Princeton: Princeton University Press, 1969.
Corrigan, Kevin. "How Did the Unmoved Mover Come to Love Everything by the End of the Ancient Pagan Tradition?" *Dionysius* 32 (2014) 82-115.
———. "Humans, Other Animals, Plants, and the Question of the Good." In *The Routledge Handbook of Neoplatonism*, edited by P. Remes and S. Slaveva-Griffin, 372-90. London and New York: Routledge, 2014.
———. "Love of God, Love of Self, and Love of Neighbor: Augustine's Critical Dialogue with Platonism." *Augustinian Studies* 34.1 (1996) 97-106.
———. *Mind, Soul and Body in the 4th Century: Evagrius of Pontus and Gregory of Nyssa*. Aldershot, UK: Ashgate, 2004.
———. "The Place and Scope of 'Participation' in the Thought of Plato and Aristotle." forthcoming 2018.
———. "The Platonist as Friend." In *Defining Platonism: Essays in Honor of the 75th Birthday of John M. Dillon*, edited by John Finamore and Sarah Klitenic Wear, 29-43. Steubenville, OH: Franciscan University Press, 2014.
———. "Plotinus, 'Enneads' 5, 4 [7], 2 and Related Passages: A New Interpretation of the Status of the Intelligible Object." *Hermes* 114.2 (1986) 195-203.
———. *Plotinus' Theory of Matter-Evil and the Question of Substance: Plato, Aristotle and Alexander of Aphrodisias*. Leuven: Peeters, 1996.
———. *Reading Plotinus: A Practical Introduction to Neoplatonism*. West Lafayette, IN: Purdue University Press, 2004.
———. "'Solitary' Mysticism in Plotinus, Proclus, Pseudo-Dionysius and Gregory of Nyssa." *Journal of Religion* 76 (1996) 28-42.
Corrigan, Kevin, and Elena Glazov-Corrigan. *Plato's Dialectic at Play: Argument, Structure and Myth in the Symposium*. University Park, PA: University of Pennsylvania State Press, 2004.
Corrigan, Kevin, and L. Michael Harrington. "Pseudo-Dionysius the Areopagite." In *The Stanford Encyclopedia of Philosophy*. https://plato.stanford.edu/entries/pseudo-dionysius-areopagite/.
Corrigan, Kevin, and John D. Turner, trans. *Plotinus, Ennead VI: On the Voluntary and the Free Will of the One*. With an introduction and commentary. Las Vegas: Parmenides Press, 2017.
D'Ancona, Cristina. "The Origins of Islamic Philosophy." In *The Cambridge History of Philosophy in Late Antiquity*, vol. 2, edited by L. P. Gerson, 869-94. Cambridge: Cambridge University Press, 2010.

Daniélou, Jean. *Platonisme et Théologie mystique*. Paris: Aubier, 1944.
Denyer, Nicholas. *Plato: Alcibiades*. Cambridge Greek and Latin Classics. Cambridge: Cambridge University Press, 2001.
Des Places, Edouard. *Numénius. Fragments*. Paris: Belles Lettres, 1973.
Diehl, Ernst. *Procli in Platonis Timaeum Commentaria*. 3 vols. Leipzig: Teubner, 1903–6.
Dillon, John M., trans. *Alcinous: The Handbook of Platonism*. With an introduction and commentary. Oxford: Clarendon, 1993.
———. *Iamblichi Chalcidensis Fragmenta*. Leiden: Brill, 1973.
———. "Iamblichus of Chalcis." *Aufstieg und Niedergang der Römischen Welt* II 36.2 (1987) 863–909.
———. *The Middle Platonists*. London: Duckworth, 1977.
———. "A Platonist Ars Amatoria." *Classical Quarterly*, New Series, 44.2 (1994) 387–92.
Dillon, John M., Elizabeth C. Clarke, Jackson P. Hershbell. *Iamblichus: On the Mysteries*. Atlanta: SBL, 2003.
Dixsaut, Monique, ed. *La Fêlure du plaisir. Études sur le philèbe de Platon*, Paris: Vrin, 1990.
———. "Ousia, eidos et idea dans le *Phédon*." In *Platon et la question de la pensée. Études platoniciennes*, 71–91. Paris, Vrin, 2000.
Dodds, Eric Robertson. *Proclus: The Elements of Theology*. Oxford: Oxford University Press, 1963.
Dover, Kenneth. *Plato. Symposium*. Cambridge: Cambridge University Press, 1980.
Ebert, Theodor. *Meinung und Wissen in der Philosophie Platons*. New York: De Gruyter, 1974.
Eijk, Philip J. van der. *Medicine and Philosophy in Classical Antiquity*. Cambridge: Cambridge University Press, 2005.
Emilsson, Eyjólfur Kjalar. *Plotinus on Intellect*. Oxford: Oxford University Press, 2007.
Ferber, Rafael. *Platos Idee des Guten*. 2nd ed. Sankt Augustin, Germany: Academia Verlag, 1989.
Fitzgerald, John T., ed. *Greco-Roman Perspectives on Friendship*. Atlanta: SBL, 1997.
Foucault, Michel. *L'herméneutique du sujet: Cours au Collège de France (1981–2)*. Edited by F. Ewald, A. Fontana, and F. Gros. Paris: Gallimard, 2001.
Fowden, Garth. *Before and After Mohammed: The First Millennium Refocused*. Princeton: Princeton University Press, 2013.
Fronterotta, Francesco. "The Development of Plato's Theory of Ideas and the 'Socratic Question.'" *Oxford Studies in Ancient Philosophy* 32 (2007) 37–62.
———. *Methexis: La Teoria Platonica delle Idee e La Particepazione delle Cose Empiriche dai Dialoghi giovanili al* Parmenide. Pisa: Scuola Normale Superiore, 2001.
Gauthier, Rene Antoine, and Jean Yves Jolif. *L'Éthique à Nicomaque*. 4 vols. Louvain: Universitaires de Louvain, 1970.
Gerson, Lloyd P. *Aristotle and Other Platonists*. Ithaca, NY: Cornell University Press, 2005.
———, ed. *The Cambridge History of Philosophy in Late Antiquity*. 2 vols. Cambridge: Cambridge University Press, 2010.
———. *From Plato to Platonism*. Ithaca, NY: Cornell University Press, 2013.
———. *Plotinus*. London: Routledge, 1994.

Gill, Christopher. "Self-Knowledge in Plato's *Alcibiades*." In *Reading Ancient Texts*, vol. 1, edited by Suzanne Stern-Gillet and Kevin Corrigan, 97–112. Leiden: Brill, 2007.
Gonzalez, Francisco. *Dialectic and Dialogue: Plato's Practice of Philosophical Inquiry.* Evanston, IL: Northwestern University Press, 1998.
Goodwin, William W. *Greek Grammar*. London: Macmillan, 1951.
Grube, G. M. A. *Plato's Thought*. London: Methuen, 1935.
Guthrie, W. K. C. *A History of Greek Philosophy IV*. Cambridge: Cambridge University Press, 1975.
———. *A History of Greek Philosophy V*. Cambridge: Cambridge University Press, 1978.
———. *A History of Greek Philosophy VI. Aristotle: An Encounter*. Cambridge: Cambridge University Press, 1981.
Hadot, Pierre. *Plotin: Traité 38*. Paris: Cerf, 1988.
Harder, Richard, Robert Beutler, Willy Theiler, and Gerard O'Daly. *Plotins Schriften*. 6 vols. Hamburg: Meiner, 1960–67.
Heil, G., and A. M. Ritter, eds. *Corpus Dionysiacum II* (*Celestial Hierarchy, Ecclesiastical Hierarchy, Mystical Theology, Letters*). Berlin: De Gruyter, 1991.
Henry, Paul, and Hans-Rudolph Schwyzer. *Plotini Opera*. 3 vols. Leiden: Brill, 1951–73.
Hermann, F-G. "*Metechein, metalambamein* and the Problem of Participation in Plato's Ontology." *Philosophical Inquiry* 25.3–4 (2003) 19–56.
Hooper, Anthony. "The Dual-Role Philosophers: An Exploration of a Failed Relationship." In *Alcibiades and the Socratic Lover-Educator*, edited by Harold Tarrant and Marguerite Johnson, 107–18. London: Bristol Classics, 2007.
Inwood, Brad, and Raphael Woolf, eds. *Aristotle. Eudemian Ethics*. Cambridge Texts in the History of Philosophy. Cambridge: Cambridge University Press, 2013.
Jayne, Sears Reynolds. *Marsilio Ficino, Commentary on Plato's Symposium*. Text, translation, and introduction. Columbia, MO: University of Missouri Press, 1944.
Joachim, H. H. *Aristotle. The Nicomachean Ethics*. Oxford: Oxford University Press, 1970.
Karamanolis, George. E. *Plato and Aristotle in Agreement? Platonists on Aristotle from Antiochus to Porphyry*. Oxford: Oxford University Press, 2006.
Kristeva, Julia. *Tales of Love*. New York: Columbia, 1987.
Kroll, G. *Procli in Platonis Rem publicam commentarii*. 2 vols. Edited by W. Kroll. Leipzig: Teubner, 1899–1901.
Laurens, P. 2012. *Marsile Ficin. Commentaire sur le Banquet de Platon, De l'Amour. Commentarium In Convivium Platonis, De Amore*, Texte et traduction, Les Belles Lettres, Paris.
Lear, Jonathan. *Aristotle. The Desire to Understand*. Cambridge: Cambridge University Press, 1988.
Leroux, G. *Plotin: Traité sur la liberté et la volonté de l'Un Ennéade VI, 8 (39). Introduction, texte grec, traduction et commentaire*. Paris: Vrin, 1990.
Lloyd, A. C. *The Anatomy of Neoplatonism*. Oxford: Oxford University Press, 1990.
Luibheid, Colum, and Paul Rorem, ed. and trans. *Pseudo-Dionysius: The Complete Works*. London: SPCK, 1987.
Majercik, Ruth. *The Chaldean Oracles*. Leiden, 1989.
Massagli, M. "L'Uno al di sopra del bello e della belleza nelle *Enneadi* di Plotino." *Rivista di filosofia neo-scolastica* 73 (1981) 111–31.

Meredith, Anthony. *The Cappadocians*. Crestwood, NY: St. Vladimir's Seminary Press, 1995.
Meyer, Marvin. *The Nag Hammadi Scriptures*. New York: Harper Collins, 2007.
Mortley, Raul. *Plotinus, Self and the World*. Cambridge: Cambridge University Press, 2013.
Motte, A., Chr. Rutten, and P. Somville, eds. *Philosophie de la Forme: eidos, idea, morphè dans la philosophie grecque des origines à Aristote*. Travaux du Centre d'études aristotéliciennes de l'Université de Liège. Louvain-la-Neuve: Peeters, 2003.
Narbonne, Jean-Marc. *Plotinus in Dialogue with the Gnostics*. Brill: Leiden, 2011.
Neumann, Harry. "Diotima's Concept of Love." *American Journal of Philology* 86 (1965) 33–59.
Nussbaum, Martha. *Aristotle's De Motu Animalium*. Princeton: Princeton University Press, 1978.
———. *The Fragility of Goodness: Luck and Ethics in Greek Tragedy and Philosophy*. Cambridge: Cambridge University Press, 1986.
———. *Upheavals of Thought: The Intelligence of Emotions*. Princeton: Princeton University Press, 2003.
Nygren, Anders. *Agape and Eros*. London: SPCK, 1957.
O'Daly, Gerard J. P. *Plotinus' Philosophy of the Self*. Shannon, Ireland: Irish University Press, 1971.
O'Meara, Dominic J., ed. *Platonic Investigations*. Washington, DC: Catholic University of America Press, 1985.
Perl, Eric. *Theophany: The Neoplatonic Philosophy of Dionysius the Areopagite*. Albany, NY: State University of New York, 2007.
Pessin, Sarah. *Ibn Gabirol's Theology of Desire*. Cambridge: Cambridge University Press, 2013.
———. "Jewish and Islamic Neoplatonisms." In *The Routledge Encyclopedia of Neoplatonism*, edited by P. Remes and S. Slaveva-Griffin, 541–58. London: Routledge, 2014.
Peterson, Erik. "Herkunft und Bedeutung des Monos pros Monon-formel bei Plotin." *Philologus* 88 (1933) 30–41.
Petty, Robert. *Fragments of Numenius of Apamea*. Westbury, UK: Prometheus Trust, 2012.
Popper, Karl. *The Open Society and Its Enemies*, Vol. 1, *The Spell of Plato*. London: Routledge & Kegan Paul, 1945.
Pradeau, Jean-François. "Introduction" and "Les formes et les réalités intelligibles. L'usage platonicien du terme *eidos*." In *Platon: les formes intelligibles*, ed., 7–16, 17–54. Paris: Presses Universitaires de France, 2001.
———, ed. *Platon: les formes intelligibles*. Paris: Presses Universitaires de France, 2001.
Pradeau, Jean-François, and Chantal Marboeuf. *Platon: Alcibiade*. Paris: Flammarion, 1999.
Pradeau, Jean-François, and Francesco Fronterotta. *Hippias majeur et Hippias mineur*. Presentations et traductions. Paris: Flammarion, 2005.
Remes, Pauliine. *Plotinus on Self: The Philosophy of the "We."* Cambridge: Cambridge University Press, 2007.
Rist, John M. *Eros and Psyche: Studies in Plato, Plotinus and Origen*. Toronto: Toronto University Press, 1964.
———. *Plotinus. The Road to Reality*. Cambridge: Cambridge University Press, 1967.

Ritter, Constantin. "Eidos, idea und verwandte Wörter in den Schriften Platons." In *Neue Untersuchungen über Platon*, 228–326. Munich: Beck, 1910.
Robin, Leon. *Platon: Le Banquet*. Paris: Vrin, 1992.
———. *Platon: Phèdre*. Paris: Vrin, 1994.
Rorty, Richard. *Philosophy and Social Hope*. London: Penguin, 1999.
Ross, W. D. *Aristotle's Metaphysics*. Oxford: Oxford University Press, 1975.
Rowe, Christopher J. *Plato: Phaedo*. Cambridge: Cambridge University Press, 1993.
———. *Plato: Phaedrus*. Warminster, UK: Aris & Phillips, 1986.
———. *Plato: Symposium*, Warminster, UK: Aris & Phillips, 1998.
Runia, David T., and Michael Share, ed. and trans. *Proclus: Commentary on Plato's Timaeus*, Vol. 2. Cambridge: Cambridge University Press, 2008.
Rutten, Christian. "La Doctrine des Deux Actes dans la Philosophie de Plotin." *Revue Philosophique* 146 (1956) 100–106.
———. "Le plaisir chez Aristote et Platon." In *La Fêlure du plaisir: Études sur le Philèbe de Platon*, edited by M. Dixsaut, 149–68. Paris: Vrin, 1990.
Saffrey, H. D., and L. G. Westerink, eds. *Théologie platonicienne*. 4 vols. Paris: Vrin, 1968–81.
Schroeder, Frederic M. "Friendship in Aristotle and Some Peripatetic Philosophers." In *Greco-Roman Perspectives on Friendship*, edited by John T. Fitzgerald, 35–58. Atlanta: SBL, 1997.
Schroeder, Frederic M., and Robert B. Todd. *Two Greek Aristotelian Commentators on the Intellect*. Toronto: Pontifical Institute of Medieval Studies, 1990.
Sharples, Robert W. "Alexander of Aphrodisias on Divine Providence: Two Problems." *Classical Quarterly* New Series, 32.1 (1982) 198–211.
Segonds, Alain. *Proclus: sur le premier Alcibiade de Platon*. 2 vols. Paris: Les Belles Lettres, 1985.
Sinkewicz, R. *Evagrius of Pontus. The Greek Ascetic Corpus*. Oxford: Oxford University Press, 2003.
Slaveva-Griffin, Svetla, and Pauliine Remes, eds. *The Routledge Encyclopedia of Neoplatonism*. London: Routledge, 2014.
Smith, Andrew. *Porphyry's Place in the Neoplatonic Tradition*. Brill: Leiden, 1974.
Smith, Nicholas D. "Did Plato Write the Alcibiades I?" *Apeiron* 37 (2004) 93–108.
Sorabji, Richard. *Animal Minds and Human Minds: The Origins of the Western Debate*. Ithaca, NY: Cornell University Press, 1993.
Stern-Gillet, Suzanne. *Aristotle's Philosophy of Friendship*. New York: SUNY, 1995.
Stern-Gillet, Suzanne, and Kevin Corrigan, eds. *Reading Ancient Texts. Volume I: Presocratics and Plato. Essays in Honour of Denis O'Brien*. Leiden: Brill, 2007.
Stewart, J. A. *Notes on the Nicomachean Ethics of Aristotle*. 2 vols. New York: Arno, 1973.
Suchla, Beata R., ed. *Corpus Dionysiacum I (Divine Names)*. Berlin: De Gruyter, 1990.
Szlezàk, Tomas A. *Reading Plato*. Translated by Graham Zanker. London: Routledge, 1999.
Tarrant, Harold. "Olympiodorus and Proclus on the Climax of the Alcibiades." *International Journal of the Platonic Tradition* 1 (2007) 3–29.
Tarrant, Harold, and Margeurite Johnson, eds. *Alcibiades and the Socratic Lover-Educator*. London: Bristol Classics, 2013.
Thesaurus Linguae Graecae. Online: http://www.tlg.uci.edu.

Thom, Johan C. "'Harmonious Equality': The Topos of Friendship in Neopythagorean Writings." In *Greco-Roman Perspectives on Friendship*, edited by John T. Fitzgerald, 77–104. Atlanta: SBL, 1997.
Thomassen, Einar, and Louis Painchaud. *Le Traité Tripartite*. BCNH. Québec: Les Presses de l'Université Laval, 1989.
Trevor-Roper, Hugh. *Renaissance Essays*. Chicago: University of Chicago Press, 1985.
Tricot, J. *La Métaphysique*. 2 vols. Vrin: Paris, 1986.
Turner, John D. *Sethian Gnosticism and the Platonic Tradition*. Québec: Les Presses de l'Université Laval, 2001.
Velásquez, Oscar. *Alcibíades, Platón*. Edición crítica del texto griego, traducción y commentarios. Santiago, Chile: Édiciones Tácitas, 2013.
Vlastos, Gregory. "Degrees of Reality in Plato." In *New Essays on Plato and Aristotle*, edited by J. R. Bambrough, 1–19. London: Routledge, 1965.
———. "The Individual as an Object of Love in Plato." In *Platonic Studies*, 2nd ed., 3–42. Princeton: Princeton University Press, 1981.
———. *Platonic Studies*. Princeton: Princeton University Press, 1981.
Wallis, Richard T. (and Lloyd P. Gerson, rev. 2nd ed.). *Neoplatonism*. Indianapolis: Hackett, 1995.
Westerink, L. G. *Olympiodorus: Commentary on the First Alcibiades of Plato*. Amsterdam: North Holland, 1956.
Westerink, L. G., and William O'Neill. *Proclus: Commentary on the First Alcibiades*. Warminster, UK: The Prometheus Trust, 2011.
Williams, Rowan. *The Wound of Knowledge: Christian Spirituality from the New Testament to Saint John of the Cross*. Plymouth, UK: Rowman & Littlefield, 1990.
Woodruff, Paul. *Plato. Hippias Major*. Translated with commentary and essay. Indianapolis: Hackett, 1982.

Index Locorum

GENERAL AND SPECIFIC TREATMENTS of works important for the arguments of this book, such as Plato's *Symposium*, *Republic* and *Phaedrus* and Aristotle's *Metaphysics*, *Nicomachean Ethics*, etc., are indicated immediately after the titles of these works before individual citations.

Alcinous

Didaskalikos

10.3	31 and nn91–92
10.6.6–7	33
33.3–4	70n67
33.187, 20ff.	54
187, 41	54

Alexander of Aphrodisias

Arabic *De Providentia*

1	1–9

(Sharples, *Alexander of Aphrodisias on Divine Providence*, 198–21)

xi, n6

De Anima

88, 26–89, 15	29n81

Aquinas, Thomas

ST, Tertia Pars, Supplement, Q.84

article 1	96n40

Aristotle

De Anima

	29n80
2.414b2	5
2. 417a16	41n115
2.421a20ff	17n44
3.429a15	ix, n1
3.429b23	ix, n1
3.430a1–16	9n19
3.430a15	22, 93n36
3.430a16–25	9n20
3.430a18	ix, n1
3.3432b5–6	5
3.433a14–15	19n47, 24
3.433a26	5

De Generatione et Corruptione

2.323a25	13n34, 22n15

De Partibus Animalium

1.645a23–36	14–15n37, 17n43
2.647b29–648a11	17n44

De Philosophia

	11n28
fr. 15 (Rose/Ross)	9n21

Eudemian Ethics (*EE*)

	17–19 and n44, 53
6.1234a27	17n44

Eudemian Ethics (EE) (continued)

7.1239a1–24	84
7.1239a17–19	85n16, 84n14
7.1239a20–21	84n14
7.1242a31–35	84, 85n16
8.1248a23–41	18–19n44

Magna Moralia (MM)

1198a2ff	17n44
1208b26–31	84, 85n16

Metaphysics

9–10, 11–12n28, 12–25, 29–33, 29n80, 30, 31, 33, 34, 36, 41, 42, 47–48, 84–86, 85n15, 90–91, 95, 96, 105, 115, 116, 122–124

1.991a8–11	29n82
1.991b3–9	29n81,
1.992a29–32	29n81
7.1033b26–1034a5	29n81
7.1041b19	90n32
9.1048b23	80n89
9.1051b24	16n41
12.1071b14–16	29
12.1072a26	31
12.1072a13	11–12n28
12.1072a24–25	11–12n28
12.1072a28	30, 47n127, 114
12.1072a35–1072b1 and 12, 15, 24, 28, 29, 32	30, 47n128, 116
12.1072b1–2	19n47, 24
12.1072b3	11–12n28, 12n31, 20n47, 24
12.1072b11	30, 114
12.1072b14 and 25; 28–29; 30	11–12n28
12.1072b13	34n98
12.1072b13–30	16, 22–23 and n59
12.1072b14–18	20n52
12.1072b18–24	21 and n53
12.1072b20–30	36
12.1072b34	30, 47n127, 114
12.1073b1–3	9
12.1074a10–17	9
12.1074b17–35	33 and n95
12.1074b20 and 33	30, 47n128, 116
12.1074b24 30	47n127
12.9.1074b34–5	12n32
12.1075a7–9	85 and n17
12.1075a8–9	30, 47n128, 116
12.1075a12 and14, 36–38	30, 47n128, 116
12.1075b2 and 8, 11	30, 47n128, 116
12.10.1075a10–15	15 and n38
12.1076a4	30, 47n128, 116

Nicomachean Ethics (EN)

19 and n46, 47, 85n16, 86–95, 105

1.1096a11–1097a14	29n82
1.1099b10ff.	84–85n14
6.1139a22–25	5
6.1139b	6
6.1139b5	91n33
6.1143a25–28	6 and n9
6.1143b	6
6.1143b6–7	6n10
6.1143b10	19n45
6.1144b32–1145a2	17n44
7.1151a15–20	17n44
7.1152b1–1154b34	86
8.1155a26–27	109
8.1154b24–28	16n39
8.1159a5–8	84, 85n16
8.1160b25–26	84, 85n16
8.1162a4–5	84, 85n16
10.1172a19–1176a29	87
10.1172b34–35	95
10.1173a18–1173b7	89n27
10.1173a29–1173b7	87
10.1173a34–1173b1	89n29
10.1173b7–20	87
10.1174a4–6	89n28, 97
10.1174a15–16	90
10.1174a17–19	90
10.1174a21	90
10.1174b5–6	90
10.1174b9	90
10.1174b11–13	90 and n13
10.1174b14ff	92
10.1174b20–23	92
10.1174b31–33	92

INDEX LOCORUM 137

10.1174b34	92	97, 110, 115, 121	105n71
10.1175a29–31	93	39, 42, 44	105n71
10.1175a30–31	88	46	107n74, 110n80
10.1175a18–19	88	135.6	113n87
10.1175a19–21	93	42	93n87, 113n88
10.1175a30–36	109		
10.1175b8–23	94		
10.1175b31–33	88		
10.1175a35–36	94		
10.1176a3–29	92		
10.1177b21	????		
10.1178a2–8	94 and n39		
10.1179a22–24	84n8		
10.1179a23ff.	84–85n14		

Dionysius the Areopagite

Divine Names

2.9.648b	9n21
4.7.704b	44
4.13.712a	67n50
4.13.712a–b	111–12 and n85
4.14–15.713a–b	111 and n84
11.2.949c–952b	112n85
11.2.952b16–17	112n85

Mystical Theology

997b3–4	45 and n124

Physics

12–23, 28–29, 47–48, 116

1.192a17ff.	31
2.194b29–30	13
3.201b16–202a12	41n115
3.202a13–21	17n42
3.202b7–8	17n43
3.2	13n34, 22n55
4.220b32–221a1	90n30
4.221b7	90n30
4.221b22–3	90n30
4.221b25–6	90n30
5.227a10–12	90n30
6.231a20–b6	90n30
8.255a33–b5	17n42
8.256b20	ix, n1
8.257b8–9	41n115

Evagrius Pontikos

Praktikos

47	4n6

Thoughts

37	4n6

Ficino, Marsilio

De Amore

Oratio Prima, cap. 3, 39	72
Oratio Secunda, cap. 8	73
Oratio Septima, cap. 2, 3, 15, 16, 17	74

Old Testament

Job 7:20	4n6
Psalm 32:15	4n6

Gnostic Texts

Trimorphic Protennoia, NHC XIII 45, 2–6

	104n65

Boethius

Consolation of Philosophy	58n24

Diogenes Laertius

Lives of the Philosophers

3.37	51n36

Tripartite Tractate, 56, 1–4

	104n65

Chaldean Oracles

1.3; 34, 4; 35, 5; 37,15; 49	93n37

Homer
Iliad
1, 73	3

Iamblichus
Anonymous Prolegomena to Platonic Philosophy
26	51n7

De Mysteriis
1.12.12.40, 12–41, 3	113n86
1.12.42.5	81
1.14.45, 4–5	113n86
1.15.46–47	106, 107
1.15.47, 5–9	106n72
4.9.192, 14–193,1	81
5.10.211, 12–13	81
5.26.238, 11–12	108
5.26.238, 6–8	81, 106
5.26.238, 12–239, 10	108
5.26.239, 5	81
5.26.239, 6	108

Life of Pythagoras
229–30	81n91

New Testament
Acts
1:24; 15:8	4n6

Hebrews
5:8	9n21

Macrobius
in Somn. Scip.
I. VIII	56n20

Olympiodorus
in Alc.
8.2–12	56–57 and n21
110, 13ff.	44n123

in Phaed.
45–49, 113–14	56n20

Ovid
Ars Amatoria
I.35–40	54 and n13

Philo
Life of Moses
II.67 and 163	84ns9 and 12

Plato
Alcibiades I
	xi, xiii, 51n26, 50–71, 79–81, 118–19, 12
103a	69
131e	58, 119
131e10–11	58n25
133b–c	55n17
133c	58n24, 80
133c8–17	55n16
133c–135c	58n24
133c–134d	71n72
133d	58n24
133d–134b	80
134a	58n24
134d	80
134dff.	58n24
134d2	57
134d4	57
134d5	57
134d7–8	57
134d–135d	55
134e1–3	57
135b7–8	57
135d3–6	57
135d7–10	57

Apology
	82, 83
18c–d	62n38
31a	83n5
40c	20n49

Gorgias
61,

Hippias Major (or *Greater Hippias*)
11, 40, 40n112, 42, 44

Hippias Minor (or *Lesser Hippias*)
40n112

Ion
20, 47, 116, 125
533d–e   20

Laws
1.631b–c   70
1.636a–637b   72n78
4.716c–e   84n12
5.726–727a   57n22
10.900d–901b   86n20

Letters

Second Letter
312e   35
312e2–3   40

Seventh Letter
341c–d   31–32

Lysis
xi, 51, 53, 58, 65, 73, 119
206c1–3   53
210e2–5   53

Parmenides
xi, 37

Phaedo
ix–xi, 3–9, 37, 39–40, 42, 44, 45–46, 51n6, 58n23, 73, 87–88, 95, 115, 119, 122, 125
58d–59a   87–88n22
60b–c   87

65c–d   8
66b   45
66e   45
67b–c   20n49
67c–d   7
67e   45
68a   20n49, 45
68a1–2   8n16
68b–69d   88
69a–b   8
69c   8
74c1–2   40
74d–75a   73, 75
75a2   8
75b1   8
96a–100a   88
105ff.   58n23

Phaedrus
ix, x1, 3, 4, 8, 9, 34, 36, 44, 45, 51, 53–57, 61, 65–75, 80, 84, 86, 98n43, 119, 120, 125
236b–d   61n34
243e–257b   73n79
244a   70
244d2–5   10n26
245a5–9   10n26
246aff.   44, 98
246b6   70n66
246b–c   84n11
246b–d   86n19
247a8   98
248d1–4   72
251a   72n78
251b   70
252c–253c   80n90
252d   35n99, 68
252e   66n49
252e–253a   66
253a   69
253a–c   66n49
254b   35n99
255a7–8   65n46
255c1–d3   67
255d5–6   56n20
255d–256b   65
255e2–256b3   65n46
255e–256e   54, 65, 120

140   INDEX LOCORUM

Phaedrus (continued)

256b-c	66n
256b7-c7	65n46
256b7-d	66n47
256b-e	98n43
256d1-2	55n15
256d2-4	66n48
256d8-e2	66
257a	54
273d4-6	72–73

Philebus

xi, 20n50, 86–89, 94, 95, 97, 122

15d–17a	25n69
21d–22a	97
24e	87
25, 1ff	97
27e	87
31a	87
31e–32b	87
32b	87n21
42c–d	87
53c–54d	87
61b–d	97
67b	87

Republic

ix–xii, 4, 5, 7, 8, 10, 11, 13, 14, 16, 19n46, 20, 22, 23–36, 36–44, 45–48, 46, 51, 57, 58n24, 61, 64, 65n44, 71–73, 76, 77–83, 84, 87, 88, 89, 92, 93, 94, 95, 97, 99, 109, 116, 118, 119, 121, 122, 125

1.327c	61n34
1.328c–331d	83 and n3
1.336b–337a	61n34
1.378cff.	77n83
4.436a	60n30
4.443c9–444a2	78–79, 119
4.444a3–5	78
5.461b	60n30
5.474c–475c	71n74
5.476d1–3	71n75
5.477d	109
5.479e	92
6.485d6–e1	5
6.485d–486a	8n14
6.485d11	8n14
6.485d12–e1	8n14
6.486a4–10	8n17
6. 486a5–6	8n14
6.489e–490a	22n58
6.490a–b	88n24
6. 490b	27
6.490c	20n50
6.493a–c	76
6.493e	72
6.494a–495a	65n43
6.494c	20n49
6, 495a–e	64n42
6.496a	60n30
6.496e	20n49
6.504e–505b	30n84
6.505a2	32n94
6.505d	43n121
6.505d–e	11
6.505d11–e2	30n85
6.506a6	30n85
6.507b– 508d	92
6.507c	92n34
6.507c8	92
6.507d–509c	27n74
6.508b–509a	34n100, 97n41
6.508b6–7	92
6.508d5	41
6.508d–509d	92
6.509b	34n100, 92
6.508d–509b	30n88
6.508e–509b	30n87
6.508e4–6	35
6.509b	28n78, 28n78
6.509a	94
6.511a–c	72n77
6. 511b5–8	21
7.517a–c	27n74
7.517b	20n49
7.517b5	34n100
7.521c–537d	30n89
7.524d5	20n48
7.531d	93n38
7.533b–534d	71n76
7.533d	27
7.534b8–10	71n76
7.534c	16n41

7.535c–536a	71n76	201b11–12	25
7.535d	60n30	201c	63n40
7.536a–b	71n76	201d1–209e4	28 and n75
7.537c	26n72, 71n73, 71–72n76	202d–204c	83n6
9.574e–575a	77n84	202e–203a	107n76
9.576a	78	203a1–2	xi, n8
9.576b	77n84	203b5	98
9.576d9–e2	77	204b8–c6	26, 112
9.576e–577b	77n82	204c2	20n47, 24
9.577a	77, 77n86	204c4	19n47, 24
9.577cff	78n87	204d–207a	24n63
9.579c	79n88	205a	43n121
9.580d7–8	4	205e–207a	26
9.581c	4	207a	61n31
9.583a	20n51	207e	112
9.583e9–10	87	208b5	19n47, 24
9.584a10	87	209e5–212a7	88n24
9.584a–b	87	209e5–212c3	28 and n77
9.585b–587a	20n51	210a–212a	93n38
9.585d–e	88n23	210a1	19n47, 24
9.586e–587a	94n39	210a6–7	105n69
9.586d–587a	94	210a4–7	59, 119
9.586e	43n122	210c1–2	24 and n67
9.588b–c	78n87	210c1–6	84n10
9. 591c–d	28n79	210 d5–6	84n10
9. 591d	79	210c1–3	59, 120
10.620c–d	83 and n2	210d1–2	59, 120
10.620d	83 and n4	210d6–7	109
		210d6–8	26

Sophist

	xi, 74
254d	103n61
260c	74

Statesman

	xi, 13
271d–274e	xii, n9

Symposium (passim)

172b	25
174b3	25n71
176a–d	89n25
176c	89n26
185a–b	63
185c	64
192c–d	30n86
195aff	86n18

210e2	119
210e3	105n69
210e4	19n47, 24, 61n33
210e6	19n47, 24
211b5–6	59, 119
211b6–d1	28n76
211b7	19n47, 24
211c2–3	19n47, 24
211d–212a	26–27
211e	50
211e–212a	59n28
212a	22n57, 41, 84n13
212a2–7	59, 120
212a3	27
212a3–6	24 and n67, 84n10
212a4–5	16n41
212a6–7	28n79
212a7	28
212c6	61n33

142 INDEX LOCORUM

Symposium (*passim*)
(continued)

212c–213a	61n32
212d–214a	59n26
213b–e	61n36
213c1	61n33
213d–e	61–62n37
214e	61n37
215a6–b3	61n35, 109
216b1–c3	61n37
216d6	61n35, 109
216e5–6	61n35, 109
217e	61062n37
219c5–6	61–62n37
219c–d	61n37
222a1–6	109
221e3–4	61–62n37
221c	58n23
222a1–6	61n35
222a8	61–62n37
222b6–7	61–62n37
227a–b8	61n37

Theaetetus

	xi, 46
176b	7

Timaeus

	xi, xii, 13, 23, 31, 36, 41, 84, 86, 102, 121,
28a–b	42
28a–37d	xii, n9
31b	32n94, 36
52b	60n30

Plotinus: *Enneads*

I.2.1, 16–21; 3, 11–19; 6, 22–27; 7, 1–6
	56n20
I.3[20]	72
I.4[46].6	114
I. 6[1].33–34	67
I. 6[1].7, 10–12	34
I.6[1].9	68–69
I.6[1].9, 7–15	34n99
I.6[1].9, 15–34	34n100
I.6[1].9, 40–41	34n100
II.9[33].10, 8	99n44

III.1[3].1, 10	42n118
III.5[50].4, 24–25	74–75n80
III.6 [26]	9
III. 8[30]	36
III.8[30].1, 8–12	68n53
III.8[30].7, 1–15.	19n45
III.8 [30].11, 22–24	10
IV.4[28].19, 1–5	96
IV.4[28].28	69–72 17n43
IV.4.28, 70–73	11
IV.7 [2].13, 3	9
V.I[10]. 6	104n62
V.1[10].7	101n51
V.3[49].10, 43	16n41
V.3[49].11	11
V.3[49].11, 5–9	11n27
V.3[43].17	68
V.4[7].2	103n60
V.4[7].2, 27–33	104n62
V.5[32].7	99
V.5[32].7, 9–10	101n50
V.5[32].12	33–34
V.5[32].12, 23–24	43n121
V.6[24].6, 8–10	101 and n48
V.8[31]	36
V.8[31].1, 5–6	68n54
V.8[31].2	67
V.8[31].2, 38–46	68n51
V.8[31].4	103n61
V.8[31].5–7	102n52
V.8[31].9, 1–7	68 and n59
V.8[31].9, 1–18	108n77
V.8[31].9.7–10	68n60
V.8[31].9.11–12.	68n61
V.8[31].9.13–18	68n62
V.8[31].12, 3	105n70
VI.2[43].8, 14–15	101
VI.2[43].18, 1–5	33–34
VI.2[43].18, 4–5	34n101
VI.2[44].21, 24–25, 50–52	102n52
VI.4[22].2, 5	42n118
VI.4[22].7	101n51
VI.7[38].1, 1–48	101n52
VI.7[38].1, 21–35	103n54
VI.7[38].1, 45–58	103ns53 and 55
VI.7[38].1, 56–58	103n55 and 59
VI.7[38].2, 1–37	103n57
VI.7[38].2, 18–19	103n56

INDEX LOCORUM   143

VI.7[38].2, 37	101	VI.9[9].6, 53–54	101 and n48
VI.7[38].12–16	103n61	VI.9[9].9, 44–45	104, 123
VI.7[38].15, 20–22	97n42	VI.9[9].11	68
VI.7[38].16, 16–22	104n62	VI.9[9].11, 22–25	101 and n49
VI.7[38].16, 19	101n51		
VI.7[38].21, 12	70n68		

Porphyry

(in) Cyril,

Contra Iulianum I.32cd, 552b1–c8   35n103

History of Philosophy, fr. 16,

TLG; fr. 222, Smith   35n102

Life of Plotinus

15, 1–17	65 and n45
16	99n44

On Abstinence

2.16	82
Sententiae 22	56n20

Presocratics

Anaxagoras DK II 12 D   ixn1
Empedocles DK 130b, 128b, 137b
    50

Proclus

Elements of Theology

Prop.13, and 1–11	37
57	44n123
100	37n104
118	58n24

in Alc.

4, 19–7, 8	51n7
25, 19ff.	63n41
26ff.	84n7
26, 2–34, 10	43n119
26, 12–27, 12	69n65
26, 16–27, 1	69
32.13ff.	69n65
34, 17ff.	69n63
35, 14–19	69n64
39, 7–9	69
42, 5–63, 11	43n120

VI.7[38].22	44
VI.7[38].22, 5–21	34–35
VI.7[38].22, 10ff (16)	98
VI.7[38]. 29, 9–10	97
VI.7[38]. 30, 14–15	97
VI.7[38]. 30, 30–32	98
VI.7[38]. 30, 34–36	99
VI.7[38]. 30, 37–38	99
VI.7.31	98n43
VI.7[38].32, 28–34	35
VI.7[38].34, 3.	70n68
VI.7[38].34, 14–22	99
VI.7[38].32, 24–38	99
VI.7[38].33, 34–39	100
VI.7[38].34, 35–38	104, 123
VI.7, 34–35	104n62
VI.7[38].35	10, 33
VI.7[38].35, 3–28	104, 123–24
VI.7.35, 19–23	100 and n47
VI.7[38].35, 19–27	10n26
VI.7[38].36, 3–25	32 and n94, 35
VI.7[38].36, 10–15	35
VI.7[38].36, 17 (15–21)	105n69
VI.7[38].37, 20	10n25
VI.7[38].37, 22–24	33 and n96
VI.7[38].39, 3–5	99–100
VI.7[38].40	100–102
VI.7[38].40, 5–18	100–101
VI.7[38].40, 46–49	101
VI.7[38].41, 27	101n51
VI.7[38].41–42	104n64
VI.7[38].42, 15–17	35
VI.8[39].6, 19–22	17n43
VI.8[39], chapters 13–21	39
VI.8[39].13, 16–19	38
VI.8[39].14, 16–31	103n57
VI.8[39].15	104n66
VI.8[39].16, 32	101n49
VI.8[39].18, 20–21	104n63
VI.9[9].3, 32–36	104n62
VI.9[9].4, 27	16n41
VI.9[9].6, 12	65n57

in Alc. (continued)

51, 16–53, 2	107n75
54–56	105
55, 17–56, 3	70
55, 18–21	71n71
56, 2–4	70n69
329, 17–330, 1	43
233, 5–7	81n91, 83
330, 2–4	43
330, 4–12	44
330, 7	44n123

in Rep.

1.271, 9–10	41
1.271, 18–29	41
1.275, 27–276, 5	41
1.278, 8–10	41n114
1.278, 13–14	41
1.286, 22–25	42
1.287, 5–10	42 and n117

In Tim.

I.212, 19ff.	110
I.213, 2–3	107
I.352, 16–27	58n24

Platonic Theology

I.18.83, 27	38
I.18.87, 10	38
I.25.110, 6–8	107n75
II.6.42.6	37
II.6.41, 27–42, 4	38 and n106
II.6.42, 20–24	37
II.6.43, 8–11	37
II.7.43, 19–20	39
II.6.95, 8–96, 11	37n105
II.7.45, 25–46, 1	40 and n110
II.7.46, 13–47, 10	40 and n113

Stoics (SVF)

III 109, 12–13	ix, n1
III 448	ix, n1

Index of Subjects and Names

activity, *energeia*, 4–6, 17, 41, 80, 89–90, 100–102, 106
  and action, 80–81, 124–25
  and contemplation, perception, thought, 6, 7–8, 12–30, 124
  and friendship, 81
  and pleasure, 16–20, 47, 92–96, 99
  and self-knowledge, happiness, 80
  beauty of, 93
  bloom, 99
  complete versus change/transition, 80, 89–90
  divine pre-inclusive, 106, 113n88
  double, 17n53, 100–102, 123
  epigenetic feature of, 95–96, 100, 122, 123
  god, act without potentiality, 12, 84, 113n88, 125
  implicate-explicate, 103ff.
  movement, *kinesis* (incomplete), 41–42, 89–90
  non-intentional vs. intentional, 101
  potentiality, capacity, *dunamis*, *dunamei*, 4n7, 6, 89–90, 92, 100
  power, *dunamis*, 92, 100–102
  prayer, 108–9
  range of, 92
  generative self-dependence vs. substrate's activity, 100–102
  single act, different perspectives, 17, 100, 101, 106, 122, 123
Adamson, P., 113n89
Agathon, 25, 61, 86, 120
agency, 5–6, 13, 39, 50
Alcibiades, 43, 55–60, 58n23, 61 and n34, 61n37, 84, 120
Alcinous, 31–32, 33, 48, 53–54, 55, 70 and n67, 118

Alexander of Aphrodisias, 29 and nn80–81, 91, 113n89, 122
Alexander of Tralles, 113n88
Al Kindi, 113n89
Allen, R. E., 22n56, 25n68, 25n70
"alone to alone", 113n88
Anaxagoras, 88
Annas, J., 58n23
Aphrodite, 80
Apollo, 82., 83
Apollodorus, 60
apprenticeship, 26
Aquinas, T., St., 96n49
Arcadia, 82
archē/originative principle, 6, 12n28, 19, 21, 29, 30, 34n98, 35, 37, 39, 40, 43, 44, 46, 91, 116
Aristodemus, 6
Aristophanes, 30, 62 and n38, 89, 120
Aristotle *passim*, but principally, 1–30, 45–49, 50–52, 75, 79–81, 82, 84–96, 102, 103–5, 114–25
  Plato-Aristotle reconciliation, 23n60
  Plotinus' criticism of the unmoved mover, 102
Armstrong, A. H., 10 and n24, 99
art, 20, 53
ascent/ ladder, 1-49 *passim*, 56–57, 100, 114, 119–12
  embodied, 28–29
Ast, J., 20
αὐτὸ τὸ αὐτό/αὐτὸ ἕκαστον, 57n23

Baltès, M., 22n56
Barnes, J., 23 and n60
Baucis, 82

INDEX OF SUBJECTS AND NAMES

beauty, beautiful (and good) [see also good, the], x, 1, 23–49
   all forms/kinds of, 28, 30, 31
   and truth, 1–2, 33–34, 118
   ascent [body, soul etc.], 26, 28
   beautiful itself vs. form of beauty, 35
   class or Platonic form, x, 24–26, 117
   form of, ix
   place of, final cause, 14n3, 34
   good, more beautiful, generates beauty, 35
   grace, 44
   itself, 28
   intelligible, 44
   Keats, 1–2, 33–34
   primary, super, 34
   supreme, 26
behaviorist, 77, 121
being (see also intellect, soul), ix, 29, 36, 37–38, 79–81, 83–113 *passim*, 107, 109, 115,
   and coming-to-be, 10, 11, 21, 22, 41, 70, 87, 89, 90, 96, 102, 123
   and having, 101n48
   and truth, 41
   and value, 30n88
   being-life-mind, 34
   beyond being, x, xii, 28
   divine, xiii, 83
   double focus of, 101–2, 115
   eros in intellect's being, 70
   implicate/explicate orders, 97, 102–10
   in search of, 10, 97
   new form of, 6, 46, 66, 68
   one's own, 79–80
   organization, axis of, 5, 7, 8, 36, 107, 109, 115
   ousia, substance, 87
   procession, conversion, 37–38 with, 26, 68
bi-unity, 106
blood, tissue, 17n44
Bodéüs, R., 11–12n29, 16n39, 18n44
Bodhisattva love, 69
Boethius, 58n24

Bonitz, H., 20, 23n62
boredom, 34, 44, 98
Brisson, L., 22n56, 25n69, 25n70
Brunschwig, J., 58n2
Burneat, M., 60n29
Bussanich, J, 39n and n109, 105 and n67, 105n68

Caesar, Julius, 14 and n36
Callicles, 61
Cameron, A., 113–114n89
care/concern, 69, 84–85n14
   divine providential, 105
causality, 10–30, 33, 34, 37–41, 46, 47, 70, 74, 84, 88, 90n32, 101, 103n55, 111–12, 116, 123–25
   and caused, 101, 103n55
   anthropomorphic, 84
   beginning of movement (see also *archē*), 15, 17–19n44, 25, 29
   coincidence of opposites vs. cause-effect, 111, 124
   coming-into-being, generative, 96, 123
   efficient, 13, 17
   exemplary, transcendent, separate, 15n38, 116
   final, goal, 13–30, 41, 47, 74, 84
   formal, 13, 46, 88, 90n32
   hierarchy of forms, 28, 47,
   inner, dynamic and external, 16–17, 29–30
   love, desire, 11–14, 22
   material, 88
   mutual implicative, 103
   procession and conversion, 37–41
   unity of, 111–12, 125
Cavalcanti, Guido, 72–73
Cephalus, 83
Chang, M. C., 30n83
Christian/ity, xi–xiii, 3, 6, 7, 55, 98–99, 107, 110, 111, 111n82, 113 and n89, 124, 125
Clarke, E. C, 113n86
Clearchos of Methydrion, 82
color, bloom, 34, 41, 69, 92–93, 99
coming-to-be (see under being)

INDEX OF SUBJECTS AND NAMES 147

contemplation (insight, *theōria*, identical with thinking as understanding, i.e., *noēsis* [as opposed to reason, discursive reason, *dianoia*, *logismos* that should work 'through,' *dia-noia*, understanding]), 10, 15, 17, 20, 21, 32n94, 36, 41, 73, 85, 91–92, 95–96, 104, 121–24
Corbin, H., 124
Corrigan, K., 38n107, 68n56, 101n51, 103n66, 105n71, 110n81, 113n88
Corrigan, K. and E. Glazov-Corrigan, 62n37, 99n55
Corrigan, K. and L. M Harrison, 111n83
Corrigan, K. and J. D. Turner, 104ns65–66, 105n67
Cupid, 73
Cusa, Nicholas of, 111n82

daimon, 74–75n80, 83, 107
D'Ancona, C., 113n89
Daniélou, J., 10n25
deliberation, 123
Delphi, 82
Denyer, N., 5n6
Descartes, R., 3
desire, ix-xii, 1–49, 51, 62, 67, 72, 73, 76–77, 85, 94, 103–4, 114–16, 120, 124
  and beautiful/good, 23–49
  and god, 106, 124
  and intellect, 9–49, 103–4
  and impulse, 17–19 and note, 44, 62
  and love, 4–8, 10–11
  and need, 26
  and passion, 5–7, 115, 120
  and pleasure, 5, 46
  and procreation, 24, 62
  and reason, 4, 45–46
  and soul, 103–4, 114
  and touch/contact, 22
  and transformability, 7–8, 26, 28–29
  and wisdom, 5
  as whole, 8n14

  correct, 5–7
  epithymia, 4, 5, 10–11, 14, 47, 115
  epithymia, *thymos*, and *boulesis*, 5, 10–11
  orexis, 5, 9, 11, 47
  ephesis and cognates, 9–10, 11
  eros and cognates, 11, 47
  extirpation vs. transformation, 7–8
  lower/higher axes of, 4–6, 7, 45, 58n23, 107, 109, 115
  not determining feature of good, 97
  positive/negative, 76–77
  pre-intellectual/pre-intellect, 11
  rational and irrational, 17–19 and n44
  reasoning desire, 6
  resource/poverty, 62
  sensible things, 73, 75
  single fount of energy, 4–5
  versus substance, 10–11
dialectic, ix, 20, 21, 71–72
  synoptic, 26, 58n24, 71n76
Dillon, J. M., 30 and n90, 92, 93, 44n123, 53–54, 113n86, 119
Diogenes Laertius, 51n6
Dionysius, the Areopagite, 83, 111–13, 124–25
Diophanes, 67
Diotima-Socrates (see under Socrates)
divine love (see under love, eros)
Dodds, E. R., 37 and n104
Dover, K., 24n65, 53n9, 80–81

Echecrates, 87–88n22
education, 26, 63–65, 69, 76
ego/self-directed vs. intersubjective self, 51–52, 57–59, 68, 119
Eijk, van der, 18n44
embodied, embodiment, 28–29, 116–17
  and disembodiment, 57–58nn23–24
Emilsson, E. K., 17n43
Empedocles, x, 50
energy see act, activity, *energeia*
Epicurus, 86, 96, 123
epigenetic pleasure, activity, 95–96, 100, 122, 123

epistemology (*Alcibiades I/Republic*, 4), 80, 121
Erasmus, 111n82
eros (see love)
  anterotic, 55, 67
  eros-daimōn, 83, 107
  pronoetikos/epistreptikos, 124
  single fount of, 4–5
Eryximachus, 61, 89
essence/essentialism, 3n3, 10, 58n24, 72, 93n37, 107, 114–18
  forms, Platonic, 57n20, 117–18

ēthos (character) vs. *plēthos* (abundance), 82
Eudoxus, 89
Eusebius, 55 and n16
eutychia, 18n44
Evagrius, ix n1, 3–4
existence, 38–39, 77–78, 118
  existence, joy of, 96–101, 123
  existence-substance, double structure, 100–102

Ferber, R., 30n88
Ficino, Marsilio, 44–45, 118, 121
flourishing, 59, 80, 89
form and participants, 71–72 and n76
form, ix–xiv, 4–49, 22n56, 71–75, 71n76, 75n81, 90–95, 99–104, 117–18
  as ideals, 30n88
  beautiful and good distinguished, 4–49
  formal cause, 13, 14n37, 46, 87–88
  classes, essences?, 24–25, 115, 117–18
  complete, 89–90,
  enmattered/ immaterial, 27–28
  final causality, 24–46
  formless infinite love, 104–5, 123
  friendship, 53–54, 66
  hierarchy of developmental form, compound, 17–19 and n44, 20, 28n76, 46–47, 90, 116
  rational desire, 5–6
  separate, 7–8, 91

three forms of soul, life, 4–5, 10–11, 80, 88
transformation, 36, 59
Platonic, ix-xiv, 19n44, 29, 35–43, 51n6, 81, 83, 87, 115, 117, 122
uniformity, 13, 37
without matter, 12
Foucault, M., 58n23
Fowden, G., 113–14n89
Frede, M., 60n29
freedom, ix, 38–39, 82–83, 123
  and friendship, 78
  choice, 6
  from passion, ix
  human-divine link, 38
friendlessness, 121
friendship (*philia*), x-xii, 42–43, 50–81, 84–85n14, 112n85, 121
  ambiguity, complexity, 52, 60–75
  and love (*eros*), 42–43, 53
  art of, 53–54, 120
  body, soul, 50
  care for, 28, 69, 70, 79, 83–86, 105–13, 117, 121, 124
  character, good will, 54
  cosmic, hypercosmic, human, interspecies, 50, 81
  divine, 109–10
  erotic, 65–67, 120
  god of, 81n91, 83
  knowledge, acquisition, and use, 54
  love of individual, xii-xiii, 53–75
  models of, 52, 76–81
  pledge, 54–55
  primary, true, 52n8, 53
  reciprocity, 54
  self and other relatedness, 52–53, 83–86
  self-realization, 57–58
  subject-object interrelational model, 78–81
  with god (s), xi-xii
Fronterotta, F., 25n69, 40n112

Galen, 113n89
Ganymede, 67
Gerson, L., 56n20, 113n86
Gill, C., 58n24

Glaucon, 94, 97n41
Glaucus-Diomedes, 8n15
Gnostic, 104–5 and nn65–66
god, 1–49 *passim*, 55–58, 66, 68, 72, 74, 75, 81, 82–113 *passim*
  in Socrates, 56
  like to, 46
  living creature, 22–23
  movement, *archē*, 12n28, 17–19n44
  thinking of thinking, 12, 17, 85, 102
  way of life, 15, 20, 47, 66, 83ff., 91, 94, 95, 122
god-beloved, xiii, 57, 83–86, 113, 121–22
Gonzalez, J., 30n88
good, the; good; goodness (see also the one), 1–49 *passim*, 50–51, 50, 59, 61, 62–63, 65, 67, 69, 70–71, 83, 85, 86, 88, 89–94, 96–105 *passim*, 111–13, 114–20, 124–25
  beautiful-good, 60, 83–84, 111, 114
  beautiful-good distinguished (*Symposium* in light of *Republic*), x, 23–49
  beyond being, intellect, beauty, x, xii, 28, 34, 43, 92, 97, 102, 104, 118
  being/form
  class or Platonic form, x, 24–26, 117
  form of, 71n76, 92, 94
  hope, 108, 110
  pleasure, 89ff.
  power, generative, 92–94, 100–102
  reciprocal, friendship, 54
  relation to beautiful (*Symposium*, *Republic*), 1–49
  self-dependence of, 102
  theurgy, 106
grace, 34, 44, 98, 105, 123, 124
Gregory of Nyssa, 6, 10n25
Grocyn, John, 111n82
Grube, G. M. A., 45–46 and n126, 81
Guthrie, W. K. C., 19n46, 77n85

habituation, divine-human, 109–10
habits, 66 and n49, 108–9
Hadot, P., 100 and n44

happiness, 26, 80, 94, 104
harmony, symphony, 78–79
health/flourishing see also virtue, 46, 81, 89, 92–93
heart, 4 and n6
Henry, P., vii
Hera, 66n49
Hermann, 22n56
Hershbell, J. P., 113n86
Hippothales, 53
Homer/Homeric, 3, 83
Hunayn ibn Ishaq/Ishaq ibn Hunayn, 113n89
Hypatius of Ephesus, 111n82

Iamblichus, 51n7, 81 and n91, 105–10, 113, 124
Ibn 'Arabi, 124
Idealism, abstract, 3, 114, 115
implicate/explicate orders, 102–10, 123
impulse, 15, 17–19n44, 44, 54, 62, 74, 115, 120
inclusion/pre-inclusion, 83–86
indivisible wholeness, 122
inspiration, 18n44, 56–57, 59, 69, 70, 119
intellect, ix, xi, xiii, xiv, 2–12, 15–23, 28, 32, 33, 56, 70, 82–83, 84, 86–110, 111–13
  above, 33
  activity, life, 23
  active, 29
  Alexander, 29 and nn80–81
  and beauty, 44
  and boredom, 34, 44
  and development, 9–12, 90–91
  and impassibility, 9–10,
  and impulse, chance, 17–19n44
  and intelligibles, 37
  and reason, 2, 3, 5, 103
  and soul, 31, 34, 45
  approach to, augmentation, 68–69
  Aristotle's active, passive, 9
  Aristotle's Unmoved Mover (s), xi, xiii, 9–10, 15–23, 47
  as final cause, 10
  bloom of, 93

intellect *(continued)*
  coming-to-be, 11, 33, 36
  convergence of reason, feeling, 5–6
  desiring intellect, 6
  divine, xiii, 9–10, 39
  divine-human, 36–39, 82
  divine loving, 111–13
  eye-sun, 41
  first/derivative in soul, 31
  freedom, choice, 38–39
  generation, procession, conversion, 32n94, 37
  joy, 96–98
  implicate/explicate orders, 97, 102–10
  in search of *ousia*, essence vs dynamic, 10, 97
  intentional/non-intentional, 100–102
  in unity, 104
  "know-thyself", 82–83
  life-mind-being, 34
  light/illumination, 27, 29, 34
  love, desire, intense, ix, 2, 5, 9–39, 47, 70
  minded, 6
  movement of, xi, 17–19n44
  our/in me, 6, 9, 10, 11, 28n79, 31, 39, 56
  perception, 6
  phronimos, 6, 9
  pleasure, 82–95
  Plotinus' critique of Aristotle's unmoved mover, 102
  practical, 5, 6
  pre-inclusion, 82–96, 105–10
  pre-intellect, 11, 47
  self-dependent power of generation, 100–102
  self-reflexivity: Aristotle and Plotinus, 102
  self-relatedness, indivisible, 83–86
  Socrates-Alcibiades, 56
  thought, 33, 36, 100–102
  two acts/powers [sober/ drunk or in love], 10, 97, 100–102, 100and n47, 123–24
  wave of, 32
  wisdom, 82–84
  worth of, 33 and ns95–96
intellectualist, 3–7, 115
Islam, 113–114 and n89, 125

Joachim, H. H., 12 and n30, 13 and n33, 19n46, 52n10
Judaism, xi, xiii, 113, 124, 125
judgment, 6, 30, 52
justice, 50, 70, 77–79, 82–83, 109 and n79, 117, 119, 121

Karamanolis, G. E., 23n60
Keats, J., 33, 48, 118

lateral, and vertical attachment, 67–69
Lear, Jonathan, 8n18
Leroux, G., 9n23
light/illumination, 27, 34, 44
  light-metaphysics, 29
Lloyd, A., 17n43
love (*eros, agapē, philia*, 98–99, 111)
  and education, 26, 69
  and friendship, 53–58
  and hate, 61–62
  and need, 26
  art (*ars amatoria/ erotikē technē*), 53–54
  chain of, 42, 43, 70
  divine loving, 111–13
  erotic friendship, 65–67
  intense, 35, 70, 99, 104, 123
  of individuals, lateral attachment, 59–65, 67–69, 73–75
  longing, 98
  moves as being loved, 12 andn28, 15, 47, 115
  nature of, 26
  passionate, 34
  providential, converting, 105–6, 111–12
  reciprocal, 84–85n14
  reflexive phenomenon of, 67–69, 73
  synoptic, 71–75
  two acts/powers [sober/ drunk or in love], 10, 100–102, 100and n47, 123–24

INDEX OF SUBJECTS AND NAMES 151

Macrobius, 56n20
magnet-stone, 19–20
Majercik, R., 93n37, 113n88
Magnesia, 125
Marinus, 56n20
Marsuppini, Christophoro, 74
Massagli, 33n97
Meredith, Anthony, 6 and n11
Middle Platonic, 31, 34, 48, 118
moira, 38, 84–85n14
Mortley, R., 68n55
Moses, 84
music, 78–79
myth, xi–xii, 44, 52, 57, 61, 66, 67, 69, 82, 86, 113, 120

Narbonne, J. M., xii n10
nature, 14n37, 15 and n38, 17–19 and n44, 20–21, 27, 29–30, 38–39, 47, 92, 94, 97, 99–103, 111n84
Neo-Kantian school, 25
Neoplatonism, vii, x, 1, 23, 29, 48, 51n6, 56, 81, 105, 111, 113, 118, 123
Neumann, 24n66
Numenius, 113n88
Nussbaum, M., 50 and n4, 51 and n5
Nygren, A., xiii n11

O'Daly, G. J. P., 68n55
Odysseus, 83
Olympiodorus, 44n123, 56 and n18–19, 119
one, the (see also the good, beauty), 1, 10, 37–40, 68, 96, 97, 98n53, 104–12
  bi-unity, 106, 124
  divine, 105–106, 107, 124
  generation of intellect from, 10
  unity beyond names, beings, of activity, causes, 37, 68, 84, 112
  subject-object in activity, 84, 95
  intellect in, 104
Origen of Alexandria, xiii
originative principle/starting point (see *archē*)
Ovid, 54

participation [community/resemblance/sharing], 7 and n13, 8, 15, 16, 20, 21–22, 23n62, 25ns69 and, 70, 47, 60, 71 and n76, 75, 77, 88, 89, 95, 99, 116
passion, ix, 4n5, 5, 7–8, 34, 45, 59, 65–66, 69, 70, 72, 74, 81, 97, 98, 115, 120
passivity, divine, 124–25
Patristic thought, ix n1, 6
Paul, St., 111n82
Pausanias, 52, 61, 62–65, 69–73, 89, 121
peace/Peace, 112n85
Peripatetic, 34, 102
Perl, E., 75n81
Pessin, S., 113n89
Philemon, 82
Philo, 84 and n9, 84n12
philosophy, ungrudging, 119
phronesis, 67
Plato *passim*, but principally, 1–30, 50–67, 75–81, 84–86, 87–98, 102–5, 114–25
  individual dialogues—see Index Locorum
  later readings of Plato, 31–45, 67–75, 105–13
  reading Platonic dialogues, 60–62, 73–75
Platonic-Pythagorean tradition, 50, 121
Platonism, xi, 2–3, 3ns3–4, 6, 7, 45, 48–49, 50–51, 60, 65–67, 70, 81, 110
  and Christian thought, 111 and n82
  intellectualist?, 7
  Plato-Aristotle reconciliation, 23n60
  Ur-Platonism, 2n2
pleasure, 19, 86–98, 122–23
  as pleasure vs. as substance, 88–89
  being vs. becoming, 89–90
  bloom, supervenient, 92–94
  cyclical exchange, pleasure-pain, 87–88
  indivisible vs. piecemeal, 90–91, 95

pleasure *(continued)*
  perfects, intensifies activity, 92–94, 96, 109
  movement vs. activity, 86–96, 98
  proper or *oikeia*, 88, 91–92, 94
  pure, 87–89
pledge, 57–58
Plotinus *passim*, but principally, 1–5, 9–11, 32–36, 67–69, 96–105
Popper, K, 50 and n2
Porphyry, 23 and n60, 35, 39, 56n20, 72, 82 and n1, 99n44, 118, 124
Postmodernism, 115
power (*dynamis*) see also under activity, 4, 9, 10, 14, 17–19n44, 20, 21, 29, 30, 35, 37, 47, 77, 79, 92–94, 96 and n40, 97, 99–102, 109, 111n84, 113, 114, 116, 118, 123, 125
  friendship, 81n91, 83
  in Plato, *Republic*, 92, 109
  of the good in intellect, 99–102, 123
practice of dying, 7
Pradeau, J-F., 22n56, 25n69, 25n70, 40n112
prayer, 81–82, 106–10, 113, 124
  habituation, 109–10
  synapse, 109
pre-intellect (in Plotinus), 11, 47
Presocratics, 83
procession/conversion, 37–38, 39, 105, 111, 124
Proclus, 33, 37–44, 51n7, 56n18, 56n20, 58n24, 83–84, 105–10, 111n82, 118, 121, 124
  trust/faith, truth, and love, 107
proper, our own, *oikeios*, 93–94
Psellus, Michael, 9n21
Pythia, 82

rational/irrational, 116
reason, reasoning, discursive (here *logos*, 5–6, but also discursive reason, *dianoia*, *logismos*), 1–12, 17–19n44, 20n50, 45, 71n76, 92, 102–3, 117
recollection, 66, 80

reflexivity, 30 and n88, 33, 36, 52, 66–69, 70, 71, 73, 79, 102
  inner disposition, 79
  inter-subjectivity, 52, 66
  panoptic, 71
  self-reflexivity: Aristotle and Plotinus, 102
  vertical relation, 70
refutation, 60
Remes, P., 68n55
Renaissance, 67
Rist, J. M., 105n67
Ritter, C., 22n56
Rorty, R., 3n3, 115
Ross, W. D., 16n41
Rowe, C. J., 8n16, 24n65, 40n111, 53n9, 53n10
Rutten, C., 17n43

Schleiermacher, F. D. E., 48, 51n6
Schroeder, F. M., 29n81, 53n10
Schwyzer, H-R., vii
scientific insight, 75
self, 3, 57 and n23, 58n24, 71, 78–80, 99, 105n70
  and soul, 57–58 and n23–24, 70–71
  augmentation, 68–69
  belonging/belongings, 58n24, 71, 80
  belongingness, ownness, 94, 112n85
  composite nature, beyond, 99–102
  embodied ascent (vs. disembodied), 28 and n79, 58n24, 71, 116–17
  in/through another, 55–59, 75
  personal vs. impersonal, 57–58n23, 58
  subject-object interrelational model, 78–81
self-knowledge, 55–57, 57–58ns23–24, 80
self-love/self-direction, 45, 75
  self-love vs. self-hate, 86n20
self-relatedness, 83–86
separation; see also transcendence-immanence, 7–8, 19
sex, xi, 30, 63–66, 120

INDEX OF SUBJECTS AND NAMES   153

Shakespeare, W., 13–14
Simplicius, 13
Sinkewicz, R., 4n6
Slaveva-Griffin, S., 2n2
Smith, N. D., 51n6
Socrates, ix, 4n7, 5, 7, 8, 11, 20–30
    passim, 35, 41–48, 53, 55–82
    passim, 87–94 *passim*, 107, 109.,
    116–20
  Diotima-Socrates, 12, 25, 26, 27,
    45, 47, 52, 59, 60, 74, 107, 112,
    116
Sorabji, R., xi n4
soul, ix, x, 2n1, 3–11, 17–19, 26–28,
    31, 34–35, 43, 44, 45, 50, 54–58,
    57–58ns, 23–24, 59, 63, 66–71,
    78–84, 87–94, 96–105, 108–9,
    114–15
  all soul/care, 70, 84, 86, 121
  and pleasure/pain, 87–94, 96n40
  and prayer, 108–109
  and thought, 100–102
  ascent, 26, 31, 105n71
  beauty in, 31
  bored by intellect, 34, 44, 98
  by itself, 7, 45
  convergence, 6
  conversion, 92
  delight, joy, 96–100
  desire/feeling, 4–49, 114–15
  enchantment, 113, 125
  eye of, 27, 55, 80, 119
  erotic love focus, 8, 35, 44, 104–5,
    123–25
  fiery, 93n37
  friendship, 81 and n91, 83–84
  generative power, 96, 115, 123
  god/daemon, 74–75n80
  intellect of, 104 and n62, 123
  intellectual, 45, 104, 123
  intense love, 104–5
  justice, 78–79
  mixed/higher, 74–75n80
  movement in, *archē* of, 17–19n44
  rational/irrational, 5
  recollection, 66

self-knowledge, 55, 57–58 and
    ns23–24
separation, 7
soul-body, 8, 26, 28n79, 50, 96,
    57–58ns23–24, 63, 70–71, 78–81,
    96 and n40
soul/compound/body, 54–55
soul-self, meaning of, 55,
    57–58ns23–24, 70–71
substance vs. desire, 10–11
three forms/pleasures/tripartite,
    4–5, 10–11, 14, 43n122
virtue/excellence, 55
whole soul, 94
world soul, xiii–xiv, 10
Speusippus, 89
Stern-Gillett, S., 52–53n8, 53n10
Stewart, J. A., 93 and n35
Stobaeus, 55n16
Stoics, ixn1, x, 1, 54
subject (see also self), 57–58n23
sublimation, Freudian, 70
sublimation/substitution, 5–6
substance/substantial being (*ousia*),
    10–11, 15, 21, 28n76, 32n94,
    33n95, 36, 442, 72, 87, 90–95, 97,
    99–102, 117
  Aristotle, 90n32, 91–93, 95
  and desire, 87
  eternal, primary, 29, 91
  pre-substantial, 11
  voluntary, 38–39
  ways of life, 88–89
Synesius, 9n21
synhypostasis, 101
Sufi tradition, 124

Tarrant, H., 51n6, 56 and n18–19, 57
theology, 11–12, 19–36
  in Aristotle, 10–11n28, 19–36,
    47–48, 85n14, 116
  greater mysteries, *Symposium*;
    Aristotle's theology, 27–30
  lesser mysteries, *Symposium*; Aris-
    totle's physics, 27–30
Theophrastus, x
theurgy, 105n71, 106, 107

thinking/thought (from our thinking to that of intellect, understanding, *noēsis, theōria* or contemplation), 100–102
    self-reflexive character, 33, 36
Thrasymachus, 61 and n34, 77
Todd, R., 29n81
touching, contact, 7 and n13, 15, 16, 20, 21, 22, 32 and n94, 88, 116
    and community, sharing, participation, 7n13, 21, 88
    generative, 22, 88
    hanging from, 20–23
    self-reflexive, 33–36, 102
transcendence-immanence, 15, 19, 37, 43, 111, 112 and n85,114, 124
Trevor-Roper, Hugh, 3n3
Tricot, J., 13n35, 16n41, 21–22 and n54, 28n76
Turner, J .D., 38n107
tyranny, 65

understanding (thinking, thought, intellect, generally *noēsis*, as distinct from reason, here *logos*, but also discursive reason or *dianoia/logismos*, and equivalent to *theōria*, contemplation or insight, though used more generally throughout of Plato, Aristotle and the later tradition), 6, 31–32, 36, 44, 73, 76–78, 92, 103, 114, 117,
    double in Plato, 73
    divine, 36
unity (see also the one), 37, 68, 84, 95, 104–8, 109–10, 112, 124–25
universalism, 115, 119
unmoved mover, xi, xiii, 9–14, 24, 27–31, 47, 83, 86, 91, 94, 96, 102–5, 111, 113n88, 115–23
    as beautiful to good, 28–30
    as being loved, 12 andn28, 15, 47, 115

indivisibly whole?, 85–96
self- and world-related?, 85ff.
thinking of thinking, 12, 17, 85, 102
way of life, 15, 20, 47, 66, 83ff., 91, 94, 95, 122

Valla, Lorenzo, 111n82
Velásquez, O., 51n6
virtue/excellence, 6, 8, 17–18n44, 22, 24, 27, 32n94, 41, 44, 55, 56–59, 63–65, 70, 72, 110, 119–20
    form of, 41
    natural, 17n44
    negative/positive ambiguity, 63–65, 72
    paradigms, 70
    political, kathartical, theoretical, enthusiastical, 56, 119
    scale, ladder of, 56–59, 119
    true vs. images, 24, 27
Vlastos, G., 50 and n3, 59, 77n85, 80–81, 119
vulnerability, 60, 82, 112, 113, 124–25

Wallis, R. T., 56n20, 113n88
well-being, 15n38, 17–18n44, 69, 81, 96
will, free will, 38–39, 78, 83
    choice, 5–6, 38–39
Williams, R., 4n5
wisdom, ix, 4, 5, 6, 7, 8, 20n50, 36, 45–47, 55, 58n24, 59, 63–65, 72, 73, 74, 76, 79, 80, 88, 94, 115–117, 120
    contemplative, philosophical, 36
    life of, 47, 88, 94
    love, desire of   5, 7, 45, 71, 94
    practical, 6, 7, 74
    virtue, 17–19n44, 64
Woodruff, P., 40n112

Xenocrates, 89

Zeus, 66n49, 67, 80, 84, 85n16

www.ingramcontent.com/pod-product-compliance
Lightning Source LLC
Chambersburg PA
CBHW031434150426
43191CB00006B/511